*Money and Monetary Policy
in Communist China*

Studies of the
EAST ASIAN INSTITUTE
Columbia University

MONEY
AND MONETARY POLICY
IN COMMUNIST
CHINA

Katharine Huang Hsiao

1971

COLUMBIA UNIVERSITY PRESS

New York and London

Katharine Huang Hsiao is Associate Professor
of Economics at Indiana State University

The East Asian Institute
of Columbia University

The East Asian Institute of Columbia University was established in 1949 to prepare graduate students for careers dealing with East Asia, and to aid research and publication on East Asia during the modern period. The faculty of the Institute are grateful to the Ford Foundation and the Rockefeller Foundation for their financial assistance.

The Studies of the East Asian Institute were inaugurated in 1962 to bring to a wider public the results of significant new research on modern and contemporary East Asia.

To My Husband

Preface

This book is the culmination of many years of interest, for it was the perplexing experience of living under the inflation in China during the Second World War that motivated me toward the study of economics. By 1963, when my dissertation project began, the pre-1949 Chinese inflation had already been capably and thoroughly examined; thus, it seemed natural for me to extend the investigation of the nation's monetary developments to a later era. That project eventually evolved into the present book.

In the preparation of this work, I became heavily indebted to many of my teachers. Special thanks are due to Professor James W. Angell, who patiently and unfailingly guided my interrupted academic career at Columbia and critically read through a variety of outlines and three complete drafts of the dissertation. In addition, Professor Franklin L. Ho, whose encouragement and counsel made possible a study in this uncharted area, carefully reviewed the dissertation as well as the final manuscript. The study was further benefited by criticism from Professors A. Doak Barnett, C. Martin Wilbur, and William W. Hollister.

From my friends and colleagues I have received much stimulation and help. Steadfast moral and intellectual support came from Professor L. L. Hsiao, my husband and colleague, who shared the burden of my mental agonies at various stages of progress, read all the drafts, and contributed in several ways. For his advice and understanding this book is gratefully dedicated to him. Professor Y. C. Yin of George Washington University and Dr. Helen Yin of the Department of Commerce freely lent their research experience and expert knowledge, went over more than one draft, and were responsible for many improvements in the final version. Professor Alexander Eckstein of the University of Michigan, Professor C. M. Hou of Colgate University, and Professor Gregory Grossman of the University of California at Berkeley were kind enough to review the manuscripts and offer valuable comments. Professors Arthur Billings and Marvin Fischbaum of Indiana State

University read or discussed portions of the book's content and gave me fresh insights. To all of them, my sincere thanks. Naturally, I alone am responsible for any flaws that remain.

The study began under a fellowship from the East Asian Institute of Columbia University in the summer of 1963 and the academic year 1963–1964. Continued research was financed by post-doctoral grants from the same Institute in the summers of 1966 and 1967. I am grateful to the Contemporary China Studies Committee of that Institute, especially to Professor A. Doak Barnett, then Chairman of the Committee, for providing this financial support, without which the study could not have been undertaken. My thanks also go to the Economics Department and the Faculty Research Committee of Indiana State University for a lightened teaching load in the spring of 1967 and for financing the clerical preparation of the final draft.

Since research dictated the use of libraries across the United States as well as in Hongkong, a large number of individuals have aided me in the quest for materials. I am particularly indebted to the Center for Chinese Studies of the University of California at Berkeley and to the Universities Service Center and the Union Research Institute at Hongkong for their courtesy in providing all necessary research facilities during the summers of 1966 and 1965 respectively. Also, the staffs at the Columbia University East Asian Library and the Library of Congress have been most cooperative. To increase the readability of the manuscripts, my friend, Mrs. Paul Fowler, gave generously of her time and attention. At the same time, Miss Doris McIntyre brought her remarkable skills to bear in typing and editing various drafts. I should like to express my deep appreciation for all these contributions.

Finally, I wish to thank my children, Georgia Angella, Gilbert Lynn, and Katharine Jean. Apart from proofreading, sorting and other chores, they contributed heavily by foregoing much that was rightfully theirs while the book was in progress. I hope that their sacrifice will not prove to have been in vain, but will, by promoting inquiries into the economic forces of a large and developing segment of the globe, help to improve the prospect of their own generation.

Terre Haute, Indiana   Katharine Huang Hsiao
February 1971

Contents

Tables

Tables

Tables

Charts

Abbreviations

CCCP	*Ching-chi chou-pao* (Economic Weekly)
CCYC	*Ching-chi yen-chiu* (Economic Research)
Central TCCT	*Chung-yang ts'ai-ching cheng-ts'e fa-ling hui-pien* (Collection of Laws and Regulations on Financial and Economic Policies of the Central Government)
CHCC	*Chi-hua ching-chi* (Planned Economy)
CHYYC	*Chiao-hsueh yü yen-chiu* (Teaching and Research)
CJCK	*Chin-jung chou-k'ang* (Financial Weekly)
CJFKHP	*Chin-jung fa-kuei hui-pien* (Collection of Monetary Laws and Regulations)
CJYC	*Chin-jung yen-chiu* (Financial Research)
CKCJ	*Chung-kuo chin-jung* (China's Finance)
East China TCCT	*Hua-tung ts'ai-ching cheng-ts'e fa-ling hui-pien* (Collection of Laws and Regulations of Financial and Economic Policies of East China)
ECMM	*Extracts from China Mainland Magazines* (Translations by the American Consulate General, Hong Kong)
FKHP	*Chung-hua jen-min kung-ho-kuo fa-kuei hui-pien* (Collection of laws and regulations of the People's Republic of China)
GAC	Government Administrative Council
HC	*Hung-ch'i* (Red Flag)
HCS	*Hsin chien-she* (New Construction)
HH	*Hsueh-hsi* (Study)
HHPYK	*Hsin-hau pan-yueh-k'an* (New China Semimonthly)
HHYP	*Hsin-hua yueh-pao* (New China Monthly)
JMJP	*Jen-min jih-pao* (People's Daily)
JMST	*Jen-min shou-ts'e* (People's Handbook)
JPRS	*Joint Publications Research Service* (Translations)

Abbreviations

NCNA	New China News Agency
NTCJ	*Nung-ts'un chin-jung* (Rural Finance)
PB	People's Bank
SC	State Council
SCMP	*Survey of the China Mainland Press* (Translations by the American Consulate General, Hong Kong)
SSB	State Statistical Bureau
SSST	*Shih-shih shou-ts'e* (Current Events)
Stat. Res.	*T'ung-chi yen-chiu* (Statistical Research)
TC	*Ts'ai-cheng* (Public Finance)
TCFKHP	*Chung-yang ts'ai-cheng fa-kuei hui-pien* (Collection of Fiscal Laws and Regulations of the Central Government)
TCKT	*T'ung-chi kung-tso* (Statistical Work)
TCKTTH	*T'ung-chi kung-tso t'ung-hsun* (Statistical Work Bulletin)
TCYC	*Ts'ai-ching yen-chiu* (Fiscal and Economic Research)
TKP	*Ta kung pao* (Impartial Daily), Hong Kong, Peking, and Tientsin

Money and Monetary Policy
in Communist China

I

INTRODUCTION

The Scope and Method

DURING THE PAST two decades, as Communist China emerged into the world scene, increasing attention has been given to the study of the Chinese economy. This new focus of scholarly interest is eminently justified in view of the nation's background and the role it plays in international relations. China is an industrially backward yet populous, large, and ancient nation that seeks to reassert her place in the modern world and to realize her potentiality. Inquiries into her economy and into the process of her economic development are of dual significance. In the first place, since China's aspirations to be a modern nation cannot be fulfilled without a sound economic foundation, such inquiries probe into a crucial facet of her national life. In the second place, the Chinese economic experience has a wider relevance; it throws light on the problems of industrialization of underdeveloped areas in general.

As a result of the awakened interest in this field, a number of major studies on the Communist Chinese economy have been published in the English-speaking world. Some of the earlier works led the way by surveying the overall economic development and centering around inquiries into her national income.[1] These were followed by studies dealing with specific topics that probed more deeply into individual facets of the economy.[2] On this level, however, much research remains to be done; the present study is an attempt to examine one central area that has not yet been covered adequately.

[1] For example: Eckstein, *The National Income of Communist China;* Hollister, *China's Gross National Product and Social Accounts 1950–1957;* Choh-ming Li, *Economic Development of Communist China;* Liu and Yeh, *The Economy of the Chinese Mainland: National Income and Economic Development 1933–1959;* Ishikawa, *National Income and Capital Formation in Mainland China.*

[2] For example: Eckstein, *Communist China's Economic Growth and Foreign Trade;*

1

Introduction

Communist China has adopted an economic system of the Soviet type. The influence and policy of money under such a system differ drastically from those in Western countries.[3] Nonetheless, money and credit have an important role to play in China; they remain essential to an understanding of the Chinese economic performance. Moreover, the significance of a study on money in Communist China is enhanced by the nation's economic history. The Chinese inflation of the 1940s, during which the Nationalist government relied mainly on price control as a cure without effectively removing the excessive money supply, resulted in economic collapse and paved the way for the Communist triumph in 1949.[4] A vivid memory of this hectic monetary experience lingers on in the minds of the Chinese people, and the new regime is inclined to be sensitive to the danger of inflation for political as well as economic reasons. This state of mind renders an inquiry into the monetary mechanism and monetary policy of Communist China all the more relevant.

Despite the importance of money in the Chinese economy, there is as yet no comprehensive study devoted solely to this subject.[5] The neglect can perhaps be explained by two factors that are applicable to studies of contemporary China in general and to monetary investigations in particular. First, there is no systematic body of source materials on money. Only widely scattered fragments of information are available, and these are buried in a voluminous collection of Chinese economic literature. Second, there is the language barrier. Neither hindrance is insurmountable, hence this present effort to weave the materials into a coherent presentation and analysis.

Kang Chao, *The Rate and Pattern of Industrial Growth in Communist China*; Perkins, *Market Control and Planning in Communist China;* Walker, *Planning and Chinese Agriculture.*

[3] For a general description of the role of money and banking in a Soviet-type economy, see Garvy, *Money, Banking and Credit in Eastern Europe* Part I-1.

[4] For the Chinese inflation, see Chang Kia-ngau, *The Inflationary Spiral: The Experience in China 1939–1950;* Chou Shun-hsin, *The Chinese Inflation, 1937–1949;* Young, *China's Wartime Finance and Inflation, 1937–1945.*

[5] One dissertation examines the Chinese monetary policy during 1949–1954. Starlight, *Fiscal and Monetary Policies in Communist China, 1949–1954.* However, it was written before the bulk of source materials used in the present study became available in the West.

2

THE SCOPE OF THE STUDY

The objective of this study is to determine the part played by money and banking in the Chinese economy, to examine the nature of China's monetary policy and to see whether the latter has contributed toward the maintenance of economic stability. The approach to this objective is naturally conditioned by the state of available information as well as by the nature of the overall economy. It would be helpful at this point to clarify several factors that are relevant to the scope of this study.

TERMINOLOGY

"Money" and "monetary policy" have specific, though not always precise, connotations in Western economies. Because China has a vastly different system, the two terms are used here in the broadest possible sense. Money refers to both currency and various types of bank deposits; together they represent almost all noncommodity assets within the Chinese framework.[6] Monetary policy refers to any centralized action or actions taken deliberately for the regulation of money supply, without regard to the form that these actions assume.[7] On the other hand, the terms "cash" and "currency" are used interchangeably in this study, referring to banknotes and coins in circulation. This usage deviates from the general Western accounting practice, which treats currency and demand deposits as cash. However, it is in conformance with the common usage in Chinese and Soviet literature.

TIME PERIOD

The focus of this study is on the period of the First Five Year Plan (1953–1957), although relevant developments in other years are also included. This concentration is both necessary and appropriate. It is necessary because those publications from Mainland China that are available in

---

[6] There is no market for commercial bills or private securities; government bonds are not negotiable, while gold cannot be sold in the market or used as a means of payment. The meaning of money supply will be further discussed in the first section of Chapter VIII.

[7] Thus, while it is true to say that there is no monetary policy in China when the term is used in the narrow, Western sense, there is monetary policy in the broad sense used here.

the United States are comparatively abundant for this period.[8] In addition, official statistics published during 1955–1957 (which often supplied back figures) were, as a rule, of relatively better quality than those of the earlier or later years.[9] Fortunately, this focus is also appropriate, since it was during these years that the nation's monetary structure evolved. During the transitional period of 1949–1952 the monetary authorities were occupied mainly with problems temporary in nature.[10] When that period ended and the country embarked on comprehensive planning, it was important to the central authority to develop an effective money and banking system as well as a policy in order to facilitate control over the economy. Hence a series of measures were implemented during 1954–1955 to overhaul the monetary structure. These measures were often regarded by Chinese monetary authorities as parts of a "credit reform," comparable to that which took place in the U.S.S.R. in the early 1930s when the present Soviet monetary system was developed. Recent literature indicates that, in spite of kaleidoscopic changes and experiments made in the Mainland since 1958, the monetary institutions and policy remain fundamentally unaltered.

AREA OF STUDY

In terms of area, this study is confined to the domestic aspects of money. This delineation is justified on the ground that in China, where both foreign trade and foreign exchange are monopolized by the state, the domestic economy is by and large insulated from economic changes in the outside world. International transactions and payments do not affect the domestic monetary situation to any significant extent. Therefore it is felt that a discussion of the international aspects of money can more logically be combined with that of other international economic problems, such as foreign trade and the balance of payments.

---

[8] The export ban imposed by Communist China on a wide range of publications in 1959 has drastically reduced the supply of materials during later years.

[9] Choh-ming Li, *The Statistical System of Communist China,* Sections VI and XIII.

[10] Measures dealing with these problems, such as the unification of various currencies and the stabilization of prices after a period of hyperinflation, have already been dealt with by other writers. For example, see Miyashita, *The Currency and Financial System of Mainland China;* also Starlight, *Fiscal and Monetary Policies in Communist China.*

Introduction

THE NATURE OF THE SOURCE MATERIALS USED

While China can be categorized as an economically underdeveloped country of the Soviet type, the nation remains unique and complex in many respects. It is a society with an ancient and distinct culture suddenly gripped by a determination for rapid change, and much of its actual development is not fully known. In the absence of clear information, there is a real danger that an economic study of China may lean on our knowledge of the U.S.S.R., prejudge the Chinese development according to the Soviet pattern or, in short, assume too much. It is to forestall this temptation that this study relies heavily on Chinese materials. The bulk of the source materials used here are taken from journals and documents published in the Mainland, in the Chinese language, and are primarily intended for circulation within Communist China among the professional and technical staff. These are supplemented, mostly for background information, by English-language literature on Communist China and the Soviet Union.[11]

Those publications from the Mainland that are available in major American libraries are piecemeal and scattered. Hence there are serious gaps for which no information can be found. This factor, coupled with the frequent fluctuations of the country's economic policies, is not conducive to an easy and systematic presentation, much less any elegance in exposition. However, care is taken to maintain objectivity throughout this study.

There is a paucity of statistical data on the Communist Chinese economy in general, but particularly in the area of money quantitative information is often withheld from publication. Therefore, this study is mainly qualitative and impressionistic. The scant quantitative data that are included here are often gleaned from figures emerging from scattered sources at different times; they should therefore be treated with caution. However, one reassuring consideration tends to compensate for the dearth of monetary statistics. While infrequently published and discontinuous, the monetary data that are available are likely to have a higher

[11] When Mainland materials are available both in the original Chinese and in English translation, the Chinese version is used. When the translated version is used for reason of availability, it is so indicated.

5

degree of reliability than other Chinese economic statistics. This can be deduced from the fact that monetary data originate primarily from the actual business records of a centralized banking network and that this network has inherited a core of competent staff and established procedures from the past. On the other hand, statistical series such as agricultural yields and industrial production involve the use of sampling and estimates, which are necessarily less reliable than a complete count. Besides, much of the collection and compilation of such data are conducted by an as yet infant organization of statistical agencies, often on the basis of primary records of doubtful value.[12] Generally speaking, then, the source data used in this study, while lacking in comprehensiveness, may be considered to be of better quality than those available in other areas of the Chinese economy.[13]

The monetary unit in Communist China is the *yuan*. In 1955 a monetary conversion took place that exchanged the pre-1955 people's currency *(jen-min-pi)* for a new people's currency at the uniform rate of ¥10,000 to ¥1. All data used in this study expressed in *yuan* are in terms of the post-1955 new currency. The new Chinese currency was officially equivalent to U.S. $2.617 in 1957.[14] Exchange rates, however, are arbitrary, since foreign exchange is completely monopolized by the state.

THE PLAN OF THE STUDY

In order to provide a frame of reference, the remaining portion of this introduction is devoted to a review of the theoretical role of money and monetary organization in the Chinese economy as seen by the central authorities. The body of the study is developed through a sequence of three steps, dealing, respectively, with the following topics: the banking institutions, the money supply, and the monetary policy. The first topic is presented in Chapters II and III; it contains a separate discussion of rural financial organizations. The second topic is covered by the four succeeding chapters, all of which concern the creation and structure of money. Specifically, Chapter IV explores the general relationship be-

---

[12] Helen Yin, *The Reporting of Industrial Statistics in Communist China.*
[13] The author is indebted to Dr. Helen Yin for this suggestion.
[14] *CHCC,* no. 12, 1957, p. 29.

tween the state bank and the supply of money, with emphasis on the way in which the credit flow is determined. This is followed by a description, in Chapter V, of the structure of bank loans, the main source of money supply. The money supply itself is then examined in the next two chapters, which study separately the bank deposit component (VI) and the currency component (VII). The third topic is discussed in Chapters VIII and IX. The former explores the overall monetary policy and its objective, while the latter evaluates the monetary performance in the light of the policy and objective. The final chapter (X) briefly summarizes the entire study and draws certain conclusions regarding the role of the People's Bank and its effectiveness in achieving monetary equilibrium.

The Conceptual Framework of Money in the Chinese Economy

Before embarking on a discussion of the diverse monetary developments in Communist China, it will be useful to provide, as background information, the Chinese central authority's view of the overall framework underlying the Chinese economy and monetary system. Thus this section briefly surveys the objectives of the economy and the theoretical role assigned to the money and banking mechanism in the economy.

Since Communist China aspires to be a modern socialistic state patterned after the U.S.S.R., her economic structure is by and large the product of a transplantation of the Soviet system. However, the cultural and institutional heritage of China is vastly different; therefore Soviet models in various areas had to be modified and adapted to the Chinese environment. In the field of money and banking, this generalization holds true. Communist China from the beginning wanted to create a system of money and banking similar to that of the Soviet Union. This was achieved, on the one hand, by a strict duplication of the basic Soviet principles and, on the other hand, by a pragmatic and flexible attitude in their application. Broadly speaking, by the end of 1955 the embryo of a Soviet type monetary structure was already in existence. The passion of the "Great Leap Forward" era of 1958–1959, with its emphasis on miraculous increases in production, on political viewpoints, and on the enthusiasm of the "massess" as against professional advice, led to an abandonment of financial disciplines. In this period economic rationality was lacking, and banking regulations disintegrated. But when the emotional disruption subsided around 1960, principles and institutions governing currency and credit similar to those of the earlier years re-emerged. Thus, in spite of a constantly shifting course of development, the basic role performed by money and banks is discernible.[15]

THE CHINESE ECONOMY AND ITS OBJECTIVES

By the end of 1952, three years after the Communist government gained control of the Chinese Mainland, the period of stabilization and rehabilitation was considered completed, and the nation began construction by means of economic planning, with "socialized industrialization" serving as the long-range goal. The First Five Year Plan of 1953–1957 aimed at achieving two things: (1) increasing production via a concentration of investment in industry, especially in heavy industry, and (2) socializing the private productive units. Industrialization and socialization were therefore the two paramount objectives of the state in these years.

The Chinese economy is essentially a monetary economy in which productive factors and commodities are valued in monetary terms and transactions are carried out mainly through the use of money. Centralized planning, by which economic activities are basically organized, is carried out both in monetary terms and in real terms, albeit the two forms are used in different degrees. While the actual planning procedures and the extent of planned activities are subjects requiring a separate investigation, the broad theoretical scheme is simple and familiar. The Five Year Plan sets the long-range targets and the annual plan is operational. Each year a centrally determined general outline of the annual plan sets the goals and priorities of different industries.[16] This draft plan provides control figures on output, input, cost coef-

---

[15] However, the effects of the cultural revolution of 1966–1967 are not yet clear.

[16] For a discussion on the scope of the economic plan and the basic decisions involved, see Yuan-li Wu, *The Economy of Communist China,* Chapters II and III.

ficient, and other operational requirements for the industries. The various ministries in charge of these industries help to put the plan in a more specific form by determining the targets for individual commodities. These targets are then broken down and assigned to the enterprises in each industry, which in turn formulate detailed plans for meeting their respective quotas.

Each enterprise, which is the basic productive unit, prepares plans covering all aspects of operations, including the enterprise production plan (consisting of labor, raw materials, production, and cost plans), the sales plan, and the financial plan.[17] The enterprise financial plan summarizes all other plans of the enterprise in value terms; it is the most important of all enterprise plans from the viewpoint of money and banking. These enterprise plans are submitted upward through the same organizational hierarchy for approval. After the plans are coordinated and modified at the top they are returned to the enterprises for implementation. In actual practice the First Five Year Plan, which began in 1953, was not completed and published until the middle of 1955. Planning in the first two and a half years was therefore limited to fixing yearly targets for individual industries.[18]

FINANCIAL PLANNING

Logically, a centrally planned economy could allocate all factors of production and finished goods in terms of physical quantities. In that case, the market mechanism and the use of money as a medium of exchange would become redundant. Because of the complexity of a national economy, however, complete reliance on physical planning is not practicable. Alternatively, the central authority could determine and control prices of all factors and commodities so as to achieve the desired allocation. In this case, there would be a market in operation and money would be required. China uses a mixture of physical plan-

[17] Before November 1957, these plans were represented by twelve targets, five of which (such as the output of major products and number of employees) were in physical terms, the rest of which (such as cost, profit, and sales) were in monetary value. Perkins, *Market Control and Planning in Communist China*, p. 100.

[18] Hooton, "The Planning Structure and the Five Year Plan in China," *Contemporary China*, vol. I.

ning and price control, plus a partial free market.[19] Thus her physical plans are far from comprehensive, and value planning expressed in monetary units and in aggregates becomes important. The latter is called financial planning; it parallels and supplements physical planning and is considered an instrument for channeling resources into the centrally determined investment projects.[20]

Financial planning consists of several component parts. These are (1) the enterprise financial plans, (2) the state budget, and (3) the cash and credit plans. In addition, there is a comprehensive financial plan for the country that integrates all three categories of plans.[21] As mentioned above, the enterprise financial plans originate from the individual state enterprises. In these plans, each enterprise sets down the expected receipts and expenditures that would be incurred if its assigned targets of production or distribution were to be fulfilled. The second and most important part of financial planning, the state budget, is compiled by the Ministry of Finance. The Ministry summarizes the government's fiscal receipts and payments. Finally, the cash plan and the credit plan are directly related to the supply of money and fall within the jurisdiction of the state bank. Thus financial planning involves all three constituents of the state sector, namely, the enterprises, the budget, and the state bank.

THE STATE ENTERPRISE, THE STATE BUDGET, AND THE STATE BANK

Ideally, the state enterprise is the primary economic unit in which production or distribution is carried out, whereas the state budget and

[19] The total number of commodities subject to direct allocation by the state was 96 in 1953, 134 in 1954, 163 in 1955, and 235 in 1956. Part of the increase in the number was a result of finer classifications. Besides, not all of these commodities were directly distributed to the consuming units. A part of each was allocated to the state commercial organizations for distribution through the market. "The Distribution of State Allocated Resources During the Past Years," *TCKT,* no. 13, 1957, pp. 29 and 31. The share of free market retail sales was generally more than one fifth of the total retail sales. Wang P'ing, "The Scope and Changes of the Free Market in Our Country," *TCKT,* no. 11, 1957, pp. 28-29.

[20] Feng Li-t'ien, "Financial Planning," CHCC, no. 8, 1956, pp. 29–33.

[21] The comprehensive financial plan is sometimes listed as a fourth part of financial planning. It is in effect an overall summary of the three types of plans mentioned above.

the state bank form two channels through which national income is redistributed. These two, the budget and the bank, are the controlling organs whereby money income is mobilized and then parceled out as money capital to state enterprises by the central authorities.

The national budget fulfills its role through fiscal receipts and expenditures. Major budgetary receipts include not only taxes but also profits and depreciation reserves of state enterprises and the sale of public bonds;[22] among these items, that of enterprise profits is the most dominant one. On the other hand, budgetary expenditures cover government administrative expenses as well as capital investments of state enterprises. Such capital investments contain two parts: (1) fixed capital, called "basic construction," and (2) working capital required to cover the regularly recurrent expenses (such as wages, fuel, and raw materials) that are necessary for the maintenance of a normal rate of operation. This is called "owned (or retained) working capital."[23] Both fixed capital and owned working capital are provided in the form of interest-free grants from the budget.

Simultaneously, the People's Bank mobilizes funds by gathering together as demand deposits all temporarily idle balances of the economy, including those from the budget, state enterprises, joint enterprises, cooperatives, and households. These funds are then used to supply that part of working capital needed by state enterprises that is over and above the average regular requirement. In other words, the Bank satisfies all temporary and seasonal demands for working capital and finances goods-in-transit. This is called "borrowed working capital" and is supplied by the Bank in the form of short-term loans, according to commercial principles.

The rationale behind this schema is that it serves to separate capital requirements of state enterprises that are constant in character from those that are not. The former are provided by the state budget; the latter, being irregular and of short duration, are more adaptable to bank financing. The momentarily unused balances of the economy,

---

[22] Bond sales and retirements are considered budgetary items; therefore they are components of the fiscal policy rather than the monetary policy.

[23] The amount of owned working capital is assessed periodically according to the changing need of each enterprise. Any excess is to be returned to the budget by the enterprise concerned.

which cannot be gathered effectively by the budget, are activated by the Bank to support these loans. The Bank's role, then, is to supplement the budget by collecting the short-term funds of the society with which to satisfy the marginal short-term capital requirements of the enterprises. This system is said to provide a degree of flexibility without imposing a heavy burden on the budget. Besides, the Bank's participation in the supply of working capital puts it in a position to supervise the state enterprises.

THE CASH PLAN AND THE CREDIT PLAN

The operations of the state bank, like other economic activities, are theoretically guided by plans. Two types of plans lie directly within the domain of the centralized state bank system. First, there is the credit plan, which indicates the expected amounts of bank loans granted and deposits received. In other words, the credit plan specifies the "credit receipts" (deposits) and "credit expenditures" (loans) of the bank. In addition, there is the cash plan, which deals with the anticipated amounts of receipts and payments in currency incurred by the bank.

The cash plan and the credit plan are separated because the money flow is divided into two distinct spheres, cash (or currency) and credit (or bank deposits), each circulating within a specified area. The general principle is that a state enterprise can use its deposits to make payment to another state enterprise only in the form of bank account transfers. Between state enterprises, then, little cash is used. However, when payments are made to individuals (e.g., payments for wages or agricultural purchases), the enterprises are allowed to withdraw cash from the bank. On the other hand, when cash is received by the enterprises (e.g., receipts from sales to the individuals), it must be deposited immediately in the bank. As a result, almost all money held by the state sector is in the form of bank deposits, while cash circulates only within the private sector and between the private and the state sectors.

The cash plan and the credit plan are intimately related. Because bank loans are granted primarily to state enterprises, which are required to keep all but a very small amount of their funds in the state bank as deposits, any change in bank loans granted to these units must result in an equal change in their bank deposits, leading to an unchanged amount in the balance of the bank's credit plan. Consequently, a rise (fall) in the balance of the credit plan can occur only as a result of cash transactions, that is, as a result of cash deposits (withdrawals) made by the enterprises. In that case, the cash receipt (payment) of the bank changes along with a compensating change in enterprise deposits. A change in the balance of the credit plan is therefore theoretically linked with an equivalent but opposite change in the balance of the cash plan. The latter change in turn represents a change in the quantity of currency-in-circulation. In short, any imbalance in the credit plan (i.e., loans larger than deposits, or vice versa) would induce an imbalance in the cash plan and a change in the volume of currency outstanding by the same amount.

The compilations of the cash plan and the credit plan are based on the expected transactional requirements for currency and credit, respectively, of the state enterprises. On the basis of the enterprise financial plan, which in turn reflects its production or distribution plan, each enterprise or organization in the state sector submits to the local office of the state bank a plan indicating its requirements for cash and for credit during the year. From these individual requirements the local banks compile credit plans and cash plans for their respective areas; the plans are then sent to the next higher banking office. As the plans are transmitted upward through a whole pyramid of banking offices, adjustments and summations take place at each level. When they reach the top, the main office of the state bank in Peking combines all the sectional plans into a cash plan and a credit plan for the entire country. These plans are then revised, coordinated with the overall national economic plan, and approved by the central government. The approved plans are then transmitted downward again through the banking system for implementation.

THE ROLE OF MONEY AND MONETARY POLICY

From the discussion above, it is clear that the use of money remains essential in the Chinese economy. Money serves as the medium of exchange and the unit of account, and a highly centralized state bank controls its total supply. These elements are similar to those in a free enterprise economy. However, in a free economy the central bank may attempt to affect the level of investment, production, and employment by influencing the supply of money, whereas in Communist China the volume of economic activities is predetermined by the planning authority. Hence the objective of monetary policy in China is not to vary money supply in order to achieve a certain level of employment; rather, it aims at supplying the appropriate quantity of money that, given the velocity of circulation and liquidity preferences, is required to realize the planned activities. In this respect, the role of money in the economy is permissive and accommodating rather than active or determining in nature. The monetary authority merely tries to satisfy the transactional requirements of money in order to allow the fulfillment of planned productions and distributions.

Viewed from the other direction, however, the supply of money has important impacts on the Chinese economy. In order to assure the smooth functioning of the general economic plan, the system must be provided with just the right amount of liquidity so that production and distribution can be financed without interruption. At the same time, the system must also be free from inflationary pressures so that the set of planned prices is not disturbed. Too small a supply of money might cause interruptions and slow down economic activities. A sudden rise in the hoarding of money by the public would have the same effect. On the other hand, given the absence of physical controls at the decentralized level, too large a supply of money could lead to competition among the enterprises in the factor market as well as excessive purchasing power in the consumer market, both tending to cause shortages and to drive up prices. Such monetary instability, if sufficiently severe, might even impinge on the drawing up of the economic plan itself, thereby indirectly affecting the volume of investment and the rate of growth. In short, monetary policy in China has a twofold objective. It must facilitate production by satisfying the transactional demand for money and at the same time maintain monetary stability.

The means by which these monetary objectives are achieved lie in planning, that is, in the cash plan and the credit plan. As mentioned earlier, the cash plan and the credit plan originate from the individual enterprises and are based on their anticipated transactional demand for money for the fulfillment of their planned tasks. At the top of the banking and planning hierarchy, the national cash and credit plans are reconciled with other financial plans and with the general economic plan. If all plans were consistent and all enterprises could accurately assess and report their monetary requirements, the financial plans would be closely geared to the overall physical economic plan, and the implementation of the cash and credit plans could roughly fulfill the monetary objectives. This, however, presupposes a comprehensive body of reliable statistical information, highly sophisticated and accurate planning techniques, and complete cooperation from the enterprises. None of these conditions was satisfactorily fulfilled in the Mainland during the period of this study.

THE ROLE OF THE STATE BANK

The state bank is a government organ responsible for the creation and control of money. In the Communist framework, the state bank has two broad functions. The first is a familiar function of central banking—it regulates the aggregate supply of money so that the monetary objectives described in the above section may be achieved. In this respect, although the instruments employed are radically different, the basic goal of attempting to sustain a desired level of economic activities without monetary disequilibrium remains similar to that of the Western nations. There is, however, a second function of the state bank that is unique in the Soviet-type economy—the supervisory function. This function stems from the centralized and monopolistic position of the state bank. Since the bank handles almost all monetary payments of the state sector, it can easily check the degree of plan fulfillment of individual enterprises. By virtue of its control over enterprise finance, then, the bank is able to scrutinize the performance and activities of each unit and to ensure conformance to plans.

There are two lines of thinking that underlie the Communist view of the state bank's role as a supplier of credit. The first is the belief that the bank merely lends out what it receives as deposits, and therefore does not create money through its credit operations.[24] From this viewpoint money is created only when the state bank lends more than it receives, that is, when loans exceed deposits. In this case, new currency would enter into circulation and the bank would be creating money in the form of currency. This type of reasoning is perhaps responsible for the state bank's preoccupation with the balance of credit (the difference between loans and deposits) rather than with the total quantity of credit. The bank also appears to be more concerned with the control of currency in circulation than with the amount of credit outstanding.

A second line of thinking is that because the state bank's resources consist of temporarily idle funds, these resources should be used only for short-term financing. Thus, in a theoretical framework, the credit function of the state bank is restricted to the provision of short-term loans, with an implied corollary that long-term credit tends to be inflationary.

[24] That bank loans could affect the amount of bank deposits (and therefore the amount of money) was last mentioned by Chinese bankers in October, 1950, in a report by the Deputy-Director of the People's Bank to the National Conference on Cash Control. *HHYP*, III, no. 3 (January, 1951), 616. Subsequent Communist Chinese literature on money only emphasized that deposits formed the major "source of funds" for bank loans. A 1962 article pointed out the two-way relationship between lending and deposits and the effect of bank loans on the total supply of money. See Huang Ta, "Principles of Bank Credit and the Circulation of Money," *CCYC*, no. 9, 1962, pp. 1–7. This view was immediately rebuked. See Lin Tsi-k'eng, "On the Function of the Law of Circulation of Money under Socialism," *CCYC*, no. 2, 1963, pp. 24–30.

II

THE BANKING SYSTEM — GENERAL

◉ THE FIRST MONETARY PROBLEM faced by the Chinese Communists when their government was established in the Mainland in 1949 was naturally one of institutional reorganization. That is to say, it was necessary for the central authority to create an appropriate banking system as quickly as possible. The priority of this task was not only emphasized in the Marxian writings that guided the Chinese authorities,[1] but was also accentuated by the economic realities of the time. When the Mainland was taken over, China had suffered twelve years of continuous wars, domestic and foreign, and the economy was collapsing under a condition of severe inflation. In fact, the Chinese inflation was considered a major factor contributing to the decline of the Nationalist government and to the concurrent rise of the Communists.[2] The new government realized that in order to consolidate its control over the country it must quickly overcome this condition. Therefore, the most pressing economic problem of the time was monetary in nature. To deal with this, it was necessary to establish an effective centralized control over the banking system.

This task of building an appropriate banking system began as early as 1948, when a State Bank was created. In 1952, three years after the regime gained control of the Mainland, all banks were effectively brought under the supervision of the State Bank. In view of the backward and confused economic conditions of the time and the fact that,

---

[1] Most Chinese authors writing about banking quoted Lenin as well as Marx and Stalin on the importance of banks in socialism. For example, see Ch'en Yang-ch'ing, "On the Nature of the State Bank," *CKCJ*, no. 21, 1953, pp. 17–18; also Kao Hsiang, "On the Function of the State Bank in Socialist Construction," *CCYC*, no. 10, 1962, pp. 12–23.

[2] Shun-hsin Chou, *The Chinese Inflation.*

17

during the early years, mainly orthodox and indirect monetary measures were used in controlling private banks,[3] the new government appears to have been fairly successful in accomplishing a basic shift to a socialistic and centralized banking system within a relatively short period of time. From 1953 on, the problem was basically one of expanding the State Bank network and strengthening this network's control over money. In this chapter the development of the overall banking system will be examined. As is the case in the Soviet Union, some institutions in China that are called "banks" are really misnamed. They are in essence fiscal agencies rather than institutions dealing with money and credit. The only real "bank" in the Western sense of the word is the People's Bank of China, which is often referred to as the State Bank.[4] It is therefore logical, as a point of departure in examining the banking system, to classify all financial institutions into two categories: (1) the People's Bank and those organizations operating under its supervision; and (2) financial institutions that are called "banks" but are under the direct control of the Ministry of Finance.[5] The first group constitutes the banking system proper, while those in the second group are, strictly speaking, not banks.

The People's Bank and Banks under Its Supervision

Monetary institutions in this category include the People's Bank itself, the Bank of China, the Joint Public-Private Bank, the Agricultural Bank, which existed only briefly but was reopened, and the credit cooperatives, which for a while became credit departments of the communes. The last two were institutions concentrating in rural finance; they will be discussed more fully in Chapter III. Of all the above-mentioned

---

[3] Y. L. Wu, *An Economic Survey of Mainland China,* pp. 407–12. These measures included the regulation of interest rates, changes in legal reserve requirements, and changes in capital requirements, and are discussed later on in this chapter.

[4] The "People's Bank of China" and the "State Bank" are often used interchangeably in Communist Chinese writings.

[5] This classification is based on that used by Hsü T'i-hsin, *An Analysis of the Chinese National Economy during the Transitional Period: 1949–1957,* p. 200.

banks, only the People's Bank and the Agricultural Bank are completely state owned; the others are nominally and partially owned by individuals or groups.

THE PEOPLE'S BANK OF CHINA

The People's Bank is the only legal money-creating organ in the country. This is true whether "money" refers to currency, to bank credit, or to both. Therefore it is in essence the all-inclusive monetary institution under the Communist government. The role and functions of this most important Bank will be discussed in Chapter IV. A short description of its organizational setup is presented here in order to throw light on its relationship to the other banks.

The People's Bank of China came into existence on December 1, 1948, as the product of an amalgamation of three Communist banks which previously existed in different areas of North China.[6] The purpose of the merger was to provide a unified Communist currency for circulation in the whole of North China, which at that time was being rapidly occupied by the Communists. Thereafter, as the Communists advanced into Central and South China in 1949 and 1950, the People's Bank took over the government banks left behind by the Nationalists, including the Central Bank of China. At the same time, the People's Bank also absorbed Communist banks scattered in these parts of the country.[7]

From the establishment of the Communist government on October 1, 1949 until the adoption of the Constitution in September, 1954, the Main Office of the People's Bank, located in Peking, was under the direct control of the Government Administration Council (GAC). The Bank's

---

[6] The three banks were The Bank of North China, the North Sea Bank, and the Northwest Peasants' Bank. Before the Communist regime was established, there were numerous Communist banks existing in the occupied areas; each bank issued a separate currency for circulation in its own area. For a discussion of these banks and currencies, and also of the process of unification of these currencies, see Tseng and Han, "Money in Circulation in the Liberated Areas, 1948–1949," *CCYC,* no. 3, 1955, pp. 109–23. A similar presentation also appears in *The Circulation of Money in the People's Republic of China* by the same authors, retranslated into English from the Russian translation *JPRS* #3317 (1960), pp. 10–29.

[7] For example, in March, 1949, Chung-chou Peasants' Bank became the regional branch of the People's Bank in Central China. *Ibid.,* pp. 114 and 10, respectively.

status paralleled that of the Ministry of Finance, the latter being also under the GAC. The GAC was the highest executive organ of the country.[8] During this period the country was divided into six administrative regions, each headed by a Military and Administration Commission that represented the central government in these regions. The People's Bank also had regional offices which were controlled by the Financial and Economic Committees of these commissions. At the provincial and municipal levels the People's Bank had branches *(fen-hang)* that were controlled by the Financial Departments of the Military Control Commissions at these levels. Within the provinces there were field branches *(chih-hang)* in counties *(hsien)* and cities, each also supervised by the local government.[9]

Under the urban branches (i.e., branches in municipalities or field branches in cities), there were offices *(pan-shi-ch'u)* located in different sections of town; these were further divided into suboffices *(fen-li-ch'u)* covering various streets. In addition, these urban divisions were supplemented, usually for the purpose of absorbing small savings, by large numbers of saving booths, mobile banks, service stations, and other devices designed to reach the mass of people. These supplementary units were located on street corners, in government buildings, or anywhere that was convenient.

Outside the urban areas, county banks (i.e., field branches in counties) were the highest level of banks in rural finance.[10] In a given rural area, one of the county banks may be designated as the "central field branch" *(chung-hsin chih-hang),* which, in addition to serving as a county bank in its own county, concurrently assumed a supervisory and coordinating role over other county banks in the area. Below the county banks, a network of business offices *(ying-yeh-so)* was created in market towns *(chen)* or centrally located districts *(ch'ü).* These business offices formed the base of the pyramid of the People's Bank's hierarchy in the country-

---

[8] There were four Committees under the GAC, each supervising a group of ministries. Both the People's Bank and the Ministry of Finance were under the Committee on Financial and Economic Affairs, which was the highest financial policy-making body.

[9] Starlight, *Fiscal and Monetary Policies in Communist China,* pt. II, chap. I.

[10] All branches above the county banks had departments of rural finance, but these higher level branches also had other important duties, whereas the county bank's main concern was with rural finance.

side. They were the hubs of rural finance, handling rural deposits as well as dispensing agricultural loans and supervising the formation of credit cooperatives. Many business offices began as agents or mobile units and gradually developed into permanent bank offices. One important responsibility of the rural banking network was to supervise credit cooperatives. These cooperatives, although not officially part of the People's Bank, were nevertheless directed closely by the Bank; in effect, they served as the Bank's local units.[11]

The constitution that was adopted in 1954 replaced the GAC with the State Council; the latter was designated as "the Central People's Government." The People's Bank and the Ministry of Finance were directly under the State Council. The regional administrative system was abolished, and to accommodate this change the People's Bank also eliminated its regional branches. The rest of the banking hierarchy remained similar to the one that existed before 1954, except that, in 1958, the previously independent credit cooperatives became officially an integral part of the Bank.

The accompanying outline summarizes the organization of the People's Bank of China after 1954.

Two features stand out in the organization of the People's Bank. The first is centralization: the Bank's network spreads downward from the national capital until it covers the urban and rural areas of the entire country. Until 1958 all major monetary and banking policy decisions were made by the Main Office of the Bank, and plans for local banking activities were coordinated and approved from above. The general decentralization of authority that took place during the Great Leap in 1958 changed the picture somewhat, but the resulting chaos forced a return to more centralized monetary and banking control.

The second feature is dual control: with the exception of the Main Office, which is directly subordinate to the central government, all banking offices are subject to a twofold supervision. Each office is responsible to the bank level immediately above it; at the same time it is also subject to the leadership of the local government, which receives

---

[11] For the organization of rural banking, see "Summary Records of the First National Conference on Rural Finance," *CKCJ,* no. 7, 1951, pp. 21–34.

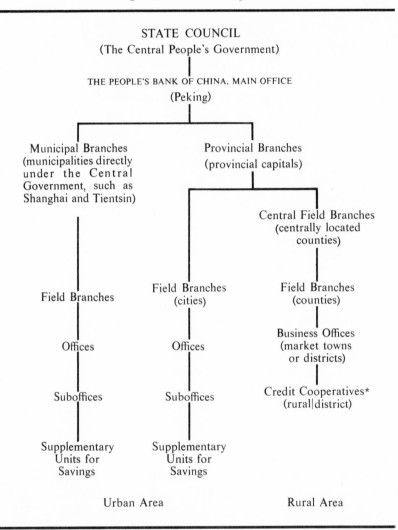

STATE COUNCIL
(The Central People's Government)

THE PEOPLE'S BANK OF CHINA, MAIN OFFICE
(Peking)

Municipal Branches
(municipalities directly
under the Central
Government, such as
Shanghai and Tientsin)

Provincial Branches
(provincial capitals)

Central Field Branches
(centrally located
counties)

Field Branches

Field Branches
(cities)

Field Branches
(counties)

Offices

Offices

Business Offices
(market towns
or districts)

Suboffices

Suboffices

Credit Cooperatives*
(rural|district)

Supplementary
Units for
Savings

Supplementary
Units for
Savings

Urban Area

Rural Area

*For the relationship with credit cooperatives, see text.

orders in turn from the central government. The 1958 decentralization
gave the local party and government administration more authority,

including complete control over local banks, but the subsequent collapse of monetary discipline soon made it necessary for the Main Office to reassert its control over the banking hierarchy.

THE BANK OF CHINA

Under the Nationalist government, the Bank of China was a public-private bank with two-thirds of its capital coming from the government and one-third from individuals. On March 22, 1950, by order of the GAC, the Bank was reorganized; the public shares which had been taken over by the Communists were represented by a new group of directors. One of the new directors was Nan Han-ch'en, then the Director of the People's Bank, who became the Chairman of the Board of the Bank of China two weeks after the reorganization.[12] From then on the Bank of China was for all practical purposes a subsidiary of the People's Bank.

The Bank of China was organized in 1908 to serve as a central bank.[13] Under the Nationalist government it concentrated on international banking activities with a network of branches and correspondents around the world. Under the Communist government it became a special bank for the management of foreign exchange and international payments. It implemented exchange control, managed all operations relating to foreign currencies and securities, and generally served as the exclusive international financial institution. Two additional business objectives of the Bank of China during the early Communist years were (1) to facilitate overseas Chinese remittances and (2) to promote foreign trade conducted by private importers and exporters.[14] In order to achieve the second goal, it probably also undertook the financing of international trade carried out by individual merchants in the early period. However, as foreign trade was gradually monopolized by the state, this function of the Bank of China became obsolete.

Throughout the First Five Year Plan period the Bank of China re-

[12] "Order of the GAC of the Central People's Government on the Strengthening of Supervision and Control over the Bank of China," *Central TCCT,* I, 267.

[13] Wu Ch'eng-hsi, *Banks in China,* p. 5.

[14] Chan (Vice-President, Bank of China), "How the Bank of China Coordinated the Drive to Develop Private Business," *CKCJ,* no. 9, September, 1951, p. 24.

tained the form of a joint public-private corporation with limited liabilities.[15] Since it was a special bank solely for international finance, its impact on the domestic money supply was negligible, being limited to the conversion of private holdings of foreign exchange into Chinese currency. By law all foreign exchange holdings within the country, including those belonging to overseas Chinese, foreign travelers, embassies, and missions, must be deposited with the Bank of China. They could be withdrawn within the country only after being converted into domestic currency at a fixed exchange rate.[16] To the extent that such conversions took place, the Bank of China was able to increase the domestic supply of money. The main source of this supply consisted of remittances from overseas Chinese, which could not have been large relative to the total domestic money supply. The Bank of China had no influence on domestic credit since all state trade inside the country, including trade in imported and exported goods, appeared to be financed by the People's Bank. The official foreign exchange rates quoted by the Bank of China were essentially arbitrary because the domestic economy was not responsive to changes in international prices.[17]

The Bank of China gained control over foreign branches in countries that had established relations with Communist China. They included offices in Hongkong, Singapore, London, Penang, Kuala Lumpur, Calcutta, Bombay, Karachi, Djakarta, and Rangoon.[18] By 1959 the Bank also had agencies and correspondent banks in France, West Germany, the Netherlands, Switzerland, Austria, Belgium, and Italy.[19]

THE JOINT PUBLIC-PRIVATE BANK

The Joint Public-Private Bank evolved from the private and semiprivate banks that existed under the Nationalist government. On the eve of the

[15] Hsü T'i-hsin, *An Analysis of the Chinese National Economy . . . ,* p. 201. Hsü was one of the directors of the Bank of China appointed by the government in 1950 during the reorganization of the bank.

[16] For foreign exchange control regulations, see *East China TCCT,* pp. 516–26.

[17] The official exchange rate announced on March 1, 1955, was £ 1 = ¥6.93.

[18] Branches in other places, among them the Bank of China in New York, remain under the Bank of China of the Nationalist Government in Taiwan. Furthermore, offices in Penang and Kuala Lumpur were closed in 1959, while those in Bombay and Calcutta were closed in 1962.

[19] Ts'ao (Director of PB), "Monetary Affairs in the Past Ten Years," *JMST,* 1960, p. 90.

Communist takeover, there were over nine hundred such banking institutions in the country. This number included traditional banking houses as well as modern banks and trusts.[20] A large portion of them did not survive the first year of the Communist rule. Their closings were a direct result of the more stringent banking regulations imposed by the new government. However, many of them might have been unsound banking institutions since they originated or grew during the period of galloping inflation.[21]

Regulations promulgated by the Communist government in 1949 placed all private banks under the supervision of the People's Bank and specified the ratios of reserves. There were two kinds of reserves to be deposited with the People's Bank; the total was around 20 percent, and later raised to 30 percent for demand deposits.[22] The 1949 regulations also limited the amount of loans made by the private banks to 50 percent of their deposit liabilities, prohibited the holding of stocks of commercial enterprises or participation in commodity speculations, and set minimum capital requirements for different types of banks.[23] These capital requirements, which were later raised to higher levels, proved fatal to many weaker banking institutions; and a large number of them collapsed early in 1950. Other banks with more solid foundations struggled on. It was difficult for the private banks to maintain their positions because the People's Bank held a monopoly over all deposits from the

[20] Tseng and Han, *The Circulation of Money in the People's Republic of China* (*JPRS* translation), p. 60. Also see Yang Yin-fu, "After Reading the New Measures on the Supervision of Private Monetary Enterprises," *HHYP*, I (November, 1949), 137. Records of the (Nationalist) Central Bank of China showed that there were 1,719 financial institutions in June, 1947. This larger figure was perhaps due to the inclusion of small money shops that, together with traditional banks, accounted for 995 of the 1,719 financial institutions. Chou Shun-hsin, *The Chinese Inflation*, p. 209.

[21] For example, of the 232 modern and native banks that existed in Shanghai at the end of 1948, half of them were established after 1945. "The Change of the Shanghai Financial Market in the Past Four Years," *CCCP*, no. 22, 1953, p. 23. From June, 1946, to June, 1947, there was a threefold increase in the number of native banks and money shops in China. Chou Shun-hsin, *The Chinese Inflation*, pp. 208–10.

[22] The two kinds of reserves may be translated as "required reserve" and "cash reserve." It is not clear what the distinction was, except that one of them was more variable; see Yang Yin-fu, "After Reading the New Measures . . . ," *HHYP*, I (November, 1949).

[23] For details of these regulations see "Temporary Measures on the Control of Private Monetary Enterprises in North China," *Central TCCT*, I, 267–70. A summary translation of these regulations appears in Starlight, *Fiscal and Monetary Policies in Communist China*, pp. 172–76. For later changes in reserve ratios and capital requirements see Nan, "Report Regarding the National Joint Financial Conference," *Central TCCT*, II, 538.

expanding public sector, which included government organs and state enterprises. Even in the private sector, the private banks had to compete with the People's Bank. As a monetary measure to stop the inflation, the People's Bank rigorously organized new ways to attract deposits from individuals and private business, leaving the private banks little room in which to expand their operations. In addition, the People's Bank controlled interest rates on loans and deposits and gradually lowered them to the prewar level. Under these conditions private banks were slowly being squeezed into an unprofitable situation. The People's Bank promised coexistence and credit assistances; at the same time, it encouraged private banks to solve their difficulties by cooperating among themselves and by pooling their resources to form loan syndicates for industrial investments. In certain cases the People's Bank participated in such joint adventures, thus converting them into public-private enterprises.[24] The sphere of cooperation among private banks expanded; by 1951 clusters of private banks consolidated into five public-private banks.[25] At the end of 1952, when private business was especially depressed as a result of the three-anti and five-anti movements[26] and when bank income again declined, a Joint Board of Directors of Public-Private Banks was organized and a combined Head Office was established to hold centralized control of the five banks. Branches of the constituent banks became branches of the new Joint Bank. It was through this process of gradual combination that all important private and semi-private banking enterprises (except for three which served overseas

---

[24] "Private Monetary Enterprises in Various Areas Formed Loan Syndicates," *HHYP*, II, no. 2 (June, 1950), 376.

[25] For the process of amalgamation and a list of these banks, see Starlight, *Fiscal and Monetary Policies in Communist China*, pp. 177–79; also Miyashita, *The Currency and Financial Systems of Mainland China* (Seattle), chap. VI.

[26] The three-anti movement was a campaign directed against public officials and contained three elements: anti-bureaucratism, anti-corruption and anti-waste. The five-anti movement had as its target the private business sector and was against (1) bribery of public officials, (2) tax evasion, (3) theft of public properties, (4) fraud in fulfilling government contracts, and (5) theft of government economic information. The net result of these campaigns amounted to the imposition of a capital levy on businessmen in the form of payments of back taxes and fines. Such payments were estimated to be 2 to 3 billion yuan, according to an unconfirmed report cited in Rostow, *The Prospects for Communist China*, p. 80.

Chinese)[27] were gathered into one single institution—the Joint Public-Private Bank. This new bank operated under the guidance of the People's Bank. When its Head Office was moved from Shanghai to Peking in May, 1953, it became, in reality, an agent of the People's Bank.

The Joint Public-Private Bank was the first socialistic institution created out of private enterprise in Communist China. Two stages of this transformation can be distinguished. The first stage involved the coordination of certain banking activities and the pooling of the banks' resources; this was referred to by the Communists as the "primary form" or "low stage" of state capitalism, under which the banking institutions were predominantly privately owned and presumably still operated for profit. The second stage witnessed a gradual movement to merge into a single bank; this was considered an "advanced form" or "high stage" of state capitalism, under which the constituent banks were paid a fixed rate of return on their invested capital.[28] This practice of paying a fixed rate of return on capital was followed later when other private business was transformed into joint public-private enterprise controlled by the state. The two-stage process also had parallels in later years during the socialization of agriculture.

The formation of the Joint Public-Private Bank in December, 1952, signified the end of the private banking era in China. This in turn meant that the supremacy of the People's Bank in domestic money and credit was established and that the basic banking structure necessary for the Soviet-type economy was built. The success in nationalizing private banks greatly increased the momentum of socialization. Beginning in 1953, private industrial and commercial firms had no source of credit and no way to transfer funds other than through channels controlled by the People's Bank. The granting or withholding of credit by the state bank became a powerful instrument for controlling these firms, thereby expediting their transformations. The socialization of industry and trade in turn curtailed the area of activities of the Joint Public-Private Bank

---

[27] Tseng and Han, *The Circulation of Money in the People's Republic of China,* (*JPRS* #3317), p. 49. The exceptions probably referred to the Overseas Chinese Investment Companies. See Miyashita, *The Currency and Financial Systems of Mainland China,* pp. 121–22.

[28] Tseng and Han, *The Circulation of Money . . . ,* pp. 60–61.

since the Bank's operations were confined to the private sector. Thus the business of the Joint Bank declined drastically after 1953.

Meanwhile, a proposal was made in a 1954 conference on urban savings to the effect that a special bank on savings should be contemplated.[29] This suggestion was consistent with the Soviet pattern of banking systems and with the spirit of the Chinese "credit reform" of 1954–1955. Experiments in creating an independent savings organization were first carried out in Peking and Shanghai; in February, 1955, they were extended to the fourteen cities where branches of the Joint Public-Private Bank were located. In each city the Joint Bank merged with the savings department of the People's Bank and became an agent devoted to urban savings.[30] Although a special savings bank had not been formally established, the major function of the Joint Public-Private Bank during the First Five Year Plan period remained the management of savings deposits for the People's Bank.[31] It is possible that the Joint Bank may eventually develop into a counterpart of the Savings Bank of the U.S.S.R., serving as a special institution dealing exclusively with deposits from individuals.

RURAL BANKING INSTITUTIONS

Certain banking institutions operated solely in rural areas. Since 80 percent of the Chinese population was engaged in farming and since the agricultural sector was less amenable to centralized control, rural banking posed a formidable challenge to the effort of the People's Bank in extending its influence throughout the country. Broadly speaking, conditions in the farm areas were not only chaotic but also subject to frequent dramatic changes, and the banking system was an important instrument for the exertion of government control and the implementation of government policy. The creation of two banks in 1951 and 1955, called the Agricultural Cooperative Bank and the Agricultural Bank,

---

[29] Hu Ching-yün (Deputy-Director of PB), "Report to the National Conference of Outstanding Worker's Representatives on Savings," *CKCJ*, no. 8, 1956, pp. 5–9.

[30] Wang Wei-ts'ai, "Guidelines for Works on Urban Savings in 1955," *CKCJ*, no. 3, 1955, pp. 5–6.

[31] Hsü T'i-hsin, *An Analysis of the Chinese National Economy . . .* , p. 202.

respectively, furnished repeated evidence of Communist China's desire to organize a bank specializing in agriculture. Neither of these banks survived for very long, and a third bank for agriculture was established in December, 1963. In addition, there were the credit cooperatives, which were officially not a part of the banking system but were nevertheless powerful supplements to the People's Bank in the management of rural finance. Because of the special significance of rural banking, and also for ease of presentation, discussion of these institutions is postponed. Chapter III will concentrate on rural banking and incidentally also provide some necessary background information about the agricultural sector.

Banks under the Supervision of the Ministry of Finance

Two banks were directly controlled by the Ministry of Finance—the Bank of Communications and the Bank of Construction. These banks were considered a part of the banking system, but in reality they functioned as fiscal agencies.

THE BANK OF COMMUNICATIONS[32]

The history of the Bank of Communications was similar to that of the Bank of China. It was another Nationalist government bank which was taken over and retained by the Communists as a special bank. The Bank of Communications was established in 1907, mainly with private capital;[33] it was reorganized by the Nationalists in 1935 to increase govern-

---

[32] This section is based on the following sources: Chou Shun-hsin, *The Chinese Inflation,* pp. 186–87; Cheng Po-pin, *The New Money and Credit System,* pp. 106–12; Hsü T'i-hsin, *An Analysis of the Chinese National Economy* . . . , p. 202; Chang P'ing-tze (Assistant General Manager, Bank of Communications), "Strengthen Financial Supervision over Public-Private Enterprises," *TKP,* September 18, 1955; Starlight, *Fiscal and Monetary Policies in Communist China,* pt. III, chap. I; Su, *Practical Dictionary on the National Economy,* p. 8005.

[33] Wu Ch'eng-hsi, *Banks in China,* p. 5. The Bank of Communications was established to handle the funds of the government-owned postal and communication systems, among other functions.

ment participation in its ownership and management. In 1949 the Communist regime assumed control of the public shares as well as of shares confiscated from "war criminals," and the bank continued to operate as a joint public-private enterprise. Through a process of reorganization identical with the one that had taken place two months earlier in the Bank of China, the Director of the People's Bank was named Chairman of the Board of the Bank of Communications in June, 1950, thereby subordinating this bank to the People's Bank. The reorganized Bank of Communications was entrusted with the management of long term investments. There were two facets to this function; until 1954, the Bank of Communications was in charge of both.

First, there were "basic construction" investments made by the state in all areas, including industry, agriculture, transportation, education, public health, government administration, and others.[34] Such investments in the early years encompassed (1) major repairs and postwar rehabilitation of capital equipment and buildings, (2) the expansion of existing state enterprises, and (3) the construction of new state enterprises. Funds for basic construction were appropriated from the national budget in the form of interest-free, nonrepayable grants. In December, 1950, the management of these appropriations was delegated to the Bank of Communications through the People's Bank by the Ministry of Finance. The duty of the Bank of Communications was to supervise their distribution and disbursements so that payments would be made only to enterprises and construction units that progressed according to plans and estimates previously submitted and approved. In fulfilling this function the Bank of Communications was temporarily serving as the Chinese equivalent of the Soviet Prombank. However, in 1954 a new state-owned bank, the Bank of Construction, was formed to take charge of funds for basic construction; and the Bank of Communications was relieved of this duty.

A second facet of the management of long-term investment was the control of government shares in joint public-private enterprises. The

[34] Basic construction investment means investment in fixed capital assets in both materially productive (industry, etc.) and nonproductive (government buildings, etc.) sectors. A fixed capital asset is defined as one with at least one year's life and a minimum cost of ¥500. Choh-ming Li, *Economic Development* . . . , p. 113.

Communists inherited from the Nationalists a great number of long-term investments in this form. They were scattered in many different fields, such as industry, mining, public utilities, and commerce, and were formerly owned and managed by the various ministries concerned. In October, 1950, the Communist government announced that the ownership of all public shares in joint enterprises was to be transferred to the Ministry of Finance and that the management of these shares was to be delegated by the Ministry of Finance to the People's Bank; the latter in turn entrusted the task to the Bank of Communications.[35] From then on, the Bank of Communications represented the state interest in these jointly owned companies. It handled dividends of public shares, supervised the internal financial management of joint enterprises, and controlled funds reserved by these enterprises for future capital expansions. Furthermore, by extending state long-term investments to private business firms, thereby transforming them into joint enterprises, the Bank of Communications gradually invaded the private sector, bringing the latter's financial affairs under its sphere of influence. As the socialization process of private enterprise proceeded toward its conclusion, the importance of the Bank of Communications began to decline. When in February, 1956, the State Council decreed that private shares in joint enterprises were to be paid a fixed rate of return regardless of the financial condition of the firms,[36] complete socialist control was in effect accomplished, and the Bank's supervisory role over joint enterprises became redundant.[37] However, the Bank continued to exist in 1958, as is evident from the fact that it was declared an administrative organ in that year.[38]

Although in the early years the Bank of Communications was con-

---

[35] Cheng Po-pin, *The New Money and Credit System,* p. 108.

[36] SC, "Regulations on the Implementation of Fixed Dividend Rate in Public-Private Joint Enterprise," *HHPYK,* no. 5, 1956, p. 70.

[37] Hsü T'i-hsin, *An Analysis of the Chinese National Economy . . . ,* p. 202.

[38] Ministry of Finance, "Report on the Nature of Organization and the Problems of Administration and Decentralization Regarding the Bank of Construction and the Bank of Communications," *FKHP,* VII (January–June, 1958), 279–80. Before 1958, the Bank of Communications charged a commission amounting to 3 percent of the net income of the public-private joint enterprises. This was eliminated in 1958, when all joint enterprise income was submitted to local government budgets, which, in turn, provided the Bank with an appropriation to cover its operating expenses.

31

sidered a part of the People's Bank system and was controlled by the People's Bank, it was later directly subordinated to the Ministry of Finance.[39] This latter organizational setup was clearly more logical since the function of the Bank of Communications had always been that of a fiscal agent, handling funds belonging to the budget and to the Ministry of Finance. In spite of the fact that it kept deposit accounts of construction units and contractors and that it managed the transfer of payments among these units, funds supervised by the Bank of Communications were actually deposited in the People's Bank. The Bank of Communications did not issue currency or grant credit of its own. Therefore, it had no direct influence on the supply of money. To the extent that it was a bank, it was one with 100 percent reserves.

THE BANK OF CONSTRUCTION

Before 1954, when the management of long-term investments for basic construction was in the hands of the Bank of Communications, a condition of general laxity of control prevailed. Estimates for construction projects (according to the approved version of which the Bank issued payments) were inaccurate and were usually too high. This resulted in such wastes as unnecessary accumulation of raw materials inventories, inefficient use of labor, poor quality of work, and even use of funds for unplanned construction.[40] In order to strengthen controls over capital investment, the State Council decided in September, 1954, to create a People's Bank of Construction of China (commonly called the Construction Bank or the Bank of Construction) directly under the jurisdiction of the Ministry of Finance.[41] The main office of the new bank and a network of branch offices began operation on October 1, when all accounts involving state long-term investments were handed over by the Bank of Communications. The fundamental objective was still distributing funds for state capital investments efficiently and economically and

---

[39] Hsü T'i-hsin, *An Analysis of the Chinese National Economy . . . ;* also Ministry of Finance, "Report on the Nature of Organization . . . ," p. 279.

[40] Ko, *The Chinese Budget during the Transitional Period,* pp. 112–13.

[41] SC, "Decision on the Establishment of the People's Bank of Construction of China," *JMST,* 1955, pp. 440–41.

ensuring a smooth progress of planned capital construction. To achieve this the Bank of Construction had to supervise the actual operation of all construction units, carefully scrutinize their budgets, enforce "economic accounting" (i.e., cost accounting), provide advance payments for the purchase of needed materials, check the progress of construction, and ensure that allocated funds were used for the specific purposes intended. In view of the complexity of this task, it is perhaps not surprising that the new Bank has been criticized for falling short of achieving its goal. It tended to operate as a supplier of funds without exercising adequate supervision over the construction projects; at the same time, its methods of making payments were complex, mechanical, and slow.[42]

The resources of the Bank of Construction, like those of the Bank of Communications before it, consisted primarily of budget appropriations. One major difference between the two banks was this: whereas the Bank of Communications allocated funds for long-term investments only, the Bank of Construction also granted short-term loans to building contractors to be used as working capital. It is not clear as to how the Construction Bank financed these short-term loans. There are several possible methods. First, the Construction Bank might have been allowed to create bank credit of its own; second, the Construction Bank might have utilized the idle balance of funds appropriated by the budget for capital investment but not yet spent; third, short-term loans might have been granted by the People's Bank to the Construction Bank, which in turn might have allocated them to building contractors, thereby maintaining a unified control over the progress of all capital constructions.

The first hypothesis is contrary to a basic tenet of the Chinese banking system—the tenet that requires the People's Bank to serve as the sole credit-creating institution in the country. The second encroaches on another fundamental principle, one that dictates a strict separation of funds for basic constructions from those for working capital. Logically, then, only the third method could have been adopted. This logical conclusion appears to be consistent with the actual regulation that required the Construction Bank to provide short-term loans "according to the

---

[42] "The Quality and Quantity of Work on the Allocation of Funds and the Supervision of Basic Construction Must Be Raised," Editorial in *TKP,* March 6, 1955; Ko, *The Chinese Budget during the Transitional Period,* pp. 113–14.

approved credit plan of the nation." This credit plan, drawn up annually by the People's Bank, determined the amounts and the allocations of credit granted by the People's Bank to various organizations. Thus it is not unreasonable to assume that, despite its power to grant short-term loans to building contractors, the Construction Bank could not actually create or affect the total money supply, and that all of its operations were financed either by the budget or by the People's Bank. Therefore the Construction Bank was probably also a bank with 100 percent reserves.

The 1958 decentralization affected the system of capital investment control and therefore also the organization of the Bank of Construction. Until that year basic construction funds were centrally controlled by the Main Office of the Bank of Construction. A State Council regulation of 1958 transferred the responsibility for the allocation of funds to the Finance Offices of the local governments. Meanwhile, in the center, the Bank of Construction was reorganized into a "Basic Construction Finance Division" of the Ministry of Finance, while retaining the Bank's name for outside dealings. Local branches of the Bank could be eliminated, retained, or reorganized at the discretion of local governments.[43]

The Growth of the State Banking System

From the foregoing description it is clear that by the end of the First Five Year Plan the monetary institutions in China had been very much simplified. The center was the network of the People's Bank, supplemented by the credit cooperatives in rural finance, by the Joint Public-Private Bank in urban savings, and by the Bank of China in international transactions. Of these the Bank of China is of less importance in this study, which deals with the domestic aspects of money. On the other hand, both the Bank of Communications and the Bank of Construction were fiscal rather than monetary organizations. Therefore, by about 1957 the framework affecting the domestic monetary structure con-

[43] PB, "Notice on State Council Regulations Regarding Improvements of Financial Administration in Respect to Capital Construction," *CJFKHP*, 1958–1960. Translated version: *JPRS* #19,499, p. 259. Similar regulations appear in *JMST*, 1959, p. 369.

The Growth of the State Banking System, 1950–1959

	The People's Bank			Credit cooperatives	Urban savings			Volunteer workers (thousands)
	Employees* (thousands) (1)	Branches		(4)	Savings offices (5)	Savings† agents (6)	Total (5) + (6) (7)	(8)
		Total (2)	Rural (3)					
Early 1950	50[a]	700[g]	—	—	—	—	—	—
Dec. 1950	75[b]	—	—	103	—	—	—	—
May 1951	165[c]	2,000[g]	1,600[g]	538	—	—	—	—
Oct. 1951	—	5,300[h]	—	—	—	—	—	—
Dec. 1952	345[d]	11,089[i]	8,456[i]	2,271	—	—	—	—
Dec. 1953	377[d]	—	—	9,418	—	—	—	—
Dec. 1955	600[e]	15,000[p]	—	159,363	4,136[k]	3,548[m]	7,684[m]	120[m]
Dec. 1956	—	—	—	102,558	7,388[n]	25,194[n]	32,582[k]	350[n]
Oct. 1957	—	20,000[j]	—	—	—	—	—	—
Early 1958	500[f]	—	—	88,368	—	—	—	—
Nov. 1959	—	—	—	—	40,000[k]	60,000[o]	100,000[o]	360[o]

—Not available.

* Figures for 1950–1951 cover employees of the People's Bank only. Figures for 1952–1958 include all financial workers employed by the state banking system.

† Savings agents were located in various state enterprises, government organizations, and schools.

Sources:

[a] John Y. W. Liu, "Monetary System of Communist China," *Proceedings of the Symposium on Economic & Social Problems of the Far East*, p. 72.

[b] PB, "The Task of the State Bank in 1950," *Central TCCT*, III, 183.

[c] Starlight, *Fiscal and Monetary Policies in Communist China, 1949–1954*, p. 166.

[d] SSB, "Communique on the Development of the National Economy and the Implementation of the National Plan for 1953," *JMST*, 1955, p. 427.

[e] "National Conference of Branch Bank Managers Convened by the Main Office of the People's Bank," *CKCJ*, no. 4, 1956, p. 3.

[f] Tseng and Yang, "On the Leap in Monetary Works," *HH*, no. 9, 1958, p. 14.

[g] Nan, "Report to the First National Conference on Rural Finance, May 10, 1951," *Central TCCT*, III, 244, 250.

[h] Wang Ching-jian, "Important Achievements in the Country's Financial Structure during the Past Three Years," *CCCP*, no. 24, 1951, pp. 463–64.

[i] P'eng and Ho, *An Outline of the Theory of Money and Credit*, p. 350.

[j] "Great Developments in the People's Financial Enterprises," *JMST*, 1958, p. 571.

[k] Computed from related figures in other columns of this table.

[l] Column taken from Table III-3.

[m] Hu Ching-yün, Deputy-Director, PB, "Report to the National Conference of Outstanding Workers' Representatives on Savings," *CKCJ*, no. 8, 1956, p. 6.

[n] "A Brief Summary of Works on Savings during the Period of the First Five Year Plan," *CKCJ*, no. 5, 1958, p. 26.

[o] Ts'ao, "Monetary Affairs in the Past Ten Years," *JMST*, 1960, p. 89.

[p] Huang Ya-kuang, "A Lecture Delivered at the Training Class for the Administration of State Budgetary Receipts and Expenditures (Excerpts)," *CKCJ*. no. 22, 1955, p. 3.

sisted of the People's Bank, the rural credit cooperatives, and the Joint Public-Private Bank. The last was turned into organs for urban savings.

As the state-controlled banking system became unified and simplified, it also spread out to exert its influence in all corners of the Mainland. The speed with which this expansion of the banking system took place in domestic areas can be seen from the steep rise in the number of banking personnel and banking offices. These figures are shown in Table II-1.

Table II-1 conveys an impression of rapid growth. In addition, it indicates three phases in the process of the banking development. In the early years the People's Bank itself expanded, with most of the new branches located in rural areas (Field-Branches in counties, etc.); after 1953 the emphasis was shifted to the creation of credit cooperatives; finally, a year or two later, the drive to increase urban saving units began, and was greatly intensified during the Great Leap.

As will become clear in later discussions, the People's Bank operated directly in the socialized sector, controlling various enterprises, while the credit cooperatives and the urban saving units dealt with individuals and other more decentralized units. Thus, supported by numerous rural and urban financial organizations, the central position of the People's Bank over the economy was by and large established. In the next chapter we shall examine rural banking before going on to study the management of money by the People's Bank.

III

THE BANKING SYSTEM — RURAL

EVEN THOUGH a major proportion of the branches of the People's Bank were devoted to rural activities, these numerous units were still insufficient to cope with the heavy task the Bank was called upon to perform in the farm areas. In these extensive areas, production organizations were less centralized, and direct control was less developed. Consequently the government had to lean heavily on monetary control through the People's Bank. In order to ease the responsibility that fell on the shoulders of the People's Bank, two types of financial institution were created that engaged exclusively in rural banking activities. One was a special bank for agriculture, the other was the credit cooperative.

Banks Specializing in Agriculture

During the 1950s, two unsuccessful attempts were made to create a special bank dealing with agriculture. As distinct from most of the other banks in the system, these special banks were newly established organizations that did not evolve directly from previously existing institutions.[1] The repeated efforts to build a special agricultural bank will be discussed separately.

---

[1] Under the Nationalist government there was a Farmers' Bank which supplied agricultural capital. No specific information about this bank is available. It is probable that, like other Nationalist government banks, the Farmers' Bank was absorbed into the People's Bank system when the Communists took over the country. If so, the personnel and facilities of the Farmers' Bank might have provided a base to be later transformed into a bank for agriculture.

THE AGRICULTURAL COOPERATIVE BANK

The first attempt to create a bank for agriculture was made in July, 1951, when the Agricultural Cooperative Bank was formed.[2] The function of the new bank was to supervise state investments and long-term credit for the development of agriculture, forestry, fishery, animal husbandry, land reclamation, and water conservation, as well as for the expansion of state farms and agricultural cooperatives. The management of state investments in agriculture, which was previously conducted by the Bank of Communications, was to be transferred to the new bank on September 1, 1951. During the period in which branches of the new bank were not yet established, the rural finance departments of the People's Bank network would serve as temporary substitutes.[3] However, it appeared that the Agricultural Cooperative Bank was never active.[4]

Judging from its assigned duties, the Agricultural Cooperative Bank was apparently a duplication of the Selhozbank in U.S.S.R.[5] The Soviet agricultural bank was an independent long-term credit institution entrusted with the task of financing the capital needs of agriculture. Two kinds of funds were handled by the Selhozbank. First, there were non-repayable grants to state agricultural enterprises that came directly from the national budget. These grants represented state investments in agriculture. Second, there was long-term credit, repayable with interest, for collectives and individual farmers. Resources for these loans consisted primarily of deposits made by the collective farms of that portion of the farms' funds that was earmarked for future capital investments.

It is not clear when the Agricultural Cooperative Bank was formally abolished. But the following developments in the 1950s indicated that the time was not yet ripe for the creation of an agricultural bank of the Soviet type.

[2] *JMJP,* July 8, 1951; also *HHYP,* IV, no. 4 (August, 1951), 875.

[3] Su, Practical Dictionary on the National Economy, p. 9015.

[4] Y. L. Wu, *An Economic Survey of Communist China,* p. 413; Starlight, *Fiscal and Monetary Policies in Communist China,* p. 171.

[5] Hubbard, *Soviet Money and Finance,* pp. 101–103. In 1959, the Selhozbank and three other long-term investment banks were replaced by a construction bank (Stroibank). See Nove, *The Soviet Economy,* p. 113.

Table III-1
Budgetary Appropriations for Basic Construction at Current Prices, Total and Agricultural, 1952-1957

Year	Total (million ¥) (1)	Agricultural (million ¥) (2)	Proportion of agricultural appropriations to total appropriations (%) (3)
1952	5,014	517*	10.3
1953	8,145	588	7.2
1954	9,592	475	5.0
1955	9,518	556	5.8
1956	14,874	1,262	8.5
1957	13,008	983	7.6

* This figure represents actual investment within the state plan rather than budgetary appropriation; the latter figure is not available. Actual investments in agriculture (including water conservation) for other years are as follows: 1953: 652; 1954: 363; 1955: 601; 1956: 1,160.
Source:
Cols. (1) and (2): reprinted from Nai-Ruenn Chen, ed., *Chinese Economic Statistics: A Handbook for Mainland China* (Chicago: Aldine, 1967; copyright © 1967 Social Science Research Council), pp. 158, 165.
Col. (3): Col. (2) ÷ col. (1).

First, during 1952-1955, capital investments allocated by the state for agriculture, forestry, and water conservation, which constituted the total budget appropriation falling within the jurisdiction of the new Bank, were relatively small. This was true both in absolute and in percentage terms, as can be seen from Table III-1. Moreover, the overall trend of intended agricultural investment up to 1955 was downward. Since there was already a special bank which supervised all state appropriations for capital investments,[6] the relatively small and declining share of such appropriations that was devoted to agriculture did not seem to justify the creation of a new and separate organization. However, the amount of the appropriation for agriculture began to rise in 1955, when renewed efforts to establish a special rural bank were made.

Second, the situation of long-term credit in agriculture was also not very favorable. Figures published in 1955[7] indicate that, in the early 1950s, long-term agricultural loans amounted to less than half of the

[6] This was the Bank of Communications and, since 1954, the Bank of Constructions mentioned in the last chapter.
[7] The figures on total agricultural loans given by the Deputy-Director of the People's

Table III-2

Proportions of Long-Term and Short-Term Agricultural Loans, 1952–1954*

	Maximum loans outstanding†		Proportions	
Year	Million ¥ (1)	Index 1952=100 (2)	Long-term % (3)	Short-term % (4)
1952	374.01	100	34.8	65.2
1953	613.44	164	45.9	54.1
1954	804.24	215	42.2	57.8

* The amounts of loans presented in the article were 37,401; 61,344; and 80,424 and the unit was the yuan. The unit given was apparently a mistake since it was unreasonably small. The customary unit used in Communist Chinese banking statistics was ¥10,000, and it is assumed here that this customary unit applied. This assumption renders the amounts of total loans the right order of magnitude. See note 8 in the text.

† Loans outstanding equal the amount of loans granted minus the amount of loans repaid. The size of outstanding agricultural loan usually reaches its maximum around the middle of the year. Tseng Ling, "The Effects of Agricultural Collectivization on Rural Monetary Circulation," *CCYC*, no. 6, 1956, p. 43.

Source: Ch'en Hsi-yü, "Notes from Studying 'Soviet Credit Reform,'" *CJCK*, no. 79, in *TKP*, June 20, 1955.

total agricultural loans outstanding. This can be seen from Table III-2, column 3. The size of the outstanding loans, though growing rapidly between 1952 and 1954, was nevertheless small when compared with figures for later years. For example, in August, 1957, the balance of the agricultural loan reached 3.58 billion yuan.[8] Thus neither the size nor the composition of the agricultural credit lent themselves to the promotion of a Soviet-type agricultural bank.

Third, the Soviet Selhozbank's resources for agricultural credit came mainly from deposits by collective farms of funds reserved by the farms for capital replacement and growth. In China during the early 1950s the rural economy was still primarily individualistic. Cooperative funds earmarked for capital improvements did not yet exist to any significant extent.

Bank (Ch'en Hsi-yü) in 1955 differ from other agricultural loan statistics released in 1956 and 1957 (see Appendix B). However, Ch'en's is the only set of statistics available which gives the percentage breakdown on long- and short-term agricultural loans. Beginning in 1955 agricultural loans were no longer classified as long-term and short-term.

[8] Yang P'ei-hsin, "Ways to Raise Funds for Agricultural Development in Our Country," *CCYC*, no. 1, 1958, p. 32. This figure is used here merely to illustrate the order of magnitude; it is not strictly comparable with figures in Table III-2.

Finally, there were also physical barriers to the development of the Agricultural Cooperative Bank. In 1951 the People's Bank was undergoing rapid expansion and was straining the supply of trained banking personnel to the utmost.[9] It was difficult to organize another network of banks throughout the country.

THE AGRICULTURAL BANK[10]

In 1955 there was a second attempt to institute a separate bank in agriculture. On March 1 a State Council Directive called for the establishment of the Agricultural Bank of China, and on March 25 the main office of this new bank opened in Peking. The objectives in agriculture at that time were first increased production and second rural socialization, and the new bank was formed to promote these objectives. More specifically, the duties of the Agricultural Bank fell into four categories: (1) to attract rural savings and deposits; (2) to promote and supervise the development of rural credit cooperatives; (3) to manage long-term and short-term loans to individual producers, producers' cooperatives and state enterprises in agriculture, husbandry, fishery, forestry, and water conservation; and (4) to supervise the allocation and use of state capital investments in these fields. Until the network of the Agricultural Bank was firmly established, the last of these duties was to remain temporarily with the Bank of Construction.

The organizational setup of the Agricultural Bank paralleled that of the People's Bank and the government hierarchy. The new bank consisted of four levels: the Main Office in Peking, branches in provincial capitals, central field branches in special districts *(chuan ch'ü)* and field branches in counties *(hsien)*. The Main Office of the Agricultural Bank was directly subordinate to the Main Office of the People's Bank;

---

[9] Main Office, People's Bank, "Major Tasks of the State Bank in 1951," *Central TCCT,* III, 199.

[10] This section is based on materials from the following articles: "The Agricultural Bank of China Formally Inaugurated in Peking," *TKP,* March 26, 1955; Po Hsiang, "Why Do We Establish the Agricultural Bank of China?," *HHYP,* no. 5, 1955, pp. 176–78; Ch'en Hsi-yü, "Notes from Studying 'Soviet Credit Reform,'" *CJCK,* no. 79, reprinted in *TKP,* June 20, 1955; "An Important Measure on the State's Support to Agricultural Production," Editorial, *TKP,* March 27, 1955.

the latter, insofar as rural finance was concerned, was in turn subject to the control of the Seventh Office of the State Council. Below the Main Office, each level of the Agricultural Bank was responsible to three organizations: (1) the level of Agricultural Bank immediately above it, (2) same level of the People's Bank, and (3) same level of the government. This triangular relationship was considered necessary for the sake of better coordination and unified policy control.

The new bank operated with an independent accounting system, but its cash plan had to be integrated with that of the People's Bank.[11] According to the State Council Directive of March 1, 1955, the Agricultural Bank's funds were derived from three sources: funds from rural savings and deposits, budget appropriations for the Bank's capital and for agricultural credit, and temporary borrowing from the People's Bank. In reality, however, the Agricultural Bank depended mainly on the third source[12] and no budget appropriation was made for agricultural credit.[13]

THE AGRICULTURAL BANK AND CURRENT DEVELOPMENTS

In view of the failure of the Agricultural Cooperative Bank in 1951, it would be interesting to explore the cause of the revived interest in a special bank for agriculture. Looking at the overall situation in the country at the time, three strands of development stand out that appear to have had connections with the resurgence of the bank in agriculture. The first development could be called money and banking reform, the second was the collectivization drive, and the third related to the general economic policy. Their impact on the creation of the Agricultural Bank require closer examination.

Money and banking reform. As previously mentioned, in 1954–1955 there was a series of endeavors to develop further a Soviet-type mone-

---

[11] The cash plan specifies the total amounts of cash receipts and cash payments of the bank. The difference between receipts and payments of the cash plan of the People's Bank represents the planned increase or decrease of currency in circulation.

[12] Ch'en Hsi-yü, "Notes from Studying 'Soviet Credit Reform,'" *CJCK*, no. 79.

[13] Ts'ao (Director of the People's Bank), "Two Links in Solving the Problems of Agricultural Funds," *HHPYK*, no. 23, 1956, p. 85. Ts'ao pleaded for budget appropriations to cover long-term agricultural credit in order to avoid "imbalance in the national cash plan." This "imbalance"·meant an increase or decrease of currency in circulation.

tary structure. The steps taken were sometimes referred to as the "credit reform" in China. Measures implemented at this time included creation of the Bank of Construction, tightening of bank control over credit, and currency conversion.[14] The birth of the Agricultural Bank could logically be considered a part of this reform. In fact, it was first suggested by Soviet banking experts who advised on other phases of the reform. In their proposal to form a separate bank for the supervision of long-term agricultural credit, these advisers explained that "if the function of granting long-term credit were left with the State Bank which also issues currency, then the possibility of issuing too large a quantity of currency in circulation would result. This cannot be allowed."[15] This explanation implied that the management of long-term credit by the People's Bank could be inflationary, and this viewpoint was in line with the Soviet emphasis on the divorce of long-term and short-term credit institutions. In other words, what the advisers wanted was a resurrection of the Agricultural Cooperative Bank of 1951.

The Agricultural Bank established in 1955 departed from the model envisioned by the reformers in two respects: (1) it dealt with both long-term and short-term agricultural loans, rather than specializing in the former; and (2), perhaps more importantly considering the advisers' viewpoint on inflationary possibilities, the Chinese Agricultural Bank depended mainly on the State Bank for financial support. This meant that long-term credit issued by the Agricultural Bank had not in effect been divorced from the People's Bank; instead it could be based on credit expansion by the People's Bank. The banking officials, in an effort to defend the new bank, stated that the modifications were merely transitional arrangements better adapted to the existing Chinese conditions; they promised that it would eventually evolve into a special bank of the Soviet type.[16]

Since the established Agricultural Bank differed quite drastically from the proposed reform model, credit reform alone could not adequately account for the rise of this bank. We must therefore turn to other developments of the time for an explanation.

---

[14] The last two developments will be discussed in Chapters IV and VII.
[15] Ch'en Hsi-yü, "Notes from Studying 'Soviet Credit Reform,'" *CJCK*, no. 79.
[16] *Ibid.*

The collectivization drive. In the fall of 1955, there was a suddenly accelerated movement towards the formation of agricultural production cooperatives. Functionally, there were three types of cooperatives in the country areas: the credit cooperative, the supply and marketing cooperative, and the producers' or production cooperative. Each of these affected the Agricultural Bank in a different way.

Credit cooperatives were atomistic, local, rural financial organizations that served to channel savings and liquid funds held by individual peasants into short-term productive uses. The drive to form credit cooperatives gained momentum in 1954 and reached its peak in 1955.[17] To consolidate and strengthen centralized control over these rapidly formed "little peasants' banks" all over the countryside was a formidable task, and the Agricultural Bank was entrusted with this task in order to relieve the People's Bank of the responsibility.

The supply and marketing cooperatives functioned as local branches of the state commercial network in the rural areas. They supplied consumer and producer goods to the rural population and concurrently served as government agents in state purchases of farm produce. By 1954, all major crops could be sold only to the state,[18] and the supply and marketing cooperatives became channels through which large sums of money were released into circulation in the farm areas as payments for state purchases. One of the devices used to drain the resulting liquidity was the formation of credit cooperatives. The banking system could also remove some of the rural supply of money by encouraging savings deposits from individuals, as well as deposits of surplus funds from collective farms and credit cooperatives. The responsibility for "absorption" of savings and deposits became another major function assigned to the Agricultural Bank. However, the working capital that was needed by the supply and marketing cooperatives to finance their commercial operations was not provided by the Agricultural Bank. Instead it was directly supplied by the People's Bank as a part of the commercial credit furnished to the entire state trading network.

The agricultural producer's cooperative was the main concern of the

---

[17] The credit cooperatives will be discussed in detail later in this chapter.
[18] *Infra,* p. 54.

1955–1956 collectivization drive. Whereas in March, 1955, only 14.2 percent of the peasant farms belonged to cooperatives, mostly of the primary type, by the end of May, 1956, 91.2 percent of the country's farming households had already joined producers' cooperatives, of which more than half were of the "advanced" type.[19] By "advanced" producers' cooperatives were meant collective farms in which "means of production"—land, equipment, and draft animals—were collectively owned, and members were paid according to the number of workdays or workpoints they contributed. During the drive, rural credit played a crucial role, and the Agricultural Bank granted loans which promoted the formation and development of the collectives. Three kinds of loans were issued: a long-term loan to individuals called the "Poor Peasant's Cooperative Fund," a long-term loan to cooperatives for capital formation, and a short-term loan to cooperatives for productive expenditures. The objectives were twofold. The first was to create momentum for the collectivization movement. This was achieved by the first type of loan, which induced the poor and lower-middle peasants to join the collectives by enabling these peasants to acquire shares of the collectives with borrowed funds. The second objective was to assure the success of the movement. This was facilitated by the last two kinds of loans, which supplied the collectives with fixed and working capital in order to enhance their productive capacity.

In view of the Agricultural Bank's contribution in bringing about this relatively swift and sweeping change in rural organization, it would appear reasonable to consider the creation of the Bank in March, 1955, to be a step taken in anticipation of the collectivization drive that began six months later. However, a careful study of the timing of the decision to collectivize indicates that this causal relationship is spurious. In the spring, when the Bank was inaugurated, the announced agricultural policy was to consolidate and improve the existing producers' cooperatives rather than to create more of them.[20] It was not until summer that the decision to socialize agriculture on a grand scale was reached.

[19] SSB, "Statistical Materials on Agricultural Collectivization and the Distribution of Products in Cooperatives in 1955," *HHPYK*, no. 20, 1956, pp. 63–65.
[20] SC, "Resolution Concerning Spring Ploughing and Production," *FKHP*, I, 368–76. This resolution was dated March 3, 1955.

Thus, although the Agricultural Bank facilitated the collectivization drive, the drive cannot in itself explain the resurrection of the specialized bank.

The general economic policy. One final plausible explanation for the birth of the Agricultural Bank in 1955 can be found in the general economic policy adopted under the First Five Year Plan. This policy favored the development of industry, especially heavy industry; hence a predominant share of state investment was directed thereto. Budgetary appropriations for investment in agriculture were insignificant and, as mentioned above, this lack of emphasis on agriculture partly accounts for the redundancy of the earlier Agricultural Cooperative Bank. The unbalanced development policy nurtured the nation's industrial growth, which in turn raised the demand for agricultural products both as raw materials and as urban consumers' goods. To meet this increased demand, the "planned purchase and planned supply" system was introduced at the end of 1953, effectively boosting the state's acquisition of essential agricultural products by means of trade monopoly and compulsory quotas.[21] However, a long-run solution required agricultural growth and, given the nation's economic policy, the farm sector had to rely on nonbudgetary investments derived either through credit expansion or through savings generated within the rural sector. The movement to form credit cooperatives in 1954 was a step to mobilize scattered money savings in the individualistic rural areas; and the creation in 1955 of the Agricultural Bank, which attempted to centralize these savings and direct them toward agricultural investment, became a logical culmination of this policy.

From this viewpoint, then, the Agricultural Bank was an instrument whereby farm production might be raised through the organization of private savings and investments; it tried to marshal resources from within the countryside to promote agricultural growth. Thus it constituted a countervailing measure to correct the agricultural lag caused by the nation's one-sided investments. Under the setup of early 1955, the nation's industry was supported primarily by the fiscal budget, whereas agriculture was left to depend on capital collected from the

---

[21] The system is more fully explained later on in this chapter.

peasants through rural banking. The latter was a more indirect, less socialistic method of financing investment; and the ownership of the invested resources, which assumed the form of savings deposits and capital shares from credit cooperatives, remained basically in private hands.

The announced functions of the Agricultural Bank tend to confirm this view of its *raison d'être*. Of the four categories of duties assigned to the new bank in 1955, three — attraction of rural savings, supervision of credit cooperatives, and management of long- and short-term agricultural loans — dealt with the channeling of rural private capital toward farm investment. The last duty concerned state investment in agriculture, but this function remained in fact with the Bank of Construction and was not carried out by the new bank.

Unlike its predecessor, the Agricultural Bank had functions closely geared to the needs and policies of the country at the time. Instead of managing long-term funds supplied by the state sector, it represented the People's Bank in the yet unsocialized countryside and exercised control over various phases of rural finance. In this light, it becomes easy to understand why the Agricultural Bank departed from the Soviet model and, furthermore, why banking officials explained that the difference was dictated by actual Chinese conditions.

THE DECLINE OF THE AGRICULTURAL BANK

Although the Agricultural Bank was given the important responsibility of mobilizing resources for rural investment, this relatively traditional method of promoting agricultural growth was not relied on exclusively for very long. Soon the collectivization began, and this signified the adoption of a much more radical solution to the problem of agricultural shortages. When the basic production unit was socialized, rural organization became more centralized and more capable of directly influencing both the amount of investment and production and the share of produce available to the state for industrial use. The roundabout approach of raising rural production via the Agricultural Bank was therefore supplanted by the more direct approach of collectivization. Under the changed environment, the Agricultural Bank was used as a convenient agent for the provision of financial support to the new movement.

The Director of the Agricultural Bank was changed[22] during the first year of its existence. In a speech given in July, 1956, the Vice-Premier of the State Council emphasized that after the collectivization drive (which was then nearing conclusion), the significance and duties of the Agricultural Bank would increase rather than decrease. He stated that "without the Agricultural Bank as a separate institution, the complex and important responsibility relating to the over-all management of rural finance could not be discharged."[23] At an annual banking conference in March, 1957, the Agricultural Bank Director pointed out several mistakes in the 1956 operations of the Bank.[24] First, the Bank had been too lenient in granting large sums for agricultural loans, thereby contributing to the nation's economic "tension;"[25] and at the same time, it had been lax in collecting overdue loans. Second, during the process of developing credit cooperatives, the Bank had employed coercive methods, to the detriment of the growth of the credit cooperatives themselves and also of government authority in the rural areas. Finally, the Bank had been careless in its decision relating to the future of the credit cooperative,[26] which had accentuated the difficulties of the moment. In the following month (April, 1957), the Agricultural Bank was abolished by order of the State Council. The reasons given for its abolition were: (1) it was difficult to distinguish between the duties of the People's Bank and those of the Agricultural Bank, especially in branches below the county level; and (2) the provision for a separate banking staff and offices increased overhead while creating problems of coordination and communication. Hence the Agricultural Bank was merged with the People's Bank.[27]

[22] When the Agricultural Bank opened, its director was Ch'iao P'ei-hsin (*TKP*, March 26, 1955). In 1956, the Director was Li Shao-yü, "Report to the National Conference of Outstanding Workers' Representatives on Rural Finance," *TKCJ*, no. 15, 1956, pp. 2–4.

[23] Teng Tzu-hui, "Speech Delivered at the National Conference of Outstanding Workers' Representatives on Rural Finance," *HHPYK*, no. 19, 1956, p. 81.

[24] Li Shao-yü, "Speech Delivered at the National Conference of Branch Bank Managers (Excerpts)," *CKCJ*, no. 6, 1957, pp. 7–9.

[25] The inflationary pressures of 1956 will be discussed in Chapter IX.

[26] This apparently referred to the fact that the Agricultural Bank considered integrating the credit cooperative with either the Bank or the agricultural collective. *Infra*, pp. 58–59.

[27] SC, "Communiqué on the Abolition of the Agricultural Bank of China," *CJFKHP*, 1957, pp. 87–88.

Judging from this scattered evidence, it may be surmised that the Agricultural Bank occupied an onerous position in 1956 and was subject to pressures from several directions. First, the urgent priorities of the collectivization drive required the Bank to grant indiscriminately large amounts of loans. Similarly, because it was desirable to allow a higher money income to the collectivized peasants, the drive prevented the Bank from collecting repayments.[28] Such a credit policy created inflationary pressures in rural areas for which the Agricultural Bank was later held responsible.

Second, the credit cooperatives, which mobilized rural savings under the guidance of the Agricultural Bank, faced two lines of resistance: from peasants who resented the semicompulsory methods often resorted to by credit cooperatives as the latter cooperatives strove to fulfill the high targets assigned to them; and from the collectives that preferred to have their members' savings contributed towards their own capital investments rather than deposited in the Bank.[29] In short, the credit cooperatives had to compete with the collectives for the savings of fundamentally reluctant individuals. This rendered doubly difficult for the Agricultural Bank the task of absorbing sufficient savings deposits.

Finally, there were duplications and conflicts of function between the Agricultural Bank and the People's Bank itself. For example, the People's Bank managed all commercial loans, including the working capital required by the rural supply and marketing cooperatives that formed a part of the trading system, while the Agricultural Bank handled other rural credit, long-term as well as short-term; yet the distinction between rural commercial credit and rural short-term productive credit was not always clear. When, at the beginning of the planting season, the supply and marketing cooperatives made advanced payments to farming collectives for state purchases, they were in effect providing the farming

---

[28] Strong friction existed between the party cadres and the banking personnel. The former were more interested in expanding the collectives than in economizing financial resources. There was evidence that party cadres dispensed bank loans and prevented the Bank from collecting repayments. They even requested the Bank to return to collective members loan repayments the Bank had already received. Yang Ming, "My Understanding of the Contradictions in the Present Rural Financial Works," *CKCJ*, no. 11, 1957, pp. 12–13. Conditions of agricultural loans will be discussed further in Chapter V.

[29] This factor was apparently at the root of the controversy as to whether the credit cooperatives should be integrated with the Agricultural Bank or with the collectives.

collectives with interest-free productive loans. Yet funds for these payments represented working capital of the supply and marketing cooperatives and were therefore furnished by the People's Bank as commercial credit. Similar problems existed in other banking functions, and the overlaps made it difficult for the People's Bank to exert centralized monetary control.

Added to these frictions arising from all sides, there was a dissipation of the original justification for maintaining a separate rural bank. The task of inducing savings and investments could now be carried out in large measure through the collectives, and these semisocialized rural productive units made it possible for the People's Bank to deal with rural finance directly. So the Agricultural Bank faded away.

In 1963, an Agricultural Bank was again created to administer capital investments in agriculture and to supervise the revived rural credit cooperatives.[30] In view of the post-Great-Leap shift in the nation's economic policy from a concentration on industrial investments to a more balanced growth of industry and agriculture, this new bank was probably closer to the Soviet prototype than the Bank of 1955.

Credit Cooperatives

In spite of the rapid extension of its network, the People's Bank could not hope to penetrate the vast area of rural China where few modern banking facilities had been present. Under these circumstances, the credit cooperative became an excellent bridge between the lowest level banks and the peasantry. Theoretically, credit cooperatives were not a part of the state banking system; they were the peasants' "own little banks," organized voluntarily and based on the principle of mutual benefits among the participants.[31] However, since all financial enterprises in Communist China were legally subject to state control,[32] credit co-

---

[30] "The First Meeting of Branch Bank Managers of the Agricultural Bank of China," *JMST*, 1964, pp. 523–24.

[31] *Talks on the First Five Year Plan (Ti-i wu-nien-chi-hua chiang-hua)*, p. 210. The credit cooperative was called "nung-min tze-chi ti hsiao-yin-hang."

[32] This was specified in Article 39 of the Common Program. *The Common Program*

operatives were supervised by the People's Bank. They became *de facto* local agencies of the Bank.

TYPES OF RURAL COOPERATION ORGANIZATIONS[33]

Rural credit cooperatives originated in the cooperative experiment which took place during the infancy of the Chinese Communist Party. By 1933 credit cooperation was practiced in certain areas under Communist rule. The early organizations were attached to other types of cooperatives and were called credit departments. It was not until after 1945 that a special type of cooperative dealing only with credit was born in the Northwest. In addition to the credit cooperative, there were traditional credit institutions, such as mutual-aid societies. Thus, by 1949 three categories of credit cooperation organizations existed in various parts of the country: the credit cooperative, the credit department (in the supply and marketing cooperative), and the credit mutual-aid team. These organizations had no direct relationship with one another although they were all subject to the control of the People's Bank.

The credit cooperative had a capital fund provided by its members; it had a representative governing body; it accepted deposits and granted loans to members; and its area of operation generally encompassed a rural district *(hsiang),* with the larger ones covering three or four districts.

The credit department was subordinate to the supply and marketing cooperative and served the cooperative's members by taking deposits and making loans. There were no capital contributions from the members, but an operational fund might be provided by the parent coopera-

---

and Other Documents of the First Plenary Session of the Chinese People's Political Consultation Conference.

[33] Materials for this and the following sections are from P'eng and Ho, *An Outline of the Theory of Money and Credit,* p. 339; Chang Yuan-Yuan, "Rural Credit Cooperatives Urgently Needed Further Development," *CCCP,* no. 8, 1952, pp. 5–6; Ta, "The Development and Functions of Credit Cooperatives in Our Country," *HH,* no. 2, 1954, pp. 31–32; "Credit Cooperative Enterprises are Rapidly Growing," *JMST,* 1955, pp. 443–44; Starlight, *Fiscal and Monetary Policies in Communist China,* pt. III, chap. IV.

tive. While keeping separate accounts, it had no independent management.

The credit mutual-aid team included a variety of small organizations which evolved from traditional credit clubs or other indigenous devices. The team usually consisted of twenty to thirty farm households which, by common agreements, contributed money to a pool. The sum was then used to grant loans to needy members. Some teams resembled miniature credit cooperatives, with capital, deposits, and loans. As its operations expanded, the credit team was expected to mature into a credit cooperative.

The credit mutual-aid team was transitional in nature and was of less importance because of its small scale. Of the two remaining types of credit organizations, the credit cooperative more effectively served the purpose of mobilizing rural funds, and was therefore considered the most important type of rural credit organization in Communist China.[34] Later development of rural credit facilities centered on the expansion of the credit cooperative.

THE DEVELOPMENT OF CREDIT COOPERATIVES

The credit cooperatives went through several stages of development. After a formative period, they burst into an era of sudden growth before entering a stage of consolidation. During the Great Leap they became credit departments of the communes, serving at the same time as local offices of the People's Bank; but this arrangement proved to be temporary. Table III-3 summarizes the growth in number and in the scale of operation of the credit cooperatives. The process of development needs further examination.

[34] A 1953 comparative study of the two types of organization in Northeast China gave the following results.
The average amount of resources (capital plus deposits):
    credit department (with no capital) ¥2,520
    credit cooperative 8,530
The average amount of loans granted:
    credit department ¥2,320
    credit cooperative 7,250
Ta, "The Development and Functions of Credit Cooperatives. . . ," *HH*, no. 2, 1954, p. 32.

Table III-3
The Growth of Credit Cooperatives, 1950–1958

	Number of cooperatives (1)	Capital (mil. ¥) (2)	Deposit balance* (mil. ¥) (3)	Loans outstanding† (mil. ¥) (4)	Total loans granted in year†† (mil. ¥) (5)
1950	103	—	—	—	—
1951	538	—	—	—	—
1952	2,271	—	—	—	—
1953	9,418	12.0	11.0	8.4	—
1954	124,068	128.8	158.9	97.7	220
1955	159,363	204.5	606.7	281.5	—
1956	102,558	280.1	1,078.7	500.5	600
1957	88,368	310.2	2,065.8	565.8	—
1958	—	415.5	4,026.1	1,698.4	3,400

*No date given. Probably refers to the deposit balance at the end of the year. This interpretation is supported by a newspaper report that rural deposits at the end of 1956 were ¥1,078.68 million, which agrees with our data for 1956. *Kuang Ming Daily,* July 18, 1957.

†This represents the maximum amount of loans outstanding during the year minus credit from the People's Bank. Therefore, it is the highest loan balance during the year that is financed with the credit cooperatives' own resources. The peak season for agricultural loans normally occurs in June.

††The total amount of loans granted during the six years of 1953–1958 is given as ¥4.9 billion. Thus the total loans granted for the years 1953, 1955, and 1957 must be less than ¥700 million.

Sources:

1950–1952: Ta, "The Development and Functions of Credit Cooperatives in Our Country," *HH,* no. 2, 1954, pp. 31–32.

1953–1958: "The General Development of Credit Cooperatives and Their Operations," *CKCJ,* September 25, 1959, p. 2.

THE FORMATIVE STAGE (1950–1953)

This period began soon after the price stabilization in March, 1950, and ended in November, 1953, when the "planned purchase and planned supply" scheme was applied to basic agricultural products. Before 1950 all previously formed credit cooperation units had perished in the inflation. Soon after price stabilization, the experimental development of credit organizations began in North China, resulting in 103 credit cooperatives and 439 credit departments by the end of 1950. Prior to the first National Conference on Rural Finance of May, 1951, the responsibility for promoting credit cooperation had been transferred to the

People's Bank.[35] Consequently, the Conference adopted a policy calling for the cultivation of all forms of credit cooperative by rural branches of the Bank through the use of technical training and advice as well as financial support. In 1953 a period of general propagation of credit groups began, but the growth of the credit cooperative per se remained gradual until the end of that year, when a new stage of development took place in the country.[36]

EXPANSION (1954)

In November, 1953, the state broadened its control over basic agricultural products by placing food grains and vegetable oils, which were previously traded in the open market, under a planned purchase and planned supply system.[37] Under this system producers first had to fill an annual quota of state purchase; the remaining produce could then be retained for their own consumption or for sale. If retained for sale it could be sold only to the state commercial network at official prices. The immediate consequence of this state monopoly on the trading of food grains was a large and concentrated increase in the payments made by the state to the rural population soon after the harvesting season.[38] Furthermore, the sudden release of currency into circulation was ac-

[35] Formerly this responsibility rested with the All China Federation of Cooperatives, although the Federation was assisted by the People's Bank. Nan Han-ch'en, "Report to the First National Conference on Rural Finance," *Central TCCT*, III, 256.

[36] In this formative period, credit departments and credit mutual-aid teams increased along with credit cooperatives. By June, 1953, there were 2,137 departments, located mainly in the Northeast, and over 14,000 credit teams, located mainly in the Northwest. However, from 1954 on, the main emphasis was on the formation of credit cooperatives. Ta, "The Development and Functions of Credit Cooperatives. . . ," *HH*, no. 2, 1954, p. 32.

[37] The "planned purchase and planned supply" system was introduced in 1950 to cover certain strategic minerals. Food grains and oils were included in 1953. In September, 1954, the program was further extended to cover cotton and cotton cloth. Other agricultural products were subject to similar control under the "centralized purchase" system. Choh-ming Li, *Economic Development. . . ,* pp. 20–22.

[38] In December, 1953, and January, 1954, the two peak months of state purchase of food grains in the 1953–1954 agricultural year, the amounts purchased doubled those of the same months in the preceding agricultural year. The total for these two months accounted for 40 percent of the annual purchase by the state. Tseng and Han, *The Circulation of Money in the People's Republic of China, (JPRS* translation) chap. III, sec. II, pp. 77–84.

companied by a lowering of the speed at which rural currency flowed back to the Bank.[39]

These conditions were indicative of a large amount of idle cash left in the hands of the farming population. Moreover, this rise in cash holding was not the result of an increase in the liquidity preference of the peasants; rather, it was a manifestation of both the compulsory state purchase and the inadequate supply of industrial goods given to the agricultural areas by state enterprises.[40] Under these circumstances, forced saving must be achieved either through price changes, which the authority was unwilling to permit, or through other more direct measures designed to absorb quickly the huge quantity of purchasing power in the countryside. The formation of credit cooperatives, ostensibly on a voluntary basis, served this purpose admirably well. They could inactivate some of the rural liquidity by turning it into capital shares and deposits. Thus the expansion of credit cooperatives took place on an unprecedentedly large scale in 1954; at the end of that year over 124,000 units existed, compared with 9,400 a year before.

The procedure for forming a credit cooperative was simple: under the leadership of a financial cadre that was chosen from among the peasants and briefly trained in a special class organized by the county bank, anyone with surplus money could join; and the capital share could

---

[39] Communist authors referred to a decrease of the "rural velocity of circulation of currency" in early 1954 and the following data were presented to illustrate this decrease: Number of days required for currency to return to the Bank in rural areas, in index form, with 4th quarter of 1952 as base

	1st Qr.	2nd Qr.	3rd Qr.	4th Qr.
1952				100.0
1953	107.7	93.9	96.0	101.5
1954	124.5	107.0		

Tseng and Han, *The Circulation of Money in the People's Republic of China* (*JPRS* translation), p. 82. It is not clear how these figures were derived. But it is clear from this illustration that "velocity" relates to the flow of currency from the state sector (the People's Bank) to the rural private sector (peasants) and back to the state sector (the People's Bank). Therefore, as this velocity decreased, the cash holding in the private sector became successively larger, exerting an inflationary pressure in this sector.

[40] Whereas previously the peasants stored products for gradual sale in the open market, they now had to exchange them for money all at once.

55

be as low as ￥1.[41] The goal was to establish a credit cooperative in every one of the 200,000 rural districts *(hsiang)* in China.[42]

The hasty expansion of the credit cooperatives in 1954 was achieved at the expense of quality. A considerable portion of these new organizations were inactive, poorly managed, or too small to be economically self-sufficient; thus losses were widespread. As a result, in March, 1955, the People's Bank called for consolidation and improvements.[44] It was at this time that the Agricultural Bank was formed under the People's Bank to supervise rural credit and to strengthen credit cooperatives. Later in the year, when large sums of rural loans were issued to promote collectivization, the Agricultural Bank employed the credit cooperatives as agents wherever this was practicable. Meanwhile, deposits received by the credit cooperatives expanded with the collectivization movement, since collective funds were now added to individual savings. All these developments tended to strengthen the infant credit cooperatives.

[41] Starlight, *Fiscal and Monetary Policies. . . ,* p. 217.

[42] Originally this goal was to be reached in 1957, but the movement proceeded more rapidly than was planned by the People's Bank; the target date was accordingly moved up to 1956. "Conference of Branch Bank Managers of the People's Bank," *CKCJ,* no. 4, 1956, p. 3.

[43] This section is based on materials from the following sources: Starlight, *Fiscal and Monetary Policies . . . ,* pt. III chap. IV; "The Mushroom Growth of Credit Cooperation Enterprises during the First Five Year Plan," *CKCJ,* no. 3, 1958, p. 22; "Striving to Develop Credit Cooperation Enterprises," *HHYP,* no. 9, 1955, pp. 132–33; Li Shao-yü, Director, Agricultural Bank, "Report to the National Conference of Outstanding Workers' Representatives on Rural Finance," (excerpts) *CKCJ,* no. 15, 1956, pp. 2–3; *idem,* "Improve Rural Financial Works and Support Agricultural Collectivization," *HH,* March, 1956, pp. 27–28; *idem,* "Speech Delivered at the National Conference of Branch Bank Managers (excerpts)," *CKCJ,* no. 6, 1957, pp. 7–9; "National Conference of Branch Bank Managers Convened by the Main Office of the People's Bank," *CKCJ,* no. 4, 1956, pp. 2–3; SC, "Directive on the Correction of Compulsory Phenomena in the Works of Banks and Credit Cooperatives," *HHPYK,* no. 15, 1956, pp. 172–73; Teng Tze-hui, "Speech Delivered at the National Conference of Outstanding Workers' Representatives on Rural Finance," *HHPYK,* no. 19, 1956, pp. 78–82; Ch'en Hsi-yü, "Report to the Conference on Financial Works during the Brisk Season," *CKCJ,* no. 18, 1957, pp. 1–5.

[44] The announcement was made at the National Conference on Rural Finance in March, 1955. The Bank was later criticized for having insisted on a complete halt to expansion. "National Conference of Branch Bank Managers Convened by the Main Office of the People's Bank," *CKCJ,* no. 4, 1956, pp. 2–3.

Collectivization affected the credit cooperatives in yet another respect. It enlarged the agricultural production units and reduced the number of rural districts, thereby facilitating the consolidation of the credit cooperatives. In 1956, mergers and reorganizations took place; the number of credit cooperatives was reduced by one-third, while nearly one-fifth of their personnel was laid off.[45] Despite the curtailments, there was a credit cooperative in almost every one of the now larger rural districts by the end of 1956. While the structure was being streamlined, attempts were made to upgrade staff training through a series of county level conferences. This was necessary because one major factor in the poor performance of the credit cooperatives had been a lack of qualified workers. The large number of financial cadres who had organized the cooperatives had been recruited from among the poor or lower-middle peasants, selected for their political zeal rather than their financial skills. The fact that they were poorly paid or even unpaid for their service with the credit cooperatives aggravated the problem. The Bank therefore tried to raise the quality of the cooperative staff and improve its remunerations.[46] At the same time, repeated emphasis was given to the "voluntary" principle, that is, the use of persuasion rather than coercion as a means of increasing membership and resources of the credit cooperatives. Evidently, compulsory devices had been widely practiced by the authoritarian staff as they strove to fulfill their excessive assigned quotas. This aroused the resentment of the peasantry and led to the hoarding of currency, which in turn caused the credit cooperatives to come to a standstill.[47]

[45] Total number of financial workers in the credit cooperatives:

1955	320,000 persons
1956	260,000 persons

"The Mushroom Growth . . .," *CKCJ,* no. 3, 1958.

[46] In some areas the salary adjustments were too high, causing heavy losses by the credit cooperatives. Han Ch'uan, "Independent Credit Cooperatives Are Still Necessary after the Agricultural Collectivization," *CKCJ,* no. 6, 1957, p. 21.

[47] For example, credit cooperatives in certain areas of Hupeh were reported to be in a state of inactivity for more than two months as a result of dissatisfaction among the peasants. *NCNA,* Wuhan, September 5, 1956; (translated version; *SCMP,* #1366, p. 24.) In mid-1956, the Vice-premier of the State Council suggested that the extension of capital subscription should be stopped. Teng Tze-hui, "Speech Delivered at the National Conference of Outstanding Workers' Representatives on Rural Finance," *HHPYK,* no. 19,

The consolidation continued into 1957, when the number of credit cooperatives was further reduced by one-tenth. However, the problems were far from being solved. Two difficulties remained to plague the banking authorities. First, the larger size of the merged cooperatives made it impossible for them to maintain easy and convenient contacts with their members without an elaborate system of subdivisions.[48] Second, a major portion of the credit cooperatives still had financial problems,[49] making it necessary to increase further the scale of operation and to reduce the staff in order to render the cooperative financially self-sufficient. It is clear that solutions to these problems are mutually conflicting, since one leads to a more complex hierarchy while the other requires simplification.

EVOLUTION DURING THE GREAT LEAP

In the period of consolidation, when reorganizations of the credit cooperatives were taking place alongside the collectivization drive, the Agricultural Bank apparently encountered sufficient difficulties to warrant a re-evaluation of the system.[50] Two proposals were current, one to subordinate the credit cooperative to the collective farm, the other to integrate it with the Bank.[51] Neither alternative was adopted;

1956, p. 81. This kind of payment must have been considered a levy by the peasants, since, unlike deposits, it could not be withdrawn.

[48] A typical credit cooperative by 1957 consisted of over 1,000 rural households; some even had 2,000 to 3,000 households. Ch'en Hsi-yü, "Report . . . during the Brisk Season," *CKCJ,* no. 18, 1957, p. 4.

[49] A study by the People's Bank covering 44,884 credit cooperatives in 12 provinces showed that only 34.8 percent of them had made profits at the end of 1956; of the remaining 65.2 percent, half suffered a loss above ¥100. *Ibid.*

[50] Difficulties were encountered in the areas of "business operations" and "cadres' renumerations,"Li Shao-yü, "Speech Delivered at the National Conference of Branch Bank Managers," *CKCJ,* no. 6, 1957, p. 85. The re-evaluation took place around February, 1956.

[51] Experiments were carried out by the Bank. One, implemented in Hupeh province, replaced the credit cooperatives with the District Bank Offices; the other, carried out in Honan and Kwangsi provinces, turned the credit cooperatives into credit departments of the collectives. (For reasons of these and other proposals, see He "Who Should Manage the Credit Cooperative?," *CKCJ,* no. 6, 1957, pp. 23–24; Han Ch'uan, "Independent Credit Cooperatives are Still Necessary . . .," *CKCJ,* no. 6, 1957.) It was found that the new Bank Offices, being subject to centralized control of the State Bank system, were ill adapted to meeting local needs of loans for individuals. Under the second experiment, the peasants, fearing their savings might be appropriated by the collectives for investment, withdrew their deposits en masse (Li Shao-yu, "Speech Delivered at the National Con-

the final decision was to retain the existing network of independent credit cooperatives for a "considerable period of time."

This policy of maintaining a separate system of credit cooperatives was reversed when in August, 1958, a sudden communization movement swept the rural areas.[52] Under this new movement, not only were the credit cooperatives (together with the supply and marketing cooperatives) merged with the collectives, but the collectives themselves were further combined into a much larger unit—the people's commune. The geographical area covered by a rural commune was much more extensive than that of a collective. The commune was all-inclusive, serving at once as the local government and as an economic unit. As an economic unit, it engaged mainly in agricultural production in the broad sense (including fisheries, forestry, etc.), but it also operated local industries; its trade department handled the distribution and exchange of goods, while its credit department managed all investment, loans, receipts, and expenditures of the commune as well as savings of individual members. The peasants, who under the collectives earned an income commensurate with each one's contribution of labor in terms of numbers of workpoints, were now paid a fixed wage and organized into work teams. The overall rural life became much more communal and regimented. During this period of rural upheaval, which came only two years after the unsettling collectivization drive, financial relationships among various units and individual peasants must have been chaotic. The situation was further confused by the release of a large sum in bank

---

ference of Branch Bank Managers," *CKCJ*, no. 6, 1957, p. 8; Teng Tze-hui, "Speech Delivered at the National Conference of Outstanding Workers' Representatives on Rural Finance," *HHPYK*, no. 19, 1956, p. 80). The Conference of Bank Managers of March, 1956, decided to retain the credit cooperatives; this policy was reaffirmed at the Conference of Rural Finance Workers of July, 1956.

[52] Individual instances of combining the credit cooperative with the collective probably continued before communization. For example, early in 1958 a Fukien local experiment of a "three-in-one" plan was declared successful; this plan merged the credit cooperative and the supply and marketing cooperative with the collective. Evidently there had been conflicts of interests between the credit cooperative and the collective, since the one encouraged savings deposits while the other wanted their members to contribute towards collective investment. *NCNA*, Foochow, March 11 and 19, 1958; (translated version; *SCMP* #1740, p. 16, and #1742, p. 13.) Also Liang, "The Condition and Problems of the 'Three Cooperatives in One' Experiment in Lientang County," *CKCJ*, no. 20, 1957, pp. 22–24.

loans for the establishment of the communes and by the general disregard of banking "rules and systems" considered restrictive, including the keeping of proper accounting records.[53]

A regulation promulgated by the State Council in December, 1958, tried to clarify some of the new credit relationships among the commune, the credit department, the People's Bank, and the commune members. In this regulation it was formally announced that the credit department served in two concurrent capacities: it was a component part of the commune, and it was also the local Business Office of the People's Bank.[54] Thus the credit cooperative became a link directly connecting the Bank to the commune during a period of financial laxity.

As an epilogue, it should be noted that the term "credit branch" evolved in 1959.[55] These were branches of the commune credit department (concurrently the People's Bank's local office) and were attached to the commune production brigade (formerly the production cooperative or collective). Assets and liabilities that had previously belonged to the credit cooperatives and had later been centralized in the commune credit departments were transferred back to the credit branches. Apparently this new unit represented a revival of the credit cooperative under a different name.[56]

The post-1960 credit organizations in the farm areas apparently reverted to conditions similar to those existing in 1955–1957.[57] One of the

[53] In 1958, when a policy of general decentralization was in effect, control of economic units was shifted from the managerial staff to the local party leadership, resulting in a downgrading of professional and technical staff, including banking personnel. Expert advice was replaced by mass participation. For background information on this period, see Schurmann, "Economic Policy and Political Power in Communist China," *The Annals of the American Academy of Political and Social Science,* September, 1963, pp. 49–69.

[54] SC, "Regulations on Several Problems Relating to the Credit Departments of the People's Communes and on the Question of Working Capital for State Enterprise," *FKHP,* VIII, 156–58.

[55] Ch'en Hsi-yü, Deputy-Director, People's Bank, "The 1958 Banking Work and the 1959 Tasks" (excerpts of a report delivered at the National Conference of Managers of Branches of the People's Bank of China), *CKCJ,* May 25, 1959 (translated version; *ECMM* #178, pp. 28–34).

[56] Rural deposits declined drastically during the 1958–1959 turmoil. At the end of 1959, rural deposits in credit departments amounted to ¥400 million. *NCNA,* February 18, 1960, quoted by Y. H. Liu, "Public Finance in Communist China, 1963," *China Monthly,* May, 1964, p. 56.

[57] Teng Tzu-huei, "The Historic Mission of the Credit Cooperative during the Present Stage of Our Country," *HC,* no. 23, 1963, pp. 21–29.

stated purposes for the recent reestablishment of the Agricultural Bank was to provide "unified leadership to the rural credit cooperatives."[58] This was a continuation of a similar function assumed by the 1955–1957 Agricultural Bank.

FUNCTIONS OF THE CREDIT COOPERATIVE

The credit cooperatives served two purposes. First, they replaced private sources of rural credit and thus prevented usury. Second, they helped the People's Bank and the Agricultural Bank in enforcing monetary policies in the countryside.

From the outset, the credit cooperative was intended to be an institution for marshalling scattered rural funds to meet local capital needs. Short-term rural credit in China, whether for production or for consumption, had been provided traditionally by landlords or other individuals rather than by banks. The interest rates for such credit had been high, ranging from 20 percent to 40 percent, with an occasional peak of 240 percent per annum.[59] The foundation of this credit system was severely undermined during the early Communist rule, when the landlords became impoverished under the land reform. The vacuum left by the collapse of private sources of credit had to be filled, and the credit cooperative was the solution to this problem. The solution was hailed as a significant step towards the socialization of the rural economy.[60] However, during the formative years of the credit cooperatives, usury continued to exist because of a shortage of short-term capital in agriculture and a lack of banking facilities in remote areas. One of the reasons for the expansion of credit cooperatives was to correct this condition. By soliciting capital contributions and savings deposits, the

[58] By the end of 1962, credit cooperatives had ¥500 million of capital plus accumulations (in plowed-back earnings) and ¥2,801 million of deposits. Hu Li-chiao, "Do Well the Rural Financial Works; Effectively Support the Collective Economic Sector," *JMST*, 1963, pp. 349–52.

[59] This was true before 1937, i.e., before inflation and war drove the interest rate even higher. *Report of the China-United States Agricultural Mission*, Nanking, 1946, quoted by Starlight, *Fiscal and Monetary Policies . . .*, p. 225.

[60] This significance was stressed by Cheng Po-pin, a (academic) monetary economist, in "The Role of State Loan on the Promotion of Agricultural Collectivization," *HCS*, no. 12 (December, 1956), 8–12.

credit cooperatives diverted the flow of surplus funds away from private loans; on the other hand, by supplying short-term production and consumption loans to the local population at an interest rate lower than that of private loans, they tended to bring down the level of rural interest rates in general. Thus the growth of credit cooperative activities, coupled with the policy of gradually lowering the interest rate on cooperative loans,[61] limited the scope and extent of rural usury and eventually uprooted it.[62] However, in 1956 it was admitted that, even though open usury had disappeared, disguised usury still remained in the form of "purchase of member's workpoints at a lower price."[63] Since members of collectives by 1956 were paid "dividends" after the harvest according to the number of workpoints, this practice amounted to a discounting of the borrower's future income.

The second function of the credit cooperative—assisting the People's Bank in implementing the overall monetary policy—did not assume importance until the end of 1953, when the disposable money income of the rural population suddenly increased as a result of the planned purchase and planned supply program discussed above. The credit cooperatives helped the People's Bank to enforce a restrictive policy by absorbing a larger total of capital plus deposits than the amount of short-term loans granted, leaving a balance that was redeposited with the People's Bank, or with the Agricultural Bank when it existed. Since most rural transactions in that period involved the use of currency, such redeposits made by the credit cooperatives caused a net flow of currency into the Bank, thereby reducing rural money in circulation. Furthermore, the increase in redeposits of the credit cooperatives represented money savings mobilized from the rural section which could be used for agricultural investment.

---

[61] For this interest rate policy, see Li Shao-yü, "Improve Rural Financial Works . . .," *HH,* March, 1956, p. 28, and "Report to the National Conference of Outstanding Workers' Representatives on Rural Finance," *CKCJ,* no. 15, 1956, p. 2.

[62] It was reported that a study covering the areas of 1,037 credit cooperatives in Fukien in early 1955 showed a decline of monthly interest rates for private loans from 10 to 15 percent before the establishment of cooperatives to 1.4 to 2 percent after their establishment. Hsü T'i-hsin, *An Analysis of the Chinese National Economy . . .,* p. 210.

[63] "There Is Still the Need for Credit Cooperatives," *TKP,* August 21, 1956; (translated version; *SCMP,* #1369, pp. 5-7. Quotation on p. 7).

The credit cooperatives also assisted the Bank in implementing other measures designed to minimize the amount of currency necessary for transaction purposes. These measures include (1) activities to smooth out the seasonal fluctuations in the transaction demand for currency, and (2) a more extensive use of "non-cash settlement" (i.e., bank account transfer) as a method of payment. They will be dealt with in Chapter VII as a part of the currency policy of the People's Bank.

Concluding Remarks

Compared with the relatively smooth transition of the urban banking structure, the development of the rural financial network in China was confused and difficult. This difference can be explained partly by the fact that the agricultural sector was inherently more decentralized and economically more primitive; besides, the formation of a comprehensive system of monetary institutions in the countryside was more or less a new venture, undertaken largely without the benefit of inherited elements.

The process of rural banking development illustrates the overall Communist Chinese strategy mentioned earlier. While attempts were made to copy the Soviet model, the Chinese system was nonetheless developed through a process of trial and error. This is especially true in the case of the bank for agriculture, although the course followed by the credit cooperatives was also determined to a large extent by the actual needs of the time. Thus doctrinairism was mixed with pragmatism. The latter led to frequent changes, while the former provided a clear sense of direction, which was to build a rural financial network capable of exerting centralized monetary control and mobilizing savings.

In striving for this goal, the Chinese appear to have been confronted with two basic difficulties. First, there was the problem of shaping the most appropriate structural hierarchy, a setup which could reach down to the peasantry but would involve neither infringements on the monolithic monetary power of the People's Bank nor heavy administrative costs to the state. The question of whether or not to retain the Agricultural Bank in 1957 and the search for the most efficient size of the credit cooperative that led to a zigzag of consolidation and subdivision were repeated manifestations of this dilemma. Second, there was the delicate task of inducing huge sums of monetary savings in the farm areas without overalienating the peasants. The constant refrains of "voluntary deposits, free withdrawals, confidential banking" and the equally frequent *de facto* violations of these principles persisted throughout the history of rural savings. In addition to these problems within the rural banking system, there were also uncertain oscillations in the role of rural banking in general. Reliance on monetary control in the farm areas tended to alternate with emphasis on other more drastic methods of control. In turn this tendency created instability and conflict.

Difficulties and confusions notwithstanding, the fact remains that a financial network was created that permeated the agricultural sector and, however haphazardly and intermittently, enabled the People's Bank to extend its control over the vast, complex, and most decentralized segment of the economy.

IV

THE MONEY SUPPLY AND THE PEOPLE'S BANK OF CHINA

ONE DISTINCT FEATURE emerges from the above description of the Chinese banking system, that is, the dominance of the People's Bank. The supply of money is monopolized and regulated by this Bank. Our next step is therefore to examine the general relationship between the People's Bank and the nation's money supply. The present chapter begins with a review of the evolution of the People's Bank into an organ for the control of money. This is followed by an examination of the structure of the money flow and the way in which bank credit, the foundation of this flow, was managed. Finally, the nature of the People's Bank is analyzed.

The People's Bank as the "Center of Cash, Credit, and Settlement"

Copying almost verbatim from the U.S.S.R., the Chinese consider the People's Bank as the "center of cash, credit, and settlement." In other words, the Bank serves as the economy's nerve center which controls the money circuits and oversees transactions in the dominant state sector. As the center of cash, it performs two functions. First, it issues banknotes and coins for circulation within the country; second, it is the custodian of nearly all cash held in the state sector. Included in this sector are government organizations, public institutions (hospitals, schools, etc.), and state enterprises. As the center of credit, the People's Bank is not only the sole banking institution from which loans originate;

it is also intended to be the unique source of credit for state units, since all forms of inter-enterprise debts, including advanced or delayed payments and time purchases, are prohibited. The term "settlement" in the present context means "non-cash settlement" and refers to the method of making payments through bank account transfers. This mode of payment is prescribed, with minor exceptions, for transactions among different entities within the state sector. Such payments are to be effected through the People's Bank; therefore, the Bank is also the center of settlement.

The development of the People's Bank toward its designated position was far from smooth. However, haltingly and slowly, progress was made. Before 1957, there were three attempts to elevate the Bank's status along the desired channels. These will be discussed separately.

CASH CONTROL

The development of the new role assigned to the People's Bank began in 1950 when certain measures known as "cash control," fashioned after the Soviet "ruble control," were implemented. These measures had the immediate effect of centralizing cash held by public units in the hands of the People's Bank, thereby reducing the amount of currency in circulation. Such a monetary policy was one of a number of weapons with which the Communist government broke the inflationary spiral in 1950.[1] But cash control also had other more permanent consequences: it began to establish the People's Bank as the center of cash, credit, and settlement, and it started an attempt to institute financial planning.

The embryo of cash control was contained in a government decree of March, 1950, specifying that cash held by government organs and state enterprises that was in excess of the amount necessary for current expenditures must be deposited in the People's Bank.[2] In April, detailed provisions were announced, under which the People's Bank was given

---

[1] Control of funds held by public units was also attempted, without success, by the Nationalist government in the 1940s. S. H. Chou, "Prices in Communist China," *Journal of Asian Studies,* XXV, no. 4, (August, 1966) footnote on p. 651.

[2] GAC, "Decision on the Unification of State Financial and Economic Work," *Central TCCT,* I, 30.

the responsibility of implementing cash control. The Bank, upon consultation with public units, was to determine a quota of currency retainable by each unit for cash expenditures; all funds exceeding this quota had to be deposited in the People's Bank, to be withdrawn when needed. The quota itself was limited to an amount equivalent to three days' operating expenses of the unit concerned.[3] Furthermore, the Bank was entrusted with the task of ascertaining that inter-unit payments in the state sector were "settled" through the Bank and that the use of cash was limited to payments for wages, agricultural product purchases and miscellaneous expenses.[4]

MONETARY CONTROL

Partly as a response to new inflationary pressures caused by the Korean conflict, the control program was broadened and strengthened in December, 1950, under the new title of "monetary control."[5] This larger program inherited cash control as one of its four parts. Thus the first component of monetary control related to cash control, under which the provisions of the earlier program were restated in a stricter and more specific form;[6] in addition, the compilation by public units

[3] This applied to units in areas where branches of the People's Bank were located. In areas without an office or agency of the Bank, the quota could amount to one month's operating expenses.

[4] GAC, "Decision on the Implementation of Cash Control over State Organs," *Central TCCT*, I, 237–38.

[5] When literally translated, as is often done, the name of this program is "currency control." However, since it regulates both currency and bank credit, the term "monetary control" is more appropriate. The principles of "monetary control" were laid down in a GAC decision on December 1, 1950: "Decision on the System of Final Accounts, the Auditing of Budgetary Estimates, Engineering Plans for Capital Investments, and Monetary Control," *Central TCCT*, II, 273. Detailed measures were worked out by the People's Bank and promulgated on December 25, 1950, by the GAC. *Idem,* "Directive on Measures for 'the Implementation of Monetary Control and Measures for the Compilation of Currency Receipt and Expenditure Plan,'" pp. 549–76.

[6] For example, it was specified in the new program that cash held by public units in excess of the retainable quotas must be deposited in the Bank either on the same day when it was received by the units or, with permission from the Bank, during the following morning. Restrictions in the use of cash were also more detailed; under "monetary control" its use was permitted for (a) dealings with private enterprises, (b) dealings with urban residents or peasants, (c) wage payments, (d) traveling expenses, and (e) interstate-unit payments which were miscellaneous and within a specific limit to be determined by the People's Bank. *Ibid.,* pp. 550–51.

of a "monetary receipt and expenditures plan" was required.[7] The second part dealt with payments through accounts—it specified the kinds of deposit accounts each type of public unit must hold open in the People's Bank and the different methods of payment through the Bank that were applicable to various categories of transactions. The third controlled short-term credit. Measures in this section forbade interunit indebtedness within the state sector, thereby placing the People's Bank in the position of a fountainhead from which all short-term loans to state enterprises emanated; principles governing bank credit were also laid down.[8] The final portion of the program concerned the supervision of capital investment. Here procedure for the use of funds appropriated from the budget for basic constructions were specified and the responsibility of control was delegated through the People's Bank to a special bank.[9]

In essence, the first three groups of measures under monetary control were intended to centralize in the People's Bank all cash flowing into the state sector, to establish bilateral—and only bilateral—credit relationships between the Bank and each public enterprise, and to direct all intrastate sector payments through bank clearings. These requirements provided the necessary conditions for the People's Bank to fulfill its role as the center of control over cash, credit, and settlement.

Despite these pronouncements, however, internal conditions and developments of the state enterprises in this period did not lend themselves to banking supervision; therefore, the control of the People's Bank was more nominal than real.[10] In early 1953, when it was attempting to restrict credit,[11] the Bank also tried to extend the practice of "settlement" by standardizing various techniques for making payments

---

[7] Under the earlier cash control program, experiments in the compilation of "cash receipts and expenditures plans" were suggested but not required.

[8] These principles required that loans should be granted as follows: (1) directly to the users, (2) according to plans and for definite purposes, (3) on the base of commodity collaterals, and (4) with specified duration, to be repaid when due. They were the same as those pronounced in 1955, *infra,* p. 86.

[9] This special bank was later directly subordinated to the Ministry of Finance; see sections on the Bank of Communications and the Bank of Construction, Chapter I.

[10] Ch'en Yang-ch'ing, "On the Work of the State Bank," *CKCJ,* no. 11, 1953, p. 1.

[11] The credit restriction of 1953 will be discussed further on in this chapter.

through the Bank. Eight types of settlement procedures were adopted.[12] But as late as 1954 the monetary control program was closer to being an expression of aspiration than a statement of reality. At that time inter-enterprise debts were prevalent,[13] the Bank granted loans freely, and public units tended to retain large amounts of excess cash holdings.[14] Outside Manchuria, only 20 percent of the sales of the state industrial enterprises was paid through transfers of bank accounts.[15]

MEASURES OF 1955[16]

Renewed efforts were made in 1955 to consolidate the Bank's position and to implement the monetary control program. Credit regulations were changed and the inventory criterion for bank loans was adopted.[17]

[12] "Regulations on State Commercial Settlements" were drafted in the National Conference on Currency Control of October, 1952, promulgated in February, 1953, and became effective on March 10, 1953. The eight technical methods of settlement were check, certified check, accreditation, planned settlement, acceptance, telegraph or mail transfer, special account, and letter of credit. "Joint Directive of the Central Ministry of Commerce and the Main Office of the People's Bank," *CKCJ,* no. 11, 1953, p. 1.

[13] Ministry of Finance and PB, "Regulations on the Abolition of Existing Commercial Credit within the State Commercial Network and between This Network and Other Organs," *FKHP,* I, 278–83; PB, "Report on the Abolition of Commercial Credit among State Industrial Enterprises and between State Industrial Enterprises and Other State Enterprises, Substituting These Credits with Bank Settlement," *ibid.,* pp. 270–73; Chao Chih-ch'eng, Assistant Director, Bureau of State Industrial Credit of PB, "Abolish Commercial Credit, Improve the Settlements of Payments of State Enterprises," *TKP,* May 7, 1955.

[14] "The Main Task of the People's Bank in 1955," *HHYP,* no. 6, 1955, pp. 142–44. For specific instances of excessive cash holdings, see Starlight, *Fiscal and Monetary Policies in Communist China,* pp. 208–10.

[15] In Manchuria, an industrial area that first experimented with cash control in January, 1950, the percentage was 50. Hu Ching-yün, "Concluding Report Delivered at the Conference on State Industrial Credit and Settlement," *HHYP,* no. 4, 1955, p. 146.

[16] Materials for this section are based on the following: Shen Chi-yen, "Strengthen the Credit and Settlement Works of State Commerce, Help Enterprises to Economize in the Use of State Capital," *CKCJ,* no. 15, 1955, pp. 5–8. Hu Ching-yün, "Strengthen Credit Supervision, Endeavor to Enforce Austerity, and Oppose Waste," *CKCJ,* no. 15, 1955, pp. 4–5; *idem,* "Improve Credit Work, Help Enterprises to Economize Capital," *HHYP,* no. 9, 1955, pp. 183–84; *idem,* "Report to the Second National Conference on the State Commercial Credit System," *HHYP,* no. 7, 1955, pp. 192–96; "The Main Task of the People's Bank in 1955," *HHYP,* no. 6, 1955; Lo Chün, "Certain Questions on the Credit System of the Supply and Marketing Cooperatives," *CKCJ,* no. 14, 1955, pp. 4–7.

[17] These changes will be reviewed further on in this chapter.

In addition, the Bank tried to eliminate inter-enterprise debts through two actions. First, these debts were replaced with special categories of bank loans, particularly with "settlement loans" that financed goods-in-transit; second, the procedures of settlement were further improved and enforced in all areas, thereby removing one major cause of interfirm commerical debts.

Furthermore, the Bank tried to reduce outstanding loans and cash holdings by abolishing the remnants of the "gold treasury" system that had continued to exist in some commercial enterprises, especially in the lower echelons and in units which dealt with agricultural purchases in rural areas.[18] Besides creating direct financial contacts with these units of state enterprises, the Bank also established credit relationships with the supply and marketing cooperatives. These cooperatives, which served as rural agents of state enterprises for the purchase of raw materials and hitherto received huge sums from various enterprises for this purpose, were now financed by local banks. Their loans and cash holdings were therefore subject to examination by these branch banks. In effect, this move amounted to an expansion of the monetary control program from the state sector into the peripheral cooperative sector.

Necessarily, the ascendency of the Bank meant an infringement on the freedom hitherto enjoyed by the enterprises. Complaints about the rigidity and complexity of banking procedures were soon heard; the Bank was accused of interfering with the internal activities of the enterprises and of copying mechanically from the U.S.S.R. a system ill-adapted to Chinese conditions.[19] Early in 1957, there was a lively discussion within banking circles on the appropriate commercial credit

[18] Under the "gold treasury" system, units had no independent accounts and received funds from their supervising organizations instead of directly from the Bank, with the result that large sums were tied up in the process of transfer from one level to another. This system was abolished in the upper stratum of the commercial network in 1952. *Infra,* pp. 81–83.

[19] The complexity of banking procedures on cash control and on the supervision of credit and settlements was first criticized by Ch'en Yun, Vice-Premier, during the Third Session of the First National People's Congress in June, 1956. This was followed by numerous articles dealing with the enterprises' resentment against the Bank's restrictions and interventions. For example, Huang Ju-chi, "A Talk on the Contradiction between the Bank and the Enterprises," *CKCJ,* no. 15, 1957, p. 15; "Listen to the Opinions of the Enterprises on the Improvements of the Credit and Settlement Systems," *CKCJ,* no. 16, 1956, pp. 19–20.

policy to follow.[20] Decisions in that year's banking conference (March, 1957) showed signs of relaxation in the regulation of commercial credit.[21] The Bank's authority suffered a further steep decline during the Great Leap, when its role as a supplier of funds was emphasized at the expense of its second major role, as an economizer and controller of funds. The accent in that period was on the Bank's function of serving, not supervising, production;[22] measures of monetary control were therefore not observed. However, the trend was reversed once again after 1960.[23]

The Money Flow

One result of developing the People's Bank into the center of cash, credit, and settlement was the creation of a double-layered monetary circuit. Within the public sector, only bank deposits could be used as a means of payment for transactions above a minimum amount.[24] As the country became more socialized, this bank credit flow, or non-cash flow, was extended to cover the cooperatives.[25] On the other hand, currency was generally employed in transactions involving the

[20] For a summary of various views and articles that appeared in February and March of 1957, see "On the Policy of Capital Supply through Commercial Credit and Other Questions," *CKCJ*, no. 6, 1957, pp. 19–20.

[21] "The Discussion of Commercial Credit Work in the Conference of Branch Bank Managers," *CKCJ*, no. 6, 1957, pp. 3–6.

[22] This theme was expounded by, among others, Hsiao Fu, "Is It the Business of Bank Credit to Serve or to Supervise?" *TCYC*, no. 5, 1958, pp. 15–17; Chiang T'ieh-shui, "Bank Credit Must Serve the Accelerated Developments of Production," *TCYC*, no. 7, 1958, pp. 36–38.

[23] For the change in emphasis, see, for example, "Correctly Develop the Supervisory Function of the Bank," *JMST*, 1962, pp. 211–12; Li Cho-wen, "From the Principle of Credit Repayment to the Supervisory Function of the Bank," *JMST*, 1962, pp. 212–13.

[24] In 1955, the minimum for non-cash settlement within the city was ￥30; for amounts below this cash had to be used. Between cities, the minimum for acceptance was ￥300 (with exceptions for certain commodities running as low as ￥100); the minimum for letters of credit, telegraphic transfers, and payments by special accounts was ￥300; there was no minimum for remittance by mail. Shu, "An Understanding of the Starting Amounts for Settlements," *CJCK*, no. 78, in *TKP*, May 30, 1955.

[25] For example, the supply and marketing cooperatives and the credit cooperatives were obliged to deposit their cash with the People's Bank; the rural collectives were encouraged to deposit their funds with the credit cooperatives.

households and the fast-dwindling private enterprises. Public units, such as the government administration and the state enterprises, paid out wages and agricultural purchase prices in cash to individual workers and peasants;[26] simultaneously, these units received cash from the households through retail sales and fiscal receipts. Payments within the private sector (i.e., among the households and between households and private enterprise) were also conducted in cash.

Thus the money circuit developed into two distinct, yet connected, levels. The size of the non-cash flow varied directly with the amount of outstanding bank credit, which in turn was dependent on the amount of bank lendings to state enterprises relative to that of loan repayments from these enterprises. As for the cash flow, its increase was affected by the total amount of wages and state purchase of agricultural products, while its decrease depended on goods and services supplied by the state enterprises to the private sector and on taxes or other fiscal payments made by the private sector. When cash held in private hands returned to the state sector and became bank deposits, the deposits might be used by the enterprises to repay outstanding bank loans. Thus, given the fiscal budget and the amount of goods and services available to the private sector, the change in the supply of money was basically influenced by the amount of outstanding bank credit. The effect of such credit on the non-cash flow was immediate; bank loans instantly became enterprise deposits and swelled the flow. However, since a part of the credit granted to state enterprises as working capital would eventually be paid out to the private sector as wages or for the purchase of raw materials, the amount of credit also indirectly determined the cash flow.[27]

---

[26] After the collectivization, agricultural payments were first made to the collectives, wherever possible by non-cash methods; the collectives then distribute dividends to the peasants, mainly in the form of cash. After the communization, non-cash payments were made to the communes, which provided group consumption commodities (food, shelter, etc.) plus some cash wages to the peasants.

[27] For a discussion on whether or not the cash flow is affected by the amount of bank loans, see articles cited, *supra*, p. 16, footnote 24. Huang believes that both bank deposits and currency constitute the supply of money and that both types of money are determined by the amount of bank loans ("Principle of Bank Credit . . . ," *CCYC*, no. 9, 1962, pp. 1–7; also *Money and Monetary Circulation in Our Socialist Economy*, p. 40). Lin considers only currency to be money and believes that the "circulation of money" is dependent on the national plan. However, he concedes that, while not a basic determinant, bank credit

Working Capital and the Flow of Bank Credit[28]

Since both components of the money supply were primarily determined by the availability of bank loans, it becomes necessary to investigate the way in which bank credit was regulated by the People's Bank. As stated earlier,[29] the conceptual role of the People's Bank was that of an organ supplementing the budget in channeling funds toward the desired direction. Whereas the budget supplied state enterprises with fixed capital and regularly incurred working capital, the Bank was to provide these enterprises with working capital that was marginal in character, used for such purposes as temporary and seasonal needs or the financing of goods-in-transit. Thus, in principle, the Bank's responsibility in the provision of working capital was clear.

In practice, however, the flow of capital originating from the Bank, which formed the bulk of the deposit flow, was indefinite. This condition was perhaps inevitable in view of two developments at the time. First, as will be shown in Chapter V, the interest rate was deprived of its traditional function as a regulator of bank credit. Second, planning, the theoretical instrument of monetary management,[30] could not provide the Bank with a sufficient guide for credit granting because financial plans in China were far from accurate.[31]

---

does have direct and indirect influences on the amount of money (i.e., currency), especially under the present Chinese conditions ("On the Function of the Law of Circulation . . .," *CCYC*, no. 2, 1963, p. 30). The intimate relationship between the amounts of bank loans and cash was emphasized also by another author. Yü Jui-hsiang, "On Several Questions Relating to the Balance of the Monetary Circulation and the Commodity Circulation," *CCYC*, no. 3, 1963, pp. 17–24.

[28] Materials for this section are based on: Ko, *The Chinese Budget During the Transitional Period;* Ko, "On the Connection between the State Budget and the Credit Plan," *TKP*, May 31, 1955; Yang P'ei-hsin, "On the Question of the Balancing of the Fiscal Receipts and Expenditures, the Monetary Receipts and Expenditures, and the Commodity Supply and Demand," *CCYC*, no. 5, 1957, pp. 50–63; Kao Hsiang, "On the Function of the State Bank in the Socialist Construction," *CCYC*, no. 10, 1962, pp. 12–25; Li Hsien-nien, "On Several Questions of Fiscal and Monetary Works," *JMST*, 1960, pp. 359–60; Ts'ai, "On the Question of Working Capital," *JMST*, 1962, pp. 208–10.

[29] *Supra,* Chapter I, pp. 11–12.

[30] *Supra,* Chapter I, pp. 14–15.

[31] The following quotation illustrates this point: "The present problem [of the Bank] is that plans are not always realistic, the planned figures of the Bank do not entirely correspond to the requirements of the enterprises. To supervise the enterprises through [the

Thus, in the 1950s, the Bank was confronted with problems arising out of uncertainties on both borderlines of the credit flow. On the one side, it was difficult to determine the "normal" need for working capital of the enterprises and thus to distinguish clearly between the responsibility of the budget and that of the Bank. On the other side, it was also difficult to separate legitimate temporary and seasonal needs of the enterprises from those caused by inefficiencies of the firms or inconsistencies in planning. These ambiguities were reflected in the history of the two categories of bank loans granted to the state sector, called quota loans and nonquota loans.[32] They were used respectively to finance two kinds of working capital, namely, quota working capital and nonquota working capital. The distinction between quota and nonquota working capital was essentially the same as the distinction between capital requirements that were constant in nature and those that were not. A detailed inquiry into the Bank's responsibilities in these two areas would illuminate the problems involved in setting limits to the total amount of bank credit.

QUOTA WORKING CAPITAL

In 1952, state enterprises in Communist China began to operate as separate and independent economic units.[33] Each enterprise was endowed with certain assets and capital, including, for the maintenance of a normal rate of business turnover, a given amount of working capital. The latter was "quota working capital." The actual amount, or quota, was approved annually by the state according to the regularly recurrent ex-

---

control of] plans is still difficult. Therefore different local banks should manage their credit plans according to the actual conditions; they should not take a partial view and blindly implement the plans." See Hsin, "Do Well in the Work of State Enterprises' Credit and Agricultural Loans," *CCCP,* no. 23, 1953, p. 6. Flexibility in credit granting was also emphasized in "The Discussion of Commercial Credit Work in the Conference of Branch Bank Managers," *CKCJ,* no. 6, 1957, p. 5.

[32] In the Chinese banking literature, the terms "nonquota" and "above-quota" are both used. There appears to be no real difference in their content when applied to bank loans or working capital.

[33] Before that time, assets and liabilities of enterprises were centrally controlled by the ministries. Bank loans were supplied to the ministries in lump sums. This was known as the capital supply system, and is discussed at a later point in this chapter.

penses (such as wages and costs of fuel or raw materials) required by the individual enterprise, which in turn depended on the planned production target assigned to it. This sum was entirely supplied by the budget, interest free, as the enterprise's owned working capital.[34]

This system was in line with the conceptual responsibility assigned to the budget. In other words, under this system the budget supplied working capital that was constantly and regularly needed by an enterprise in order to carry out its normal rate of activities. The Bank, then, would not grant loans to cover this kind of working capital; it would grant only nonquota loans covering any additional working capital requirements which occurred over and above the quota.

However, this theoretical separation in the financing of the two kinds of working capital was not always adhered to. The Bank was, in fact, often required to supply a portion of the quota working capital. The result was that, in the 1950s, there were constant shifts in the regulations that governed the Bank's share of quota working capital. This can be seen from Table IV-1.

As stated, in 1952 there was an attempt to determine the quota working capital for each enterprise and to provide this quota entirely through the budget. However, it was soon discovered that quotas tended to be excessive.[35] Apparently, as a means of self-protection, the enterprises were inclined to overestimate their normal requirements.[36] To correct this condition, in 1953, the budget provided only 85 percent of the quota working capital, leaving a balance of 15 percent to be covered by "quota loans" from the Bank as the need arose, thereby giving the Bank an opportunity to check on the use of quota working capital. On top of this, the Bank continued to supply nonquota working capital in the form of nonquota loans.

This arrangement proved to be confusing because sources of funds for the enterprises' regular and irregular requirements were no longer clearly separated. The budget and the Bank encroached on each other's juris-

[34] Hsü Yi *et al.,* "On the Present System of Management of Working Capital," *CCYC,* no. 12, 1958, p. 61.

[35] Ko, "On the Connection . . .," *TKP,* May 31, 1955.

[36] Enterprises were concerned about three things, all of which could be alleviated by inflating the estimates of their quota working capital needs: (1) bank supervision, (2) failure to fulfill plan, and (3) burden of interest payments. Shen Chi-yen, "An Opinion on the Present Work of Loans to the State Commercial System," *CKCJ,* no. 11, 1953, p. 8.

Table IV-1
Proportions of Quota Working Capital from the
Budget and the People's Bank
(industrial enterprises)*

	Percent	
	Budget	People's Bank
(1) 1952	100	0
(2) 1953–1954	85	15
(3) 1955–1957	100	0
(4) 1958	70†	30†
(5) 1959-July, 1961	0	100
(6) From July, 1961, on	80	20

*Figures for 1958 and after July 1961, applied specifically to state industrial enterprises. Other figures were for "state enterprises" without specification. However, because loans to commercial enterprises are known to be different, these figures apparently were applicable only to industrial enterprises. Working capital of commercial enterprises contained two categories, commodity (i.e., inventory) and non-commodity, and the former category comprised over 90 percent of the total (*TKP,* May 19, 1963, p. 1). The budget supplied all non-commodity working capital and a small portion of commodity working capital, while the Bank supplied a large share of commodity working capital (in 1953, it was 90 percent). Beginning in 1958, a minimum amount of commodity working capital was provided by the Bank with long-term loans, additional commodity working capital was provided with short-term loans. Non-commodity working capital was from the budget. (Fei, "Help the Commercial Department to Implement Quota Control," *CKCJ,* no. 5, 1958, pp. 15–16.) Since 1959, all working capital for commercial enterprises was supplied by the Bank, as was the case in industrial enterprises. Beginning in September, 1962, non-commodity working capital again came from the budget.

†During the 1958 decentralization, local governments were given a degree of fiscal autonomy and certain enterprises were transferred from the central government to the local governments. These figures applied only to centrally controlled industrial enterprises. Enterprises under local governments received 30 percent from local budgets and 70 percent from the Bank. "Excerpts of Discussions on This Year's Bank Tasks in the National Conference of Branch Bank Managers," *CKCJ,* no. 2, 1958, p. 3; SC, "Directive on the Compilation of the 1958 State Draft Budget," *FKHP,* VI, 330.

Sources:

Line (1) Hsu Yi *et al.,*"On the Present System of Management of Working Capital," *CCYC,* no. 12, 1958, p. 61.

Line (2) Ko, "On the Connection between the State Budget and the Credit Plan," *TKP,* May 31, 1955; Chao Chih-ch'eng, "On the Question of Credit to State Enterprises," *CKCJ,* no. 10, 1953, p. 3.

Line (3) Ko, "On the Connection . . . ," *TKP,* May 31, 1955; Hu Ching-yün, "Concluding Report to the Conference on State Industrial Credit and Settlement," *CKCJ,* no. 5, 1955; reprinted in *HHYP,* no. 4, 1955, p. 147.

Line (4) Wang Ken-shu, "The Significance of the Granting of Quota Loans to Industrial Enterprises by the Bank," *CKCJ,* no. 5, 1958, p. 21.

Line (5) SC, "Regulations on Several Problems Relating to the Work of Credit Departments of the People's Commune and on the Question of Working Capital for State Enterprises," *FKHP,* VIII, 158; SC, "Supplementary Regulations," *FKHP,* IX, 122.

Line (6) "An Important Measure on the Strengthening of Control over Enterprise Working Capital," *JMST,* 1961, pp. 216–17.

diction, resulting in duplication and, again, excessive working capital in the hands of the enterprises.[37] Therefore in January, 1955, along with other reform measures that generally tightened credit control, the Bank returned to the granting of only nonquota loans.

In 1958, the plan to accelerate industrial production led to the Bank's renewed participation (30 percent) in the supply of quota working capital. When the change was introduced in January, 1958, the stated objective was again to economize funds by promoting more efficient use of working capital through bank supervision and also through the imposition of an interest charge on part of the quota working capital.[38] However, during that year the decentralization plus the feverish pursuit of higher production forced a compromise in the desire to exercise monetary restraints. The Bank became a captive of the enterprises, local governments, and rural communes; these units demanded loans not only for working capital but also for fixed capital, thereby undermining even the fundamental role of the Bank as a supplier solely of short-term credit.[39] Quotas for working capital became meaningless; the distinction between budget funds and bank loans was blurred; and the Bank in fact served as an unlimited supplier of monetary capital. Under the circumstances, the dual system of shared responsibility and control of working capital by the budget and the Bank was unnecessarily complex and cumbersome.

It was in recognition of this reality that, beginning January, 1959, the

[37] There were instances in which nonquota capital was granted by the budget, while the budget's share of quota capital was supplied by the Bank. Ko, "On the Connection . . .," *TKP,* May 31, 1955. A study covering 50 industrial enterprises of the central government showed that in the 3rd quarter of 1954 about 11 percent of their quota working capital was regularly idle, while nonquota inventory accumulation (supported by nonquota loans) amounted to 18 percent of their quota working capital. "The Main Task of the State Bank in 1955," *HHYP,* no. 6, 1955, p. 143.

[38] Wang Ken-shu, "The Significance of the Granting of Quota Loans to Industrial Enterprises by the Bank," *CKCJ,* no. 5, 1958, p. 21; "Excerpts of Discussions on This Year's Bank Tasks in the National Conference of Branch Bank Managers," *CKCJ,* no. 2, 1958, p. 3.

[39] Although the principle of divorcing long-term and short-term investments had never been implemented in agriculture in China (*supra,* Chapter III), it had been upheld in the industrial sector until 1958. However, pressures from the passion for the Leap were so great that even economists and bankers who consistently and vocally advocated this principle moderated their position and wrote in 1958 that, under certain circumstances, the use of bank credit for some basic construction was permissible. For example, Tseng and Yang, "On the Leap of Monetary Works," *HH,* no. 9, 1958, pp. 14–15.

Bank was entrusted with the task of "unified management," under which it supplied the whole of working capital, quota and nonquota alike. This new "100% credit" system[40] at least had the advantage of providing the Bank with a total view of the working capital situation even though the Bank might not be able to limit its size. The system also turned out to have a second effect that may or may not have been intended originally; it relieved the budget of its share of the burden and thus ensured the appearance of a budgetary surplus by means of credit inflation during a period of high fiscal investment.[41]

The "100% credit" system was abolished in the post-Leap era. After July, 1961, the budget again supplied the bulk of the normal requirements of industrial working capital while the Bank participated at the margin (20 percent) with quota loans and shouldered all nonquota loans.[42]

Thus the actual course of development of the Bank's responsibility in supplying working capital to state enterprises was tortuous; it often deviated from the theoretical scheme. In view of the many changes and the explanations given for these changes, it may be concluded that there was in practice a lack of a well-defined demarcation between the budget and the Bank in the financing of working capital. The shoreline of this part of the bank credit flow was therefore indistinct.

A second generalization may be drawn from the historical survey of the quota working capital. While changes in regulations were made

[40] Literally translated, the system was called "credit for entirety." For explanation of the change and conditions of the time, see Hsü Yi *et al.,* "On the Present System . . .," *CCYC,* no. 7, 1958; Yin Yi, "On the Experimentation of '100% credit,'" *TCYC,* no. 8, 1958, pp. 9–11.

[41] Theoretically, funds covering the quota working capital of enterprises were still to be provided by the budgets (central and local) and transferred to the Bank, the latter in turn granting loans to enterprises. SC Communiqué, Ministry of Finance and the People's Bank, "Supplementary Regulations on the Transfer to the People's Bank of the Unified Management of State Enterprise Working Capital," *FKHP,* IX, 121–27. That this had not been effectively carried out was evident in state directives of late 1959 that provided detailed explanation of the procedure and urged the transfer of funds. Ministry of Finance and the PB, "Notice on the Disposition of Several Major Problems . . .," *FKHP,* X, 252–53; PB, "Notice on the Question of Covering the 1959 Quota Working Capital of Local Enterprises with Budgetary Grants," *ibid.,* pp. 270–71.

[42] For commercial enterprises, the "100% credit" system was continued until September, 1962. *Supra,* Table IV-1, first footnote.

throughout the decade, as shown in Table IV-1, these changes fell into two cycles. Before 1957 there was first a movement toward providing a portion of the quota working capital through the Bank and later a retreat from this policy. A similar cycle occurred after 1957. There was, however, a difference in the motives underlying the changes for the two periods.

Until the end of 1957, one major concern of the central authorities was how to reduce the "normal" working capital requirement of each enterprise to a minimum consistent with the rate of economic activities assigned to it. In this respect there was a natural divergence of interests between the individual enterprises and the state. To the former, the possession of abundant working capital meant freedom of action and protection against possible bottlenecks in production; they therefore tried to inflate their estimated capital needs. To the latter, the main task was to maximize the nation's production with a given amount of capital funds, and this required the prevention of excessive quotas. The change in monetary regulation in 1953 that led to the Bank's participation in supplying 15 percent of quota working capital was motivated by a desire to solve this problem. It attempted to reduce the amount of quota working capital held in the hands of an enterprise by 15 percent, while at the same time it ensured that the entire quota was available to the enterprise in case of real need. In addition, the change also enabled the Bank to scrutinize a little more closely the financial condition of each individual enterprise.

In 1955, the Bank withdrew from supplying quota loans. An examination of the prevailing conditions of the time suggests that one or more of the following three reasons might have been responsible for this reversal: (1) The 1955 credit reform might have dictated a return to the theoretical separation in the financing of the two kinds of working capital; (2) the annual quotas estimated by the state enterprises might have become more realistic and less inflated as a result of the Bank's participation and investigation during the previous years, thereby removing the need for continued participation by the Bank in the supply of quota working capital; (3) the Bank might have failed to exert sufficient restraint and supervision over the enterprises, thus rendering the 1954 system ineffective as a measure for the reduction of quota working capital. The second and third propositions are contradictory, but they could have applied simultaneously to different enterprises.

The second cycle of changes in quota working capital began in 1958. The Bank again supplied quota working capital, in increasing proportions. However, the main cause for repeating this policy was no longer a desire to minimize funds supplied to the enterprises or to strengthen bank supervision. Instead, it was an attempt to stimulate a "Leap" in production through an ample supply of bank credit to the enterprises. In other words, monetary stability was disregarded in favor of production. The turning point of this cycle came in 1961, when the Bank sought to re-establish a measure of financial order and reduce its share of quota working capital.

NONQUOTA WORKING CAPITAL AND CREDIT PRINCIPLES

Nonquota working capital referred to capital requirements of the enterprises over and above the quotas allowed. The supply of this type of capital was the main responsibility of the People's Bank and hence formed the major component of the credit flow. Conceptually, the People's Bank functioned so as to provide a flexible revolving pool of resources to meet only temporary and fluctuating capital requirements, thereby supplementing the more rigid budget in the "redistribution of funds." Thus all temporary and seasonal needs of the enterprises plus goods-in-transit were to be financed by the Bank with nonquota loans. However, errors or malpractices in either overall planning or in individual enterprise would result in unexpected capital needs, as would the overfulfillment of plans. Unlike the above-plan outputs, which were encouraged by the authorities, capital needs arising from errors or malpractices were undesirable and tended to become perpetuated. For example, inventories might grow because of shortages in complementary products (due to poor planning coordination) or because of defective products (due to inefficiency of the firm). Such accumulations of unmarketable goods, along with other enterprise losses, might be shifted to the Bank in the form of continuous loans. Furthermore, bank credit might be used to cover unrealized planned profit or even tax payments.

In such cases, budgetary receipts from state enterprises would, in effect, be derived from the Bank.

That the People's Bank had to combat this type of situation was evident from its efforts to establish criteria through which bank lending might be limited. Broadly speaking, the development in this respect consisted of several stages, which will be reviewed below.[43]

CAPITAL SUPPLY SYSTEM (1949–1952)

Until the end of 1952, all capital requirements of state enterprises were provided by the central ministries in charge. The role of the Bank in this rehabilitation period was (1) to consolidate and extend its network in order to absorb and centralize quickly huge sums of deposits from public units and individuals, and (2) to support the central ministries with loans, the bulk of which were for commercial activities. This was called the "capital supply system" or "gold treasury system" under which state enterprises operated with funds belonging to the supervising ministries without separate independent cost accountings. The Bank did not have direct credit relationships with these enterprises, nor did it attempt to limit the amounts of loans to the ministries.

This system was said to have had several drawbacks. First, individual enterprises, since they were not being held responsible for losses, were unconcerned about their own financial condition; inventories of unsalable goods accumulated, as did bank loans to the ministries. Second, under this system liquidity had to travel up in the pyramid of the People's Bank and then down again through the state commercial complex,

---

[43] Materials in the following sections are based on: Li Shao-yü (in 1955, Li was the Head of the Bureau of Commercial Credit of the People's Bank), "Several Questions on Credit to State Commerce," *TKCJ*, no. 17, 1955, pp. 9–11; Shen Chi-yen, "An Opinion on the Present Work of Loans . . . ," *TKCJ*, no. 11, 1953, pp. 7–11; "The Present Conditions of Loans to the State Commercial System (Summarized Report)," *TKCJ*, no. 11, 1953, pp. 17–18; Hu Ching-yün, "Speech at the Conference of Monetary Workers for the Exchange of Advanced Experiences," *TKCJ*, no. 8, 1953, pp. 6.–7; Tseng Ling, "Special Features of the 1953 Economic Conditions and the Bank's Task in Planning," *TKCJ*, no. 10, 1953, p. 1; Chao Chih-ch'eng (Assistant Head, Bureau of State Enterprise Credit, People's Bank), "On the Question of Credit to State Enterprises," *TKCJ*, no. 10, 1953, pp. 3-4; Bureau of State Enterprise Credit, PB, "How to Begin to Implement the 'Temporary Measures on Short-Term Loans to State Commerce,'" *TKCJ*, no. 8, 1953, pp. 14–15; "On the Goal and Functions of Credit to State Commerce," *CKCJ*, no. 5, 1957, pp. 13–15; Hsü T'i-hsin, *An Analysis of the Chinese National Economy . . .* , pp. 206–207.

with large sums being tied up in the process of transfer. Third, the Bank, having no direct connection with the enterprises, could neither supervise these units nor exercise any control over the loans it issued.

To remedy these conditions, in late 1952 assets and liabilities of state enterprises were thoroughly checked; these units were then put under the "business accounting" system, each responsible for its own profit or loss. The business accounting units were endowed with certain capital and assets and assigned various norms relating to the use of working capital. In addition, they established direct contact with local offices of the Bank. Outstanding credit, granted earlier in lump sums by the Peking Bank to the ministries, was converted into local bank loans to individual enterprises. Thus, the Bank was in a position to examine the loans it granted and, through credit control, to spur the enterprises to greater efficiency. Besides, the firms now had to shoulder interest charges as a part of their production costs.

CREDIT RESTRICTIONS (EARLY 1953)

While these transformations were under way, the Bank stipulated in February, 1953, that existing loans to state commercial enterprises be separated into quota loans and temporary loans.[44] Quota loans were to cover 90 percent of the quota commodity working capital;[45] the residuals were temporary loans. Accumulated inventories, labeled "above-quota commodities," were covered by temporary loans.[46] Under the

[44] "Temporary Measures of the People's Bank of China on the Management of Short-Term Loans to State Commerce" was promulgated on February 22, 1953. This was supplemented on May 13, 1953, by "Practical Regulations Relating to Certain Questions Arising from the 'Temporary Measures of the . . . ,'" see "Joint Directive . . . ," *CKCJ*, no. 11, 1953, pp. 1–5.

[45] Quota commodity working capital referred to the quota working capital assigned for the financing of a normal amount of commodity inventory. Commodity inventory accounted for the major part of capital requirements of commercial enterprises. The first Joint Directive of the Bank and the Ministry of Commerce specified that 70–90 percent of quota commodity working capital was to be provided by the Bank. Subsequently the enterprises received only 10 percent of the quota from the Ministry of Commerce as owned working capital; thus the Bank was forced to provide 90 percent of the quota, which was then specified in the supplementary regulations of May. Chao Chih-ch'eng, "On the Question of Credit . . . ," *TKCJ*, no. 10, 1953, p. 4.

[46] In 1953 large amounts of loans were long overdue, making possible inventory accumulations. Hu Ching-yün, "Speech at the Conference of Monetary Workers . . . ," *CKCJ*, no. 8, 1953, p. 6.

Bank's regulations, such commodities had to be liquidated and their loans completely repaid before the end of 1953.[47] In this way the Bank attempted to eliminate the excessive commercial credit that accompanied the piling up of unmarketable goods. It also intended, as a second step, to compartmentalize loan accounts in order to gain a better control of credit and to prevent illegitimate uses of working capital.[48]

However, the immediate cause of the Bank's policy of credit contraction in 1953 lay in certain monetary developments. First, the transitional rapid growth of deposits from public units and individuals was leveling off. Second, the 1953 planned budget drew on the previously accumulated budgetary surplus, resulting in a reduction of budgetary deposits in the Bank. Both factors contributed to inflationary pressures early in the year, and the Bank was compelled to tighten credit.

The Bank's desire to contract credit and to exert a degree of influence over a major component of the credit flow was never realized. At this time, a turmoil was caused by several simultaneous financial changes, and the Bank encountered from the start numerous frustrations as the enterprises sought to circumvent its supervision with various devices.[49] In addition to administrative difficulties caused by resistance from the enterprises, there was a more basic, though evidently unforeseen conflict within the state sector. It was said that the forced liquidation of commercial inventory "disturbed the stability of the market,"[50] while the restriction of commercial loans affected the progress of state industrial production, since it limited the capacity of the commercial enterprises to purchase all goods produced by these industries.[51] The Bank's policy was also denounced on the ground that it reduced the share of

[47] The supplementary regulation allowed some items to be liquidated in 1954.

[48] There were five kinds of loans under the new regulations: quota loans, seasonal loans, settlement loans, temporary loans, and major repair loans.

[49] The enterprises in this period were subject to a thorough examination of their assets, the determination of various quotas, the transfer and separation of bank accounts and the classification of inventory. For the confusion and problems of the Bank and the enterprises, see Shen Chi-yen, "Strengthen the Credit and Settlement Works . . . ," *CKCJ,* no. 15, 1955; and "The Present Condition of Loans . . . ," *CKCJ,* no. 11, 1953.

[50] It is not clear whether this statement means a decrease in prices or a decrease in commodities controlled by the public sector or both.

[51] Ko, *The Chinese Budget in the Transitional Period,* p. 158; *idem,* "The Nature of the National Budget in Our Country and Its Function in the Transitional Period," *CCYC,* no. 3, 1956, p. 78.

market controlled by the state sector and consequently allowed an unwarranted expansion of the capitalistic trade that was contrary to the national objective of socialization.[52]

As a result of this resistance and criticism, the Bank had to reverse its position abruptly in July, 1953. Thus the brief attempt on the part of the Bank to restrict commercial credit ended as a failure.

BALANCE OF FINANCIAL RECEIPTS AND EXPENDITURES SYSTEM (JULY, 1953 THROUGH 1954)

The Bank resumed the policy of unrestrained credit in July, 1953. Under the new lending criterion, called the "balance of financial receipts and expenditures" system, the Bank provided whatever amount that was necessary to balance an enterprise account. As a result, all financial outlays of state enterprises that were not covered by budgetary grants were loaned by the Bank. These loans carried no specifications as to their use or duration; they could be used as working capital, as payments of unrealized planned profit, or for any other purpose. Nor was there any attempt by the Bank to separate the enterprise's owned capital (from the budget) and borrowed capital (from the Bank); they could be used interchangeably to defray all expenses.[53] In brief, bank credit assumed the nature of subsidies or grants rather than that of loans.

This new system differed from the capital supply system of the early years in that it applied to state enterprises with independent accountings.[54] Hence the Bank loaned directly to these units instead of indirectly through their supervising ministries. However, from the monetary point of view, under both systems the Bank provided an unlimited amount of loans. Insofar as there was any difference at all, credit under the new balance system was easier because enterprises had direct access to the Bank and were therefore freed from whatever restraints that might have come from the supervising ministries. On the other hand, the process of a roundabout transfer of funds was eliminated under the new system, thereby helping to reduce the amount of money in transit.

---

[52] "On the Goals and Function . . . ," *CKCJ,* no. 5, 1957, p. 14.

[53] "The Main Task . . . ," *HHPY,* no. 6, 1955, p. 142; Hsü T'i-hsin, *An Analysis of the Chinese National Economy . . . ,* p. 206.

[54] Enterprises which have not changed into "business accounting" units continued to use the capital supply system.

COMMODITY INVENTORY SYSTEM (1955–1957)[55]

As the country embarked on more comprehensive planning in 1955, a major effort was made by the Bank to overhaul the credit system. The new credit regulations were complex, taking into account the conditions and needs of various types of commerce; their implementation was gradual, applying in 1955 only to a group of more important commercial enterprises.[56] Despite this differentiated and partial approach, which indicated caution bred from the 1953 experience, the general direction of the reform measures was clear. The objective was to allow the People's Bank to assume its conceptual role as a supplier of the fluctuating portion of working capital and at the same time to attempt to set limits to this flow. To begin with, the Bank once again enforced the separation of the enterprise's owned and borrowed working capital with the budget providing the owned part.[57] The use of borrowed working capital, that

[55] Additional materials in this section are from: "The Main Task . . . ," *HHYP,* no. 6, 1955, pp. 142–44; Hu Ching-yün, "Report to the Second National Conference . . . ," *HHYP,* no. 7, 1955, pp. 192–96; *idem,* "Concluding Report Delivered at the Conference . . . ," *HHYP,* no. 4, 1955, pp. 146–49; *idem,* "Improve Credit Work . . . ," *HHYP,* no. 9, 1955, pp. 183–84; Bureau of State Industrial Credit, PB, "Summary of Work on the Experimentations of the New Draft Regulation on Industrial Credit and on the Classification of Loans," *CKCJ,* no. 11, 1955, pp. 11–13; Liu Cho-fu (Vice-Minister of Commerce), "Concluding Report to the Second National Conference on the State Commercial Credit System (excerpts)," *HHYP,* no. 7, 1955, pp. 196–99; Li Shao-yü and Ch'en Shih, "Correctly Implement the New State Commercial Credit System," *JMJP,* August 7, 1955; Ch'en Yang-ch'ing, "On the Work of the State Bank from the Viewpoint of Materialism," *CKCJ,* no. 12, 1955, pp. 12–22. Shen Chi-yen, "The Superiority of Socialist Credit Principles Was Revealed through the Implementation of New Measures on Commercial Loans," *CKCJ,* no. 13, 1955, pp. 7–9.

[56] The commercial loan regulations were drafted in mid-1954 with the help of Soviet advisers. They were first applied to the Coal Construction Equipments Company in the 4th quarter of 1954, extended to the Monopoly Trading Company (which dealt with such products as tobacco), the Chemical Products Company and the Petroleum Company in July, 1955, and then to the Cotton, Yarn and Cloth Company in October, 1955. The combined working capital of these five firms amounted to 30 percent of the capital of the entire state commercial system; Their combined sales represented 45.6 percent of the total sales of the system. The group was representative in that it included enterprises dealing with industrial products, agricultural products, products under complete state monopoly as well as imported products; Hu Ching-yün, "Report to the Second National Conference . . . ," *HHYP,* no. 7, 1955, p. 193. Industrial loan regulations were first applied to eight industries in October, 1954, then extended gradually to all industries in July, 1955. *Idem,* "Concluding Report . . . ," *HHYP,* no. 4, 1955, p. 148. Bureau of State Industrial Credit, PB, "Summary of Work . . . ," *CKCJ,* no. 11, 1955, p. 11.

[57] The 1955 budget message showed that a sum of ¥1.69 billion was allocated from the 1954 budget surplus to state enterprises as working capital. This sum was used to repay

is, bank credit, was restricted to the financing of the above-normal or nonquota inventory in the case of industry[58] and to the financing of a major share of commodity inventory in the case of commerce,[59] but state or cooperative trading units dealing with agricultural purchases in the rural areas received full bank financing for their stocks. Next, certain "credit principles" were reaffirmed. According to these princi-- ples, loans should be granted as follows: (1) directly to the users, (2) according to plans and for definite purposes, (3) on the base of commodity collateral, and (4) with specified duration, to be repaid when due. Although the application of these principles varied with different categories of enterprises, in general the Bank was placed in as strong a position as was practicable at the time without conflicting with the state commercial policy. As in 1953, loans were compartmentalized; there were five kinds of loan to industry, six to state commerce, and many more to supply and marketing cooperatives. All were strictly separated and each served a specific purpose.[60]

One result of the reform was that credit became broadly tied to inventory and goods-in-transit. The purpose was to limit the credit flow so that it not only closely followed the commodity flow in direction, but also fluctuated with the latter in size. This policy was founded on a Soviet postulate akin to the classical idea of "monetary veil." Soviet economists believe that money is a mere reflection of goods, and, therefore, monetary circulation should be determined by the circulation of commodities. From this the conclusion is drawn that as long as credit is granted on the basis of commodities it will not lead to inflation or deflation.[61] The upshot was that the People's Bank, in 1955, transplanted

---

a part of their previously accumulated debts to the People's Bank. Li Hsien-nien, "Report on the 1954 Final Budget and the 1955 Draft Budget," *JMST,* 1956, p. 162. This sum was given to commercial enterprises. Lu Han-ch'uan, "On the Equilibrium of Budgetary Receipts and Expenditures, Credit Receipts and Expenditures, and the Supply of Commodities," *CKCJ,* no. 10, 1957, pp. 2–5. The sum was probably used to repay bank loans granted in past years that either were not supported by inventory or were supported by unmarketable inventory accumulated through the years.

[58] In 1955, the whole of quota working capital for industry was provided by the budget, *supra,* Table IV-1.

[59] In general the Bank would provide 85 percent of commodity inventory.

[60] The structure of loans in 1955 will be presented in Chapter V.

[61] Yü Jui-hsiang, "On Several Questions . . . ," *CCYC,* no. 3, 1963, pp. 17–24.

from the U.S.S.R. a policy similar to the "real bills" or "productive credit" principle of the early Western commercial banks, under which loans were granted rather passively on the basis of inventory.

AFTER 1958

The banking situation in 1958 and 1959, when credit was in fact unlimited, has been described above. The principles governing working capital and bank lending reiterated in 1960 were almost identical with those announced in 1954–1955,[62] but it was not until 1961 (for industry) and 1962 (for commerce) that a portion of the enterprise working capital again came from the budget.[63] While no detailed information is available for this later period, it appears that the Bank once more relied on the amount of inventory assets as a guide to lending.

In summary, the Bank's responsibility in supplying nonquota working capital, as in the case of quota working capital, followed an uneven course of development. Before 1953 and again during the Great Leap, the flow of nonquota loans was unrestricted. It covered all requests for working capital, and even some for fixed capital, that were made by state enterprises. The beginning of the planned era (1953) witnessed a brief but ill-fated attempt by the Bank to restrain and regulate credit. This was followed by a period of retreat in which the Bank served as an unlimited supplier of residual funds required by the enterprises and not covered by budgetary grants. The only years with a more narrowly, albeit cautiously, defined flow of nonquota loans were 1955–1957, when bank loans were used to finance a large share of the commercial inventory plus seasonal and temporary requirements and goods-in-transit.[64] Broadly speaking, the goal was to grant both industrial and commercial loans on the basis of stocks of raw materials or finished goods, thereby allowing total credit to ebb and flow passively with the value of inventory.

---

[62] For example, Li Hsien-nien, "On Several Questions of Fiscal and Monetary Works," *HC,* no. 1, 1960, pp. 9–11.

[63] *Supra,* Table IV-1.

[64] In addition, the Bank granted agricultural loans and loans to private sectors. These were relatively unimportant and were not guided by any specific lending criterion.

The Nature of the People's Bank

Developments described above indicate that, despite constant changes, the general functioning of the People's Bank was fairly clearly established by 1955. This section examines the characteristics of the Bank and its responsibilities in the economy.

MAJOR ASSETS AND LIABILITIES

The nature of a financial institution can best be judged through a review of its assets and liabilities. Even though data for the financial statements of the People's Bank are unavailable, a glance at the skeleton items would be helpful.

Instead of the traditional balance sheet of assets and liabilities, the two sides of the People's Bank statement were labeled "uses of funds," and "sources of funds," and items were grouped according to economic sectors.[65] On January 1, 1955, a major revision of the Bank's accounting classifications came into effect. The essentials of the revised contents are presented in Appendix A. Judging from this classification the important components of the Bank's assets and liabilities, stripped of the semantic differences, appear familiar to the Western student.

Among the Bank's assets, the major item was loans, which were classified according to economic sectors and functions. Short-term loans constituted the lion's share, but agricultrual loans were partly long-term. A second group of assets consisted of precious metals and foreign exchange.[66] These were treated as commodity assets of the Bank; while they could be used as, or turned into, international currency, they apparently had little proportionate relationship to the domestic supply of money. Other assets of the Bank included cash on hand[67] and the

---

[65] Hsüen, "The 1955 Accounting Classification of the State Bank," *CKCJ,* no. 23, 1954, pp. 15–16.

[66] Though not listed in the classification presented in Appendix A, which includes only domestic items, foreign exchange is held by the People's Bank. Kao Hsiang, "On the Function of the State Bank . . . ," *CCYC,* no. 10, 1962, p. 15.

[67] Cash on hand, or till cash, was considered a part of the currency in circulation and was held by the Operation Cash Office of the Bank. This was limited to an amount de-

Bank's owned capital equipment, including budgetary appropriations and depreciation reserves for such equipment.

The Bank's liabilities included currency in circulation and deposits. Banknotes issued by the People's Bank constituted the only legal currency in the country; they had a well-defined economic area of circulation. Deposits included those from the state and other sectors; they were predominantly demand deposits but also contained savings deposits from rural and urban individuals. In addition to these two important kinds of liabilities, the People's Bank had certain amounts of capital and earnings. Beginning in 1955, the Bank also received an annual budgetary grant as "credit funds."[68]

In Chinese terminology, then, the main "sources of funds" of the Bank consisted of currency issues, deposits, and budgetary grants, while the major "use of funds" was loans.

A HYBRID INSTITUTION

When its various duties are examined, the Bank appears to possess features of different types of Western organizations. It may therefore be considered a hybrid institution that functioned in several capacities. First, the operations of the People's Bank were in part reminiscent of those of a Western commercial bank. It accepted deposits, cleared payments, and granted short-term productive loans according to the amount of eligible working capital assets held by the state enterprises. It had little discretion in determining the total quantity of outstanding credit. However, unlike the Western commercial bank, the People's Bank was monopolistic; it was expected to keep nearly all enterprise funds as deposits. These features, plus the fact that there was no legal

---

termined by the Bank's normal requirements. Any excess in cash holding must be transferred to the Issue Reserve Fund (formerly an independent system, but since March, 1955, a part of the Bank) and such transfers represented formal retirements of currency from circulation. When more till cash was needed, it was transferred from the Fund to the Cash Office and treated as note issues. Tseng and Han Lei, *The Circulation of Money . . .* (*JPRS* translation), pp. 127–28.

[68] Kao Hsiang, "On the Function of the State Bank . . . ," *CCYC,* no. 10, 1962, p. 17; *infra,* Table VI-7.

reserve requirement, gave the Bank an infinite ability to expand credit as long as such credit was not used for wages or agricultural payments. Loans granted by the People's Bank were coupled with enterprise deposits in the same bank. When enterprise deposits were withdrawn in the form of cash for payments to the households, bank loans turned into circulating currency, which was subject to a quota set by the government.

Besides functioning as a monopoly commercial bank, the People's Bank was, quite naturally, a government bank. It not only served as the fiscal agent and the treasury, with a major portion of its total deposits coming from the budget,[69] but also stood ready to provide the government with loans whenever the need arose.[70] There is thus a close relationship between the budget and the Bank.

In addition, the People's Bank assumed certain characteristics of central banking, albeit not in the sense of a bankers' bank.[71] The People's Bank issued domestic currency, held the nation's reserves of precious metals and foreign exchange and, more important, it was concerned with the total supply of money, particularly with the quantity of currency in circulation.

Finally, the People's Bank was also considered a supervisory organ. This is a unique function of the Communist state bank and stems from its monopolistic status as the center of cash, credit, and settlement. If all measures of the monetary control program were effective, the People's Bank would, as a by-product of daily banking operations, have a complete record of transactions within the state sector except those carried out through barters. The Bank would be, therefore, in a strategic position overseeing the activities of the state enterprises. By watching over their financial conditions and transactions, the Bank could detect in each enterprise any inefficiency or departure from planned performances; by granting or withholding quota or nonquota loans, the Bank

---

[69] Budgetary deposits will be discussed in Chapter VI.

[70] For example, a large portion of the 1956 budget deficit was covered by a bank overdraft. Li Hsien-nien, "Report on the Implementation of the 1956 State Budget and the 1957 Draft Budget," *FKHP,* VI, 109.

[71] Its relationship with the credit cooperatives might be construed as that of a bankers' bank; however, it is perhaps more appropriate to treat the credit cooperatives as semi-independent local agents of the Bank.

could exercise a measure of discipline. Thus it could become a convenient vehicle for the supervision of the enterprises. At the same time, the Bank could also serve as a "barometer" of the nation, reflecting the overall economic weather in the nation.[72]

Inside the Mainland, the mixed nature of the People's Bank had been discussed in different terms. There the question centered on whether the Bank should be considered a state enterprise or a government organ.[73] The People's Bank resembled an enterprise in that it operated on commercial banking principles, with business income derived from interest,[74] and was responsible for its own profit or loss. However, unlike an enterprise, its performance was judged neither by profit achievements nor by the scale of operations. Its major function was the implementation of government policies in the field of money. It was, therefore, according to Communist students, a government organ.

THE FUNCTIONS OF THE PEOPLE'S BANK

Summarizing these characteristics of the Bank, it may be said that, like its Soviet counterpart, the People's Bank was intended to serve two broad types of functions, the one microfinancial in nature, the other macromonetary. These functions are interrelated; both are important to the economic development of the nation.

THE MICROFINANCIAL FUNCTION

The microfinancial, or supervisory, function refers to economic surveillance over individual enterprises via careful scrutiny of the financial conditions of each unit. In this respect, the Bank is to act as a central accounting and auditing agency that can check the performances of the firms, thereby spurring them to greater efficiency and adherence to plans. This banking function is closely related to detailed economic

---

[72] Kao Hsiang, "On the Function of the State Bank . . . ," *CCYC,* no. 10, 1962, p. 18.

[73] Ch'en Yang-ch'ing, "On the Nature of the State Bank," *CKCJ,* no. 21, 1953, pp. 17–18, 26; *idem,* "On the Work of the State Bank from the Viewpoint of Materialism," *CKCJ,* no. 12, 1955, p. 13; Wu Ch'ing-you, "Is the Socialist State Bank an Organization or an Enterprise?," *HH,* no. 1, 1957, p. 8.

[74] Interest will be discussed in Chapter V.

planning. In Communist China, the institutional foundation for this function was laid under the monetary control program; further progress was made in the 1955 reform. However, generally speaking, the People's Bank was not yet in a position to control state enterprises effectively. Thus, during the period of this study the microfinancial function of the Bank was by and large secondary to the Bank's other major function.

THE MACROMONETARY FUNCTION

The macromonetary function of the People's Bank is more traditional; it is similar to that of a noncommunist banking system. The fundamental role of the banking system in a modern nation is to act as an intermediary between saving held in the form of bank deposits and investment made through bank lendings. When an economy is at equilibrium, total saving approximately equals total investment. However, it is possible for the bank, through its decision to extend more or less loans, to cause too large or too small an amount of investment relative to saving. Under full employment, such disequilibrium would lead to changes in the general price level before equality between saving and investment could be restored; in other words, equality would be realized by forced saving via price fluctuations. Thus in order to avoid price instability, the banking system must strive to ensure an aggregate supply of money which is consistent with the requirements of money in the economy at a particular price level. This function of controlling the supply of money so as to achieve a stable or other desirable price level is the macromonetary function. In the West, the responsibility is vested in the central bank, which attempts to influence the amount of commercial credit available by manipulating various instruments of monetary policy.

In Communist China, the People's Bank in fact served as the entire banking system; its monetary function was therefore comprehensive. It channeled saving towards investment, and supplied loans for working capital; it also had to control the total supply of money so as to avoid inflationary or deflationary pressures, especially the former. The preeminence of the macromonetary function of the People's Bank was perhaps due to two conditions. First, the elementary state of planning in China and the underdeveloped nature of the economy rendered aggregative control more realistic and practicable than specific financial control. Second, there was the lingering apprehension of inflation in China. Since the Bank had contributed much towards containing the hyperinflation in the early Communist years, it was only natural that this aspect of control was given continued emphasis.

Concluding Remarks

Paradoxically, the People's Bank's position vis-a-vis the money supply was at once strong and weak. On the one hand, the Bank was the sole creator of money in the economy, and its lending operations fundamentally determined the supply of both deposits and currency. On the other hand, the Bank was required to finance certain types of working capital for state enterprises and its control over credit granted for this purpose was rather loose. Even after 1955, when the inventory criterion was adopted, the influence of the Bank on the quantity of loans, and therefore on the money supply, was passive.

Under the circumstances, how could the Bank perform its macromonetary function, which was considered important? How could monetary stability be maintained? In search for an answer to these questions, we shall first turn to an examination of the major operations of the Bank; that is to say, the condition and development of loans, deposits, and currency will be our next area of exploration.

V

BANK LOANS
AND THE RATE OF INTEREST

THE RELATIONSHIP between bank credit and money supply, as well as the general condition of the credit flow, has already been discussed in the previous chapter. Here bank loans and the rate of interest are surveyed in detail. The institutional structure, quantitative development, and basic policy for each major type of loan are presented and analyzed; an effort is made to gauge the size of aggregate loans; finally, the function of the interest rate is examined.

The presentation of bank loans would be facilitated by dividing credit into two categories according to the nature of the recipients. The first of these, loans to the state sector, includes credit granted to state enterprises and supply and marketing cooperatives. The second category, loans to the nonstate sector, refers to those granted to private and semiprivate units of the economy as well as to the agricultural cooperatives.[1] This classification is useful because the two sectors roughly correspond to the spheres in which the two forms of money, deposits and currency, circulate.

Loans to the State Sector

The quota and nonquota loans described in the last chapter were loans granted to socialized enterprises; thus the credit flow discussed therein was primarily that of the state sector. This sector had priority of access to bank loans, and it normally received by far the predominant share

[1] Loans to the credit cooperatives, however, do not fall into either group because these cooperatives functioned as a part of the banking system itself.

of total credit. Within the state sector, industrial enterprises were most adequately furnished with working capital by the budget; their share of loans was correspondingly small. On the other hand, commercial enterprises, whose working capital mainly consisted of inventory, relied heavily on bank financing. Therefore a distinction between commercial loans and industrial loans should be made.

COMMERCIAL LOANS

The state commercial network, consisting of the public trading companies and the supply and marketing cooperatives, occupied a leading position among recipients of bank credit. This was due to two reasons. First, a large proportion of commercial working capital was supplied by the Bank, as is indicated by the fact that 73.5 percent of the total increase in commercial working capital during the First Five Year Plan period consisted of bank loans.[2] Second, the size of the commercial working capital was considerable because of the extensive functions performed by the state trading network. This network undertook to purchase and store the bulk of goods produced, as well as raw materials required, by state industrial enterprises; thus, in effect, it carried a large part of the industrial inventory. Moreover, it bought and distributed nearly all centrally-controlled agricultural crops and a major share of products made by private firms.[3] Furthermore, it managed the "state commodity reserve" which was held as a buffer stock for the stabilization of essential prices.[4]

THE STRUCTURE OF COMMERCIAL LOANS

The composition of commercial loans underwent several changes; in general, it varied with the organizational hierarchy that governed the nation's trading activities. In the early Communist years, all trade, domestic and foreign, was under the jurisdiction of the Ministry of

---

[2] Sun and Kuo, "Why Is It Necessary to Adjust the Interest Rates," *CKCJ*, no. 24, 1957, pp. 17–18.

[3] Private enterprises generally served as contractors to state commercial enterprises for processing commodities.

[4] Ko, *The Chinese Budget during the Transitional Period*, p. 117.

Trade, and a number of state trading companies were successively organized by this Ministry to deal with specific commodities. In these years, commercial loans were loans to the Ministry of Trade. In 1952, the Ministry of Trade was replaced by the Ministry of Commerce, which administered domestic trade, and the Ministry of Foreign Trade. "Loans to state commerce," then, referred to loans granted to the first Ministry alone. This means that total commercial loans in the state sector had two components: loans for state (domestic) commerce, and loans for foreign trade. Later, as the agencies engaging in state trading multiplied, so did the subgroups in the category of commercial loans. By 1955, in addition to the two ministries for domestic and foreign trade, there were the Ministry of Foodgrains, which monopolized the trading of the most essential consumer's goods, the Ministry of Agricultural Purchases, which controlled the acquisition of certain important agricultural and subsidiary products, and a system of supply and marketing cooperatives in the rural areas. A Ministry of Urban Services was added in 1956, and further changes in the trading hierarchy took place in later years. Since the classification of commercial loans varied accordingly, it is important to bear in mind these organizational developments when examining commercial credit.

As mentioned in Chapter IV, bank credit to state enterprises, commercial loans included, was, except for a brief interlude, unlimited before 1955. Commercial loans were at first supplied to the Ministry of Trade in lump sums, and after 1952 granted directly to various state trading companies. However, this direct contact between branches of the People's Bank and units of the trading network was confined to the upper hierarchy. Commercial units in the lower echelon, especially those below the county level in rural areas, depended on the higher-level firms instead of local banks for funds. These lower trading organs dealt with the population at large; they were the retail stores and cooperatives that supplied consumer's goods and agricultural equipment and simultaneously purchased farm products for the state. Under the post-1952 setup, large sums of working capital, much of it in the form of cash, were held by these decentralized units. The Bank could exercise no immediate control over these funds in spite of the fact that they originated from bank credit granted to the upper trading echelon.

In 1955, coordinated with other reform measures, an attempt was made to extend bank control to cover these local trading units. The Bank tried to loan directly to these units and to ensure that such loans were tied to inventory. This led to a multiplication of regulations and a complex system of commercial credit.

Loans to state commerce. The first type of commercial credit, called loans to state commerce, was a continuation of the pre-1955 domestic commercial loans. The loans were granted directly to various state trading enterprises at the top segment of the commercial pyramid. To tighten these loans, a new set of regulations was experimented with in one important commercial enterprise in 1954 and extended to several others in 1955.[5] Under the new regulation, loans to state commerce were classified into six groups: (1) planned commodity inventory loans, (2) above-plan commodity inventory loans, (3) loans for prepayments of commodity purchase, (4) settlement loans, (5) special loans, and (6) loans for major repairs.[6] The objectives of this compartmentation of commerical loans were to ensure a close relationship between the commodity movements and the flow of loans, to restrict or at least to identify inventory accumulations, and to prevent the use of loans for illegitimate purposes.[7] Similar goals and procedures appeared in other types of commercial loans.

Loans to the basic-level supply and marketing cooperatives.[8] The system of supply and marketing cooperatives formed the lower half

[5] *Supra,* Chapter IV, p. 85, footnote 56.

[6] Li Shao-yu (Director, Bureau of Commercial Credit of the People's Bank) and Ch'en Shi (Deputy-Director, Bureau of Finance of the Ministry of Trade), "Correctly Implement the New State Commercial Credit System," *JMJP,* August 7, 1955; Kao Chi-min and Wang Chung-ho, "Views on the Revision of Loans for Prepayments of Commodity Purchases," *CKCJ,* no.' 15, 1955, pp. 11–13.

[7] When a company ordered goods which could be purchased only with a prepayment, that company was first provided with a loan for this purpose. This loan would be replaced with a settlement loan when the goods were shipped. The settlement loan in turn would be replaced, upon the arrival of the goods, by a planned commodity-inventory loan, which would be repaid when the goods were sold. Should the company fail to sell the goods, it would be forced to apply for the stricter above-plan commodity-inventory loans before it could make further purchases. Special loans were for other unexpected or temporary needs, while major repair loans were for capital maintenance, to be supplied out of a pool of the enterprises' major repair reserves.

[8] This section and the next one are based on the following sources: Lo Chün, "Certain Questions on the Credit System of the Supply and Marketing Cooperatives," *CKCJ,* no. 14,

of the commercial pyramid. Within this network, the above-county-level cooperatives were mainly wholesale distrubutors of manufactured goods. These were granted loans by the People's Bank in the same way as the trading companies were; in other words, they received loans to state commerce.[9] On the other hand, the basic-level cooperatives,[10] which were located in rural areas and performed two distinctive functions of retail sales and state purchases, received two separate kinds of loans for the two functions. The first of these, simply called "loans to the basic-level supply and marketing cooperatives," financed the supply of finished products to the rural population. It was subdivided into three groups: loans for commodity turnovers, settlement loans, and temporary loans.[11] These loans were granted by the county banks directly to various rural cooperatives.[12] The cooperatives themselves were expected to provide at least fifteen percent of the commodity working capital and all of the noncommodity working capital.[13]

Loans for agricultural purchases. The second kind of loans received by the basic-level cooperatives was for the purchase of important agricultural products other than foodgrains. These "loans for agricul-

---

1955, pp. 4–7; T'ieh, "An Understanding of the Three Lending Procedures Under 'Temporary Measures on Short-Term Loans to Basic-Level Supply and Marketing Cooperatives,'" *CKCJ,* no. 11, 1955, pp. 7–8; Wang Tzu-ch'in, "The Role and Functions of Credit and Settlement of the State Bank in the Rural Market," *CKCJ,* no. 10, 1955, pp. 4–7; Jen and Kung, "An Understanding of the Measures on Loans for Agricultural Purchases to Basic-Level Supply and Marketing Cooperatives," *CKCJ,* no. 10, 1955, pp. 8–9.

[9] However, instead of being subject to six groups of loans, these cooperatives had only five; loans for major repairs were eliminated.

[10] In 1955 there were over 30,000 basic-level supply and marketing cooperatives on or below the county level.

[11] Loans for commodity turnovers were for the regular financing of planned sale of products. Temporary loans were to cover any unplanned increase in inventory or other departure from plan that was due to circumstances beyond the control of the cooperatives. Settlement loans were for goods-in-transit.

[12] However, in order to be eligible for direct loans from the county bank, the local supply and marketing cooperative had to satisfy four requirements. (1) It could have suffered no business losses during the preceding three months; (2) it could compile a plan for commodity turnover and a financial plan on time; (3) it could keep accurate accounts and regularly submit them to the Bank; and (4) its average monthly sale was above an assigned quota. Local cooperatives which could not fulfill these requirements could borrow only indirectly from the Bank through the county-level cooperatives.

[13] Non-commodity working capital included the "four expenditures"—petty cash, packaging, goods of negligible value or short life, and advance payment. These could not be covered by bank loans.

tural purchases" were granted by the local business office of the Bank rather than by the county bank. The reason for this closer contact was to ensure a prompt and flexible supply of funds to the rural cooperatives in response to fluctuating deliveries made by the peasants. Because the purchase of some important products, such as cotton, was conducted through advanced contracting that involved partial prepayments to the peasants, two subdivisions for this type of loan were necessary: loans for advance payments and loans for actual purchases.[14] In addition, since rural payments were made in cash, local cooperatives had to be provided first with loans for a cash reserve and then with further loans to replenish the reserve. Thus the classification of loans for agricultural purchases multiplied.[15]

Loans for foodgrains.[16] Among the agricultural products monopolized by the state, foodgrains, the basic daily necessity, were of special importance. The output of foodgrains was large, and so was the amount of credit required for their distribution. Their purchase and sale were administered by a separate countrywide system managed by the Ministry of Foodgrains. The rural foodgrains stations, assisted by the local supply and marketing cooperatives serving as agents, purchased grains from the peasants. The grains were then transferred up the system for storage, then down again for rationed sales in urban areas and in rural districts of industrial crops.

Under the 1955 structure, operations of the foodgrains network were financed in two ways. In rural areas, county banks granted loans to

[14] The practice of granting advance payments (or deposits) for agricultural purchases was discontinued in 1961 on the ground that loans for such payments were not backed by commodities. Ko, "The Arrangement and Control of Budgetary Funds and Credit Funds," *JMST,* 1961, p. 216.

[15] In 1955, there were (1) loans for the reserve funds of advance payments, (2) loans for advance payments, (3) loans for the reserve funds of agricultural purchases and (4) loans for agricultural purchases. In 1956, a new regulation governing short-term loans for agricultural purchases specified five kinds of loans: (1) loans for purchases, (2) loans for advance payments, (3) expenditure loans, (4) settlement loans, and (5) major repair loans. Tai, "A Discussion of the Purchase Loan and Expenditure Loan under the Regulation of Loans for Agricultural Purchases," *CJCK,* no. 111, in *TKP,* June 11, 1956.

[16] This section is based on the following articles: Lin Lang-t'ien (Deputy-Chief, Division of Finance and Accounts, Ministry of Foodgrains), "Do Well in This Year's Work on Foodgrains Credit," *CKCJ,* no. 12, 1955, pp. 23–24; Tai Ch'en-ting and P'eng Wang-p'ei, "An Understanding of the Regulations on Short-Term Loans to State Foodgrains Units," *CKCJ,* no. 12, 1955, pp. 25–28.

local foodgrains units on the basis of the balance of financial receipts and expenditures system.[17] In practice this meant that the supply of credit was neither limited nor necessarily tied to inventory. In urban areas, however, the principle of specialized loans was adopted, giving rise to four groups of loans: inventory, advance payments, settlement, and special. The purpose was, again, to create a direct correspondence between inventories and loans.[18]

Loans for foreign trade. Another type of commercial credit was granted to state enterprises for foreign trade. By 1955, such trade was already monopolized by the state, and bank loans were used to finance the inventories and goods-in-transit for export and import.

THE DEVELOPMENT OF COMMERCIAL LOANS

There is little information available in absolute magnitudes that would indicate the quantitative development of commercial loans in the state sector. However, it is possible to outline roughly the growth and importance of these loans in relative terms. For the years between 1950 and 1954, there is a series of published data on loans to state commerce which is expressed in percentages. This is shown in Table V-1. But systematic data, even in index form, broke off in the year of the credit reform; thereafter the broad trend of development could only be mapped on the basis of scattered references. Despite the meager information, two aspects of commercial loan development may be discussed further.

The proportion. Column 1 of Table V-1 shows that, of all loans granted by the People's Bank in the early years, between 75 and 80

---

[17] *Supra,* Chapter IV, p. 84.

[18] The system of specialized loans was instituted in 1955 in 96 larger cities (each with a population of over 100,000) under "Temporary Measures of Short-Term Loans to State Foodgrains Unit." (Lin Lang-t'ien, "Do Well in This Year's Work . . . ,", *CKCJ,* no. 12, 1955) However, judging from the article by Tai and P'eng "An Understanding of the Regulations . . . ," *CKCJ,* no. 11, 1955), the Bank apparently had intended to implement this regulation in the entire country and to eliminate all loans granted on the balance system. This discrepancy in viewpoints in their presentations of the same regulation is interesting since Lin represented the Ministry of Foodgrains whereas Tai and P'eng obviously wrote from the position of the Bank. The divergence indicates the obstacles confronted by the Bank in its struggle to limit bank credits to state enterprises and the resulting gradual approach adopted by the Bank.

Table V-1
Loans to State Commerce, 1950–1957

Year	As percent of total loans from the People's Bank (1)	Percent change from preceding year (2)	Index 1950 = 100 (3)
1950	80.36	—	100
1951	75.38	+228.60	329
1952	79.03	+ 76.37	580
1953	76.45	+ 21.01	701
1954	80.16	+ 44.05	1,010
1955	—	—	1,140
1956	—	—	—
1957	—	—	1,740

Sources:
   Cols. (1) and (2): Li Shao-yü, "Several Questions on Credit to State Commerce," *CKCJ*, no. 17, 1955, p. 10.
   Col. (3): 1950–1954: computed on the base of col. 2. 1955: Ko, *The Chinese Budget during the Transitional Period*, p. 21. 1957: Ts'ao, "Monetary Affairs in the Past Ten Years," *JMST*, 1960, p. 88. In this source it was stated that loans to state commerce increased by more than two times in the five years between 1953 and 1957. Accordingly the index for 1957 is indicated here as three times the 1952 index.

percent were loans to state commerce. Thus commercial loans were by far the most important form of bank credit. Certain additional data are available that supplement those in the table. It was said that: (1) for the three years of 1953–1955, 85 percent of all bank loans were commercial loans granted to the trading departments, including commerce, foreign trade, supply and marketing cooperatives and foodgrains;[19] (2) loans to the Ministry of Commerce and those to supply and marketing cooperatives amounted to 56 percent of all loans granted;[20] (3) for the period of the First Five Year Plan, the Bank gave approximately 65 percent of its loans to support state commerce and supply and marketing cooperatives.[21] The first of these percentages (85 percent) is larger than those given in column 1 of Table V-1, even though both appear to refer to the share of total commercial loans. One possible explanation for the discrepancy is that data in the table represented loans to the Ministry of Commerce, which at first handled all state trade

[19] Wang Lan, "Financial Planning in the Past Three Years," *CKCJ*, no. 14, 1956, pp. 3–5.
[20] *Ibid.*
[21] "Great Developments in People's Monetary Affairs," *JMST*, 1958, p. 571.

101

but since 1952 managed domestic trade alone. Thus figures for 1953 and 1954 in Column 1 of the table (76.45 and 80.16 percent) were exclusive of foreign trade, while the 85 percent mentioned above included it. This explanation seems reasonable in view of the institutional development.[22]

On the basis of the above information, certain generalizations on the size and composition of commercial loans during the period of the First Five Year Plan could be made. First, broadly speaking, total commercial loans accounted for over 85 percent of all bank loans granted; of these approximately one-tenth was for foreign trade, two-tenths for foodgrains, and the rest was for state trading companies (Ministry of Commerce) and supply and marketing cooperatives. The last component tended to grow within the five-year period. Second, a large proportion of loans from the People's Bank, probably higher than 50 percent, was devoted to the financing of rural products. This can be deduced from the fact that, besides loans for foodgrains, loans for foreign trade primarily supported the purchase of agricultural products for exports.[23] In addition, one of the main functions of the trading companies and cooperatives was to purchase agricultural and subsidiary products so as to provide the industries with raw materials and the urban population with consumer's goods.

The growth. Besides the large proportion, Table V-1 also shows a continuous growth in commercial loans. There were two reasons for the steep rise. In the first place, it was a deliberate policy of the government to expand state trading so as to replace gradually private commercial activities. As state trading expanded, so did commercial loans, since the former was essentially supported by the latter. In the second place, the growth in commercial loans was partly the result of a growth in inventory. Table V-2 compares the rate of change of commercial inventory and that of commercial loans. Both series increased together. For 1951–1952, the percentage growth in loans was much larger than that

[22] In addition to the Ministry of Foreign Trade, the All China Federation of Supply and Marketing Cooperatives and the Ministry of Foodgrains were established in 1954; thus in 1955 these also became separate commercial departments. However, these were domestic trading units. Their loans were probably not excluded in the data of col. 1 of Table V-1.

[23] Imports in this period were mainly capital goods that were subject to direct physical distributions.

Table V-2
Indexes of State Commercial Inventory and Loans to
State Commerce, 1950–1956

Year	Percent change from preceding year		Index 1950 = 100	
	Inventory* (1)	Loans (2)	Inventory (3)	Loans (4)
1950	—	—	100	100
1951	+83.6	+228.60	184	329
1952	+49.7	+ 76.37	275	580
1953	+20.0	+ 21.01	330	701
1954	+44.4	+ 44.05	476	1,010
1955	+23.0	—	586	1,140
1956	−16.1	—	491	—
1957	—	—	—	1,740

*In the source, the inventory data are labeled "commodity inventory of state commercial departments," without further specification. The data may or may not include the state commodity reserve.
Source:
Col. (1): Jung, "On the Balance of State Budgetary Receipts and Expenditures, State Credit Receipts and Expenditures, and Commodity Supply and Demand," *TC,* no. 6, 1957, pp. 1–2.
Cols. (2) and (4): Table V-1.
Col. (3): Computed on the basis of col. (1).

in inventory (see columns 1 and 2) while, for 1953–1954 the two series were quite close.

Part of the annual increase in inventory was a natural result of the expansion in state trading itself. However, the periodic emphasis given to inventory liquidations leads to the suspicion that some of the large increase represented accumulations caused by inefficiencies in the planning or production processes.[24] The developments in 1956 and 1957 tend to confirm this suspicion. Since a few absolute figures, so rarely available, were published for these years, a review of the conditions in this period would be worthwhile. Besides lending support to the above-mentioned conjecture, such a review would provide a glimpse on the magnitude of changes in commercial loans and inventory.

In 1956, high investments, increased wage rates, and loans granted

---

[24] For example, *JMJP* editorial, "Stop the Accumulations and Wastes of Commodities," *JMJP,* May 21, 1955. Reprinted in *HHYP,* no. 6, 1955, pp. 102–103.

to the nonstate sector to stimulate socialization led to a sudden increase in the money supply. The resulting inflation was partially kept in check by drawing on the commercial inventory, including the buffer stock.[25] Consequently, the state's holding of commodities declined by about two billion yuan,[26] while loans to state commerce contracted by "more than one billion yuan."[27] The condition was reversed in 1957, when the nation contracted. Inventory held by the trading network greatly expanded and commercial loans climbed accordingly. Between January and August, loans granted to state commerce (excluding those for the purchase of foodgrains) rose by 1.4 billion yuan.[28] The increased inventory reflected by these loans contained, in the most part, producer's goods;[29] it was apparently an aftermath of the sudden deceleration in the rate of investment.[30] The total increase in commercial loans for 1957, however, was obviously very much larger than 1.4 billion. This can be seen from two sets of information. First, the total of industrial and commercial (including foodgrains) loans of 1957 was said to be ¥3.46 billion above the planned figure[31] while industrial loans increased by ¥0.4 billion.[32] Assuming that the planned figure for 1957 was at least as large as the 1956 realized amount[33] and that the 1957 planned

---

[25] Ch'en Yün, "Speech in the Third Meeting of the Second Plenary Session of the Chinese People's Political Consultative Conference," *JMJP*, March 10, 1957, p. 2, quoted by Ko, "On the Inter-Connection and Equilibrium of Budget, Credit, and Material Goods," *CCYC*, no. 1, 1958, p. 14. This source specifically mentioned a decline in 1956 of both the state commodity reserve and the inventory of the commercial departments.

[26] Here it is not clear whether the decline in holding took place in commercial inventory only, or in both the inventory and the state commodity reserve. The Chinese phrasing permits both interpretations. Li Hsien-nien. "Report on the Implementation of the 1956 State Budget and the 1957 Draft Budget." *FKHP*, VI, 115. The same phrasing is used by Ko after the quotation mentioned in the above footnote (Ko, p. 15).

[27] *Ibid.*, p. 13. These loans included those to different state commercial departments, including foodgrains, agricultural purchases and domestic commerce.

[28] Ch'en Hsi-yü, "Report to the Conference on Financial Works . . .," *CKCJ*, no. 18, 1957, pp. 1–5.

[29] *Ibid.* Stocks of essential consumer's goods, such as coal, cloth, sugar, and oil, remained low. Li Hsien-nien, 1958 Budget Report, *FKHP*, VII, 120.

[30] "Conditions in the Past Half Year; Requirements for the Next Half Year," *CKCJ*, no. 14, 1957, pp. 1–2.

[31] Li Hsien-nien, 1958 Budget Message, *FKHP*, VII, 120.

[32] Bureau of State Industrial Credit, PB, "The Condition of Industrial Credits in 1957 and the Arrangements for 1958," *CKCJ*, no. 3, 1958, pp. 11–14.

[33] The assumption appears reasonable in view of the unusually low (and way below-plan) commercial loan figure for 1956.

relative shares of industrial versus commercial loans remained similar to those of the previous year, the commercial loans must have increased by at least ¥3.06 billion in 1957 compared with 1956 (that is, the difference between ¥3.46 billion and ¥0.4 billion). Second, this estimate is consistent with another set of data that show that commercial inventory, the bulk of which was financed with bank credit, rose by ¥3.83 billion in 1957, of which ¥2.57 billion was for consumer's goods and ¥1.26 billion for producer's goods.[34]

THE POLICY AND PROBLEM OF COMMERCIAL LOANS

The structural description of commercial loans reflects the credit policy of the Bank in 1955. By creating a multitude of direct flows of loans from the banking system to the immediate credit users, and by regulating these flows through detailed classifications and attachments to inventories, the Bank was trying to satisfy the transactional demand for money in commerce while at the same time keeping the amount of outstanding credit to the minimum. If the regulations for commercial loans were strictly enforced, each movement of goods would be accompanied by a special kind of credit designed to finance only that particular step of the commodity journey.

It is also clear from the classification and development of commercial loans that farm products occupied a uniquely important position among the nation's trading activities. This mirrored the rural character of the economy, in which agriculture was the prime source not only of consumer's goods, but of industrial raw materials and exports as well. The purchase of rural products was therefore one of the most important functions of the commercial network, and it was necessary for the Bank to support it. On the other hand, while it was important for the Bank to restrict excessive commercial credit in general, it was particularly crucial for the Bank to curtail the part that flowed into the farm areas; for that part would immediately affect the volume of currency in circulation. Since agriculture was by nature more difficult to control or predict, the Bank could not set accurate quantitative limits to commercial credit

---

[34] "Commodity Turnover in the Domestic Market in 1957," *Stat. Res.,* no. 4, 1958, p. 24. In the budget message of 1958 (Li Hsien-nien) the increase in commercial inventory was given as approximately ¥3.5 billion without breakdowns.

for each local area. Thus the attachment of bank loans to inventory furnished a logical solution to reconcile the conflicting requirements. It gave a measure of restraint over commercial credit without rigidly limiting funds available for rural purchases.

However, although the inventory criterion provided a flexible guide to commercial loans, it could not, without a detailed investigation into the operations of individual enterprises, solve the problem of inventory accumulations arising from lack of coordination or other reasons. Following the 1955 reform, the commercial enterprises reacted strongly against the Bank's stringent control of credit and periodic checking of inventory.[35] The trading network was especially agitated over the restriction placed on inventory accumulations. By 1957 commercial credit was relaxed and the detailed regulations were simplified. Loans were granted to trading companies and basic-level units according to their purchases, without regard for the progress of their sales.[36] In 1958, the policy of providing ample financial supports to the commercial network was intensified.[37]

INDUSTRIAL LOANS[38]

The tightening of industrial credit also began in 1955. In that year a new regulation on short-term industrial loans was implemented. Following

[35] *Supra,* Chapter IV, p. 70. The dilemma of the Bank regarding commercial credit was also discussed in Ts'ao, "Summary Report at the Conference of Branch Bank Managers," *CKCJ,* no. 7, 1957, pp. 1–3.

[36] Hsin, "Contradictions in the Works of Commercial Credits," *CKCJ,* no. 13, 1957, pp. 9–10; "The Discussion of Commercial Credit . . .," *CKCJ,* no. 6, 1957, p. 5.

[37] Shih Tzu-kuang (Assistant Head of the Bureau of Commercial Credits, People's Bank), "The Main Task of State Commercial Credits and Settlements in 1958," *CKCJ,* no. 2, 1958, pp. 9–10.

[38] This section is based on materials from the following sources: Articles on industrial loans cited in Chapter IV, note 55; "Thoroughly Implement the Policy of Economy, Further Improve the Works on Industrial Credit and Settlement," *CKCJ,* no. 16, 1955, pp. 3–4; "Extend the New System of Credit and Settlement for State Industry: Promote Enterprise Economic Accounting," *TKP,* February 17, 1955; Shen Yü-chieh (Chief of Bureau of State Industrial Credit of the People's Bank). "Work on the Extension of the New Regulations of State Industrial Loans," *CJCK,* #97, in *TKP,* December 22, 1955, and "The Meaning and Functions of the Special Loan for Accumulated Inventory to State Industries," *CJCK,* #98, *TKP,* December 29, 1955; Shao Ch'iu-ming, "The Management of Industrial Loans for Major Repairs," *CKCJ,* no. 2, 1956, pp. 19–20; Ho Chuan, "An Opinion on the Improvement of State Industrial Loans, *CKCJ,* no. 18, 1956, pp. 20–21.

a policy similar to the commercial credit policy, this regulation classified industrial loans into five caregories.[39] The first and most important of these was the nonquota loans, which were to cover above-normal financial needs of state industries. They were primarily intended for the financing of the above-average portions of seasonal increases in inventory. Other excessive inventory that could not be attributed to the seasonal factor fell into three groups and received different treatment. (1) Previously accumulated inventory for which nonquota loans had already been granted were to be disposed of by the enterprises as soon as feasible so that these loans could be repaid. (2) Inventory accumulations arising out of conditions beyond the control of the enterprises concerned were eligible for nonquota loans. Such accumulations included those caused by changes in the production plans or technology, by off-schedule deliveries of imported or centrally allocated goods, or by overfulfillment of planned production. (3) Inventory accumulations caused by inefficiencies in the enterprises themselves were not eligible for bank financing.

The second category of industrial loans, called settlement loans, served to finance goods-in-transit. The expansion of these loans, which helped to discourage inter-enterprise debts by replacing them with bank credit, was considered an essential ingredient of the 1955 reform. The settlement loans tended to strengthen the Bank's supervisory role over the enterprises and to synchronize the flow of bank credit with the flow of commodities. Therefore they were assigned an important status among commercial loans as well as among industrial loans. Into the third category, temporary loans, were grouped all existing bank credit against which the borrowing firms held no inventory. These might be loans that the enterprises could not repay immediately because of interfirm debts (i.e., because goods were sold to other enterprises on credit), or they might be loans for other temporary or transitional purposes. The fourth category contained special loans that were for making advance payments by industrial enterprises to either rural trading cooperatives or the peasantry toward the purchase of industrial raw materials. Like temporary loans, special loans were not backed by

---

[39] In 1955 the budget provided all quota working capital for the state industry, therefore the Bank abolished quota loans. *Supra,* Table IV-1.

107

commodities. Obviously, they overlapped with the commercial loans for agricultural purchases and were perhaps intended to be transitional in nature. Finally, there were loans for major repairs. They were similar to those granted to commercial enterprises bearing the same name.

All five kinds of industrial loans were, theoretically, short-term. In practice, however, some of the accumulated industrial inventory could not be eliminated in less than a year. Since budgetary grants were insufficient to cover these accumulations, the Bank was forced to grant longer-term loans to the enterprises. But it tried to separate them from the current flow of short-term credit. Therefore a "special loan for accumulated inventory of state industry" was instituted at the beginning of 1956 that financed above-quota inventory not disposable within one year.[40] These loans were to be repaid as soon as the goods were sold. They had a two-year limit, expiring December, 1957, with an interest rate amounting to half of the rate for the regular nonquota loans.

Statistical data for industrial loans were even more meager than those for commercial loans. Evidently, the size of industrial loans was relatively small. This was so because, first, a large share of industrial inventory was carried by the commercial network, and second, state industries were more generously endowed with working capital from the budget. However, the available scattered figures show a long-run growth trend for industrial loans. During the First Five Year Plan period, total industrial loans increased 2.3 times.[41] The rise during these years was not smooth; it was obviously interrupted by the credit stringency and reform in 1955. However, the Bank's control over industrial credit was not as effective as desired, for the industry's total indebtedness again

[40] Accumulated inventories were eligible for special loans only if they were caused by the following factors: (1) Accumulations of raw materials, semimanufactures and finished products caused by a change of the approved production plan, a lack of production plan, or inconsistencies in various plans; (2) accumulations of semimanufactured and finished products caused by a lack of balance or of coordination in productive facilities; (3) accumulations of finished products caused by a lack of balance between productions and sales or by an overfulfillment of the production plan; (4) accumulations of raw materials caused by a change in blueprint designs or in the quality of the product; (5) accumulations caused by early or delayed arrivals of imported resources; (6) unmarketable inventory taken over from previous owners during the socialization of private industry. Ho Chuan, "An Opinion on the Improvement . . .," *CKCJ,* no. 18, 1956, and Shen Yü-chieh, "Work on the Extension . . .," *CJCK, #*97, in *TKP,* December 22, 1955.

[41] Ts'ao, "Monetary Affairs of the Past Ten Years," *JMST,* 1960, p. 88. More than half of the industrial loans were granted to heavy industries.

climbed "a great deal" in 1956.[42] This climb was prompted by the inflationary pressures and the subsequent scarcity of goods that prevailed at the time. Industrial enterprises, in an effort to forestall shortages, competed to purchase and stock up either raw materials or other useful commodities that could be used to barter for the needed materials. In this scramble for goods, the industry's process of liquidating old inventory was halted, while new bank borrowing grew.[43]

The expansion of industrial loans continued in 1957. In that year the abrupt decline in state investments and the consequent changes in production plans left an accumulation of producer's goods in the hands of the firms. To cover the increased inventory, bank loans were granted. Between January and August, state industrial loans rose by 0.4 billion yuan, whereas the planned increase for this type of loan was 0.15 billion yuan for the entire year.[44] At the end of 1957, the total increase remained about the same (¥0.396 billion) as that in August.[45] The fact that state industries received additional working capital from the budget during 1957, and that this was used partially to cover the swollen inventory, was perhaps responsible for the stability of industrial loans during the closing months of the year. In general, the Bank's industrial credit policy of 1955 was maintained in 1957; loans were limited to the financing of nonquota and temporary needs. At the same time, the Bank struggled to recall the special loans for accumulated inventroy.[46]

The abandonment of monetary caution in 1958 necessarily affected

[42] Shao Ch'iu-ming, "Prevent Industrial Enterprises from Purchasing and Stocking Materials Blindly," *CKCJ,* no. 4, 1957, p. 13. It is also known that in 1956 some bank loans were used, contrary to regulations, to cover quota working capital. Ch'en Hsi-yü, "Report to the Conference of Branch Bank Managers on Last Year's Conditions and This Year's Tasks." *CKCJ,* no. 6, 1957, pp. 1–3.

[43] The "commodity scare" and the enterprises' competition for raw materials began in September, 1956. Bureau of State Industrial Credit, PB, "The Condition of Industrial Credits . . .," *CKCJ,* no. 3, 1958. The situation was also mentioned in a communiqué of the National EconomicCommission concerning the inter-enterprise inventory accumulation, *FKHP,* V, 87–90. Since both the inventory and bank borrowing of the commercial enterprises declined steeply in 1956, part of the growth in industrial loans might represent a shift of inventory from the commercial to the industrial enterprises.

[44] Ch'en Hsi-yü, "Report to the Conference on Financial Works . . .," *CKCJ,* no. 18, 1957, p. 1.

[45] Bureau of State Industrial Credit, PB, "The Condition of Industrial Credits . . .," *CKCJ,* no. 3, 1958, p. 11.

[46] Ch'en Hsi-yü, "Report to the Conference of Branch Bank Managers . . .," *CKCJ,* no. 6, 1957, p. 3.

industrial credit, and the Bank resumed the granting of quota loans to cover quota working capital. During the first eight months of the year, industrial loans increased by 1.75 billion yuan[47] even though the planned increase for the whole year was only 0.65 billion yuan.[48] By November, total industrial credit amounted to ¥9.35 billion, of which ¥7.47 billion was to finance the development of local industries.[49]

Loans to the Non-State Sector

Compared with loans to the state sector, those to the nonsocialized sector were rather minor. However, there was an important exception to this rule; in 1956, bank credit was used to encourage the socialization of private productive units, causing the non-state sector to receive a large share of loans. There were two types of borrowers in this sector— agriculture and nonsocialized commerce or industry. Thus the two main flows of bank credit were agricultural loans and loans to private or semi-private enterprises.[50]

AGRICULTURAL LOANS

Agricultural loans were bank credit to the rural productive units, including individual farmers and cooperatives.[51] They were granted by the People's Bank through the Agricultural Bank when it existed, or

---

[47] Ts'ao, "Repeated Leaps in Bank Works," *TKP,* October 1, 1958. In 1958 there was a decentralization of industries. Most of the increase in industrial loans (¥1.67 billion out of the ¥1.75 billion) was granted to local industries. The Bank had to provide 70 percent of the quota working capital for these industries.

[48] Bureau of State Industrial Credit, PB, "The Condition of Industrial Credits . . .," *CKCJ,* no. 3, 1958, p. 12. This planned figure excluded quota loans. Of the ¥0.65 billion planned increase in industrial loans, ¥0.5 billion was intended for centrally controlled industries, ¥0.15 billion for locally controlled industries and handicrafts.

[49] "The Glorious Performance of Fiscal and Financial Work in 1958," *JMST,* 1959, p. 360. The iron and steel industry alone received ¥2.0 billion of new loans in 1958. Ts'ao, "Monetary Affairs in the Past Ten Years," *JMST,* 1960, p. 89.

[50] Loans to credit cooperatives are not included here because, as mentioned, these units are a part of the financial system.

[51] State farms were insignificant in this period. Their loans were negligible and belonged to the state sector.

through the credit cooperatives which served as bank agents. These loans did not represent the entire supply of credit in the rural areas. In addition to agricultural loans, the farm sector received advance payments for agricultural purchases which originated as commercial loans while the credit cooperatives also granted loans with their own funds.

THE STRUCTURE OF AGRICULTURAL LOANS [52]

Agricultural loans included both production and consumption credit as well as long-term credit. In the very early period, they were extended directly to individual farmers. Thus, between 1949 and 1952, 70 to 80 percent of the rural credit was granted to poor peasants who had acquired land under the land reform but lacked both working capital and living maintenance, while the remainder went to middle-class peasants.[53] From 1953 on, the emphasis was shifted to the socialized sector that was beginning to take form; as a deliberate policy measure, an increasing share of loans was directed towards the agricultural mutual-aid teams and cooperatives. Therefore, by 1955, eighty percent of the agricultural loans was received by these semisocialized units for productive purposes.[54] Meanwhile, the rural credit cooperatives were gathering force and supplementing the Bank in the provision of credit to individuals, either for consumption or for production. A large share of the Bank's rural loans of 1956 was extended to individual peasants, but the purpose was to enable them to join the collectives. In 1956, rural lendings suddenly gained importance; at the same time the structure of

[52] This section is based on materials from the following articles: Tseng Ling, "The Effects of Agricultural Collectivization on the Rural Monetary Circulation," *CCYC*, no. 6, 1956, pp. 39–58; The Agricultural Bank of China, "Temporary Measures on the Management of Loans to Agricultural Collectives." *FKHP*, II, 545–46; "The Actual Policy of Basic Construction Loans to the Agricultural Collectives," *CKCJ*, no. 7, 1956, p. 2; "How to Manage the Productive Expenditure Loans to the Agricultural Collectives," *CKCJ*, no. 7, 1956, p. 3; "The Objects, Uses, Amounts, and Durations of the Poor Peasant Cooperation Fund Loans," *CKCJ*, no. 7, 1956, pp. 3–4; "On Public Welfare Loans to the Agricultural Collective and Individual Members," *CKCJ*, no. 7, 1956, p. 5.

[53] Ts'ao, "Monetary Affairs in the Past Ten Years," *JMST*, 1960, p. 89.

[54] Yang P'ei-hsin, "Rural Finance," *Peking Review*, no. 16, 1964, p. 18. The share of total agricultural loans granted to Agricultural Cooperatives (excluding mutual-aid teams) rose from 21.4 percent in 1954 to 43.5 percent in 1955. "The State Bank Granted Eight Billion Yuan Agricultural Loans during the Period of the First Five Year Plan," *CKCJ*, no. 2, 1958, p. 23.

loans also became more complex. There were five kinds of agricultural loans granted by the People's Bank. The first three of these assumed a crucial role in stimulating the collectivization drive and were therefore the most important.

Loans for basic construction. The first kind of agricultural loans supplied fixed capital to the collectives; these loans might be used for financing the purchase of farm implements, livestock, etc., or for projects involving irrigation or virgin land development. While the duration of loans was generally three to five years, with exceptional cases extending to a maximum of ten years, the repayment began within the first year. The amount of this type of loan was not to exceed the sum of the expected "accumulation fund" of the borrowing collective during the period of indebtedness.[55]

Loans for productive expenditures. The collectives could use this kind of loan only as working capital, to cover such items as seed, fertilizer, insecticide, animal feed, and small farm tools; they were short-term loans, expiring within one year. The ceiling of such credit was 20 percent of the "productive expenditure fund" of the borrowing collective if the latter were a newly formed unit. This ratio was lowered to 10 percent when the collective became more than one year old. By the "productive expenditure fund" was meant the amount of capital necessary for short-term turnovers.[56]

Loans for the Poor Peasants' Cooperation Funds. The formation of collectives during the socialization drive was based on a "capital share" system under which a collective held two "capital share funds." The first, called productive expenditures capital share fund, was a pool

---

[55] Out of its income, the collective set aside each year a reserve to cover capital depreciation and growth, called the accumulation fund.

[56] There have been three interpretations of the term "productive expenditure fund": (a) the actual amount of turnover capital, (b) the productive expenditures of the collective during the year, and (c) the "productive expenditure capital share fund" of the collective. The Agricultural Bank of China pointed out that only the first interpretation was correct. In areas producing only one crop a year, the rate of turnover would be one and the first two interpretations would coincide. But in areas producing two or three crops a year, then (a) would be much smaller than (b). Item (c) referred to the amount of capital shares earmarked for productive expenditures when the collective was formed; it might or might not correspond with the actual need of working capital during the year. "How to Manage the Productive Expenditure Loans . . .," *CKCJ*, no. 7, 1956.

of working capital; the second, named capital share fund, was really fixed capital. To form the two pools of capital for the new unit, all rural "means of production" were transferred from private hands to the collectives; in return, individual owners acquired shares in the two funds. The number of shares to be contributed by each member was allotted according to his labor power. A relatively well-to-do peasant whose possession of means of production might exceed the value of his allotted capital shares, would receive compensation from the collective for the excess either in a lump sum or by installments. On the other hand, a poor peasant who might have neither real nor monetary capital to pay for his shares would be given state assistance in the form of credit from the People's Bank. These were the loans for "poor peasants' co-operation funds." They were long-term loans, granted at a low rate of interest. They matured in three to five years, with repayments starting at the end of the second production year. This type of credit could be granted only once to each borrower, and the size of the loan was restricted to the amount necessary for the peasant to acquire his allotted shares during the first year of the collective. In 1956, a sum total of more than 700 million yuan was granted to 40 million households.[57] The functions of this kind of loan were multiple. First, it made possible the use of the capital share system during the collectivization, thereby avoiding a policy of outright confiscation even though private rural capital was in fact being eliminated. This indirect approach lessened the antagonism of the middle-class peasants and possibly prevented the type of large scale sabotage that occurred during the Soviet collectivization. Second, the loans supplied an inducement to the poor peasants to support the drive; moreover, they strengthened these supporters' economic and political status inside the collectives by transforming them into fully participating members who paid in their shares. Finally, the loans in effect provided money capital to the collectives while leaving the debtors' obligations with individuals, since the borrowing peasants had to pay the principal plus interest out of their future income.[58]

[57] Yang P'ei-hsin, "Ways to Raise Funds . . .," *CCYC,* no. 1, 1958, p. 32.

[58] In 1959, after the collectives were further combined into communes, all outstanding loans for poor peasants cooperation funds were to be repaid by the communes.

113

Loans for public welfare expenditures. These loans, granted to the collectives only in exceptional cases, were limited to the financing of welfare expenditures directly contributive to the growth in productivity (e.g., expenses for medical facilities and children's nurseries). They were not to exceed one year's duration and were to be repaid with the accumulation fund.

Loans for individual members. This kind of loan was extended to members of the collectives for either production or consumption. Productive loans were used to finance subsidiary occupations (such as handicrafts) of individual farmers while consumption loans were for personal contingency expenses (such as funerals or house repairs). Generally, this type of credit came from the credit cooperatives. The Bank would grant it only in areas where there was no credit cooperative or in cases where the loans required were long-term.

THE DEVELOPMENT OF AGRICULTURAL LOANS

Statistics for agricultural loans, while far from satisfactory, are nevertheless the most generously available among all credit data. The relevant data are presented together in Appendix B. Like commercial loans, the development in agricultural loans can be analyzed along two lines, one in terms of the relative share, the other in terms of the overall growth.

The proportion. The proportion of bank loans that went to agriculture was relatively small in the years before 1956, amounting to "about ten percent."[59] However, in order to support the rapid countrywide socialization movement, agricultural loans rose steeply in 1956.[60] This sudden surge of rural indebtedness, which occurred while the dominant commercial loans were declining, temporarily raised the share of agricultural credit to 45.9 percent of all bank loans during that year.[61]

The behavior of agricultural loans in 1956 was erratic in yet another

---

[59] Ko, "On the Inter-Connection . . .," *CCYC,* no. 1, 1958, p. 13.

[60] The credit plan for 1956 expected an increase of ￥1.12 billion in agricultural loans, while the actual increase was ￥2.03 billion. Po I-po, "Report on the Implementation of the 1956 National Economic Plan and the Draft 1957 National Economic Plan," *FKHP,* VI, 152.

[61] Ko, "On the Inter-Connection . . .," *CCYC,* no. 1, 1958, p. 13.

respect. As was mentioned earlier, a portion of farm credit from the People's Bank was long-term; this portion had been below 50 percent of the outstanding agricultural loans in earlier years.[62] In 1956, however, out of the large increase of 2.03 billion yuan in agricultural loans, 1.4 billion, or over two-thirds, was long-term.[63] The sharp rise in agricultural credit plus the shift toward long-term commitments were considered by the Bank as contributing factors to the inflationary pressures of the time.[64] The monetary policy of 1957 was one of contraction and agricultural loans granted in that year were confined to short term.[65] In 1958 the Bank once again allowed the granting of long-term credit with the stipulation that such credit was not to exceed 40 percent of rural loans.[66]

For 1953–1957 as a whole, over eight billion yuan of agricultural loans were granted. They were distributed as follows:[67]

Loans for productive expenditures	43.1%
Loans for capital construction	21.8
Loans to individual members for consumption or subsidiary production	16.0
Loans for relief of disaster	8.0
Residual	11.1
	100.0

The residual share of 11.1 percent was not specified. It probably included the poor peasants cooperation funds of 1956 and certain loans for reclaiming virgin land.[68]

---

[62] *Supra,* Table III-2. For the First Five Year Plan period as a whole, 40 percent of the agricultural loans granted were long-term. Li Shao-yü, "Tasks of Rural Finance in 1958," *CKCJ,* no. 2, 1958, p. 7.

[63] In 1956, the "poor peasants cooperation fund" loans and the agricultural loans for "basic constructions" amounted to ¥1.4 billion; both were long-term loans. Ch'en Hsi-yü, "Report to the Conference of Branch Bank Managers . . .," *CKCJ,* no. 6, 1967, p. 1.

[64] *Ibid.*

[65] "Conditions in the Past Half Year . . .," *CKCJ,* no. 14, 1958, pp. 1–2.

[66] "Excerpts of Discussion of This Year's Bank Tasks in the National Conference of Bank Managers," *CKCJ,* no. 2, 1958, p. 1.

[67] "The State Bank Granted Eight Billion . . .," *CKCJ,* no. 2, 1958, p. 23.

[68] *Ibid.*

Table V-3
Agricultural Loans of the People's Bank, 1950–1958
(million yuan)

Year	Total loans granted (1)	Loans outstanding (End of year) (2)	Planned target for total loans (3)
1950	212.4	94.9	—
1951	399.5	204.8	302.2
1952	966.2	481.6	693.2
1953	1,051.4	666.2	1,127.1
1954	788.2	782.7	1,134.0
1955	1,004.2	1,000.7	1,434.0
1956	3,408.4	3,029.5	3,000.0*
			3,700.0
1957	2,257.4	2,759.5	4,000.0
1958	3,837.4	—	4,400.0

*The original target for 1956 was 3,000 million yuan. It was revised upward during the year.
Sources:
Col. (1) "Agricultural Loans of 1950–1958," *CKCJ,* September 25, 1959, p. 2.
Col. (2) 1950–1956: Yang P'ei-hsin, "Ways to Raise Funds for Agricultural Developments in Our Country," *CCYC,* no. 1, 1958, p. 32. 1957: Li Hsien-nien, 1958 Budget Report, *FKHP,* VII, p. 119.
Col. (3) 1951–1956: "The State's Important Assistance to the Peasants," *SSST,* no. 7, 1956, p. 39. 1956–1958: Li Hsien-nien, 1958 Budget Report, *FKHP,* VII, pp. 119, 137, 130.

The growth. Table V-3 and Chart 1 present three series as indicators of the broad trend in agricultural loans.[69] An examination of their behavior and interrelations reveals certain interesting phenomena. To avoid confusion, the three series are discussed separately.

(1) Total agricultural loans granted. The series on the aggregate amount of agricultural loans granted each year by the People's Bank, like the other two series, followed an upward trend. However, its movement formed two distinct cycles. The first cycle began with a rapid growth in 1950–1952, then slowed down and reached its crest in 1953. The next year (1954) was a year of tight credit and the amount of agricultural loans extended actually declined. The second cycle again started with a slow rise in 1955, then a spectacular threefold increase in the collectivization year (1956) was followed by a severe contraction in 1957. In 1958 the series resumed its steep climb. Thus, compared

[69] There are discrepancies in different series of agricultural data (see Appendix B). However, they do not affect the trends.

116

Chart 1
Agricultural Loans of the People's Bank, 1950–1958

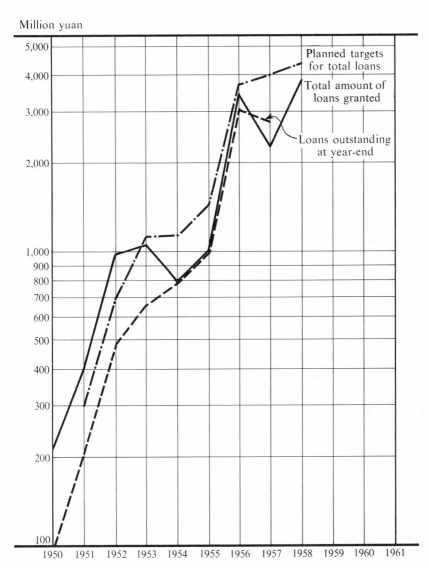

Million yuan

Planned targets
for total loans

Total amount of
loans granted

Loans outstanding
at year-end

Source: Table V-3

117

with the almost continuous rise in commercial loans, the growth in agricultural loans granted was more erratic. It had two peak years, 1953 and 1956, and the latter was the single year of decline for commercial loans. It is interesting to note that the two years in which agricultural loans fell were years of contractions in the overall economy, both having been preceded by periods of strong inflationary pressures. It thus appears that agricultural credit was used more than commercial credit as an instrument to stabilize the economy.

(2) Outstanding agricultural loans at year-end. The amount of outstanding agricultural loans at year-end behaved somewhat differently from aggregate loans extended. The former enjoyed a sustained climb until 1957, when it decreased. Compared with total agricultural loans granted, outstanding loans were at first (1950–1952) very much smaller in size. This was due to the fact that short-term agricultural loans were generally granted in the spring and repaid after the harvest in the fall, so that by year-end the amount of outstanding rural loans was low. However, in 1954, it caught up with total agricultural loans and the two series moved close together. Finally, in 1957, the outstanding rural loans outstripped the total agricultural loans. Thus for the 1950s as a whole, the series of outstanding loans grew at a much faster rate than total loans granted, as is witnessed by the steeper line for the former in Chart 1. This gradual accrual of outstanding agricultural loans was probably a reflection of two factors: the growth in the long-term component of agricultural loans and the accumulation of bad debts. The latter will be discussed further in the next section.

(3) Planned total agricultural loans. Finally, Table V-3 and Chart 1 also show the planned targets of loans. It can be seen that there have been varying degrees of discrepancies between the targets and the total amount of loans actually granted each year. For 1951–1952, actual loans granted were above the planned amounts. These were the years when the People's Bank was not yet firmly established and systematic planning had not yet begun. From 1953 on, actual loans extended were persistently below the corresponding planned targets, and the difference varied widely from year to year; for 1954 and 1957, the two series even moved in opposite directions. How could this difference be accounted for? What determined the actual amount of loans granted if they were

not guided by planned targets? It is difficult to answer these questions fully, but certain information is relevant. First, the Bank often granted rural loans according to the amount of goods, particularly agricultural producer's goods, available in the supply and marketing cooperatives. In other words, the Bank was at times required to coordinate its loans with the trading cooperatives so as to facilitate sales of farm equipment.[70] Second, the annual planned target was rather flexible; it could be revised from time to time as the need arose. For example, the original planned target for agricultural loans in 1956 was 3.0 billion yuan; this eventually became 3.7 billion.[71] Third, the two years in which the planned and actual series moved in opposite directions were years of overall contraction, when the People's Bank applied a tight monetary policy in the rural areas in an attempt to control inflation. When this evidence is combined with the divergency between planned and actual loans granted, the impression is created that rural loans were not really determined by premeditated plans. Instead, they were often influenced by the amount of producer's good available at the rural retail outlets or by discretionary actions of the local or central authorities.

THE POLICY AND PROBLEM OF AGRICULTURAL LOANS

It follows from the above discussion that, as in the case of commercial loans, the extension of agricultural credit was not subject to an effective quantitative criterion. The actual loans granted for productive expenditures, the major component of rural credit, were more-or-less dependent on inventory available for sale in the local supply and marketing cooperatives; while the aggregate agricultural loans granted could also vary widely according to the tempo of the rural socialization drive or the necessity to maintain monetary stability.

The management of agricultural lendings was beset with much dif-

---

[70] "Improve the Supply of Producer's Goods Through Works on Bank Credit," *NTCJ*, no. 10, 1956, pp. 18–19.

[71] It was said that the planned increase in agricultural loans for 1956 was ￥1.12 billion while the actual increase was ￥2.03 billion. Po I-po, "Report on the Results of Implementation of the 1956 National Economic Plan and on the Draft 1957 National Economic Plan," *FKHP*, VI, p. 152. These figures apparently referred to planned and actual increase in outstanding loans since the actual increase in outstanding agricultural loans at the end of 1956 (col. 2, Table V-3) was precisely ￥2.03 billion.

ficulty and confusion. Problems arose in both the extension and the collection of credit. Several central decrees, issued around the two cyclical peaks of agricultural loans, revealed the chaotic condition of rural credit.[72] The first, promulgated in 1953, indicated that loans were sometimes tendered by zealous cadres to unwilling borrowers for the purchase of farm equipment and supplies so as to raise the rural productivity. Some of these producer's goods, supplied through the rural network of supply and marketing cooperatives, were defective or not adapted to local conditions, while others were left idle as a result of the peasants' reluctance to adopt new tools or their lack of skill to use and to maintain the equipment and supplies. Certain loans were used to finance water conservation projects that were poorly designed, with little or no yield. All loans for such unproductive undertakings became uncollectable, especially in cases where the peasants themselves did not initiate the borrowing. The Bank was therefore forced to cancel these debts wholly or partially.

The problems in 1956 were basically similar to those in 1953.[73] This time, loans were granted loosely for the promotion of the collectives, sometimes by party cadres rather than by the banking staff.[74] A portion of these loans consisted of short-term productive credit to the collectives that expired within the year. Recalling such loans when they became due would divert the collectives' financial resources and thus would reduce the amounts available for income distribution to the members. Since the prevailing state policy called on the collectives to assure increased monetary earnings to 90 percent of the collectivized farmers, the Bank found it difficult to collect these loans. In short, loans to the collectives were not repaid; instead, they were transformed into a temporary subsidy for boosting the money income of participating

[72] GAC, "Directive on Certain Questions Relating to the Settlement of Agricultural Loans," *JMST,* 1955, pp. 441–42; SC, "Directive on Certain Questions Regarding Rural Finance Works," *FKHP,* IV, 302–05; SC, "Directive on the People's Bank's Report Relating to the Settlement of Agricultural Loans," *CKCJ,* no. 23, 1957, pp. 4–5.

[73] For conditions of rural bank loans in 1956, see, for example, Ch'ü, "Problems and Conditions of Rural Credit Works," *CKCJ,* no. 13, 1956, p. 8. "Endeavor to Recall Expired Agricultural Loans and to Absorb Rural Deposits," *CKCJ,* no. 24, 1956, pp. 2–4; Wu Yi-t'ang *et al.,* "The Slow Progress in Rural Financial Works Must Be Changed," *CKCJ,* no. 24, 1956, p. 7; "Quickly Correct the Phenomenon of Wasting Agricultural Loans," *NTCJ,* no. 8, 1956, pp. 6–7.

[74] *Supra,* Chapter III, pp. 48–49.

peasants in order to demonstrate the superiority of the new organization. As mentioned, the subsequent inflationary pressures forced the Bank to take emergency measures to recall rural credit at the end of 1956, but the result was poor.

The collectivization drive created other problems relating to rural credit. Because the movement involved intricate transfers of capital ownership among the individuals, the mutual-aid teams, and the collectives, the responsibility for loans that had been previously granted to finance capital equipment became indeterminate. In addition, frequent shiftings of the rural cadres who led and organized the drive accentuated the disorders and ambiguities in the records of loan accounts. The condition was so chaotic that in 1957 the State Council, acting upon a request by the Bank, ordered a thorough recheck of rural credit. The purpose was to clarify debtor-creditor relationships, to call in overdue loans, and to cancel uncollectible credit. Among the numerous problems faced by the Bank at this time, an especially thorny one originated from the unwillingness of the cadres, who formed the rural leadership, to repay their personal loans from the Bank.[75]

Underlying all these specific real factors that made the collection of rural loans difficult, there was an additional pervasive force of economic incentive that induced the borrowers to delay loan repayments. For both 1953 and 1956 were periods of inflation, under which it would be especially advantageous to remain debtors. On this count, the People's Bank was facing a problem familiar to all central banks under similar situations.

LOANS TO PRIVATE AND SEMIPRIVATE ENTERPRISES

Since private enterprise was to be discouraged in Mainland China, its share of bank credit was, generally speaking, negligible. Although the

[75] SC, "Directive on the People's Bank's Report . . .," *CKCJ*, no. 23, 1957; Chiang Shih-Tsi, "Pay Attention to the Problem of Loan Repayments from the Cadres," *NTCJ*, no. 24, 1956, pp. 14–15; Wang Chao "Contradictions in the Work of Collecting Bank Loans," *NTCJ*, no. 14, 1957, pp. 19–20; Ts'ao, "Summary Report . . .," *CKCJ*, no. 7, 1957, pp. 1–3. The political significance in collecting overdue personal loans from the rural cadres was also mentioned in the following editorial. "Continue to Struggle for the Fulfillment of the Bank's Tasks during the Brisk Season," *CKCJ*, no. 22, 1957, p. 3.

absolute magnitude of this type of loan might have grown somewhat during the 1950s, large increases took place only under special circumstances. There were three periods when credit to private enterprises was expanded.[76] The first took place in June, 1951, and the objective was to establish a financial relationship with the private firms so as to exert control over them.[77] The second occurred in 1952 when, as a result of the heavy fines imposed on the then still important private firms under the three-anti and five-anti movements, business was depressed for lack of working capital. In order to revive the economy, the People's Bank extended a relatively large amount of loans to the business firms.[78] The final wave of increased credit to this sector came in 1956 when, parallel to the rural collectivization, socialization was carried out in urban areas. Under this movement the remnants of private industrial and commercial concerns were converted into public-private joint enterprises or organized into cooperatives. The transformation was once again brought about through the extension of bank credit to the semisocialized units.[79] By the end of that year, the amount of outstanding loans to this sector increased by 0.94 billion yuan although the planned increase was only 0.29 billion.[80] Prior to 1956, the total amount of loans to handicraft industry and joint enterprises accounted for approximately 5 percent of total bank credit; in 1956, this ratio rose to 22.7 percent.[81]

Aggregate Loans of the People's Bank

Direct information on total credit from the People's Bank is almost completely lacking. In order to indicate the order of magnitude of

[76] Kuan and Tai, "The Great Monetary Achievements in China under the Guidance of Marxism-Leninism," *CJYC*, no. 1, 1958, p. 57.

[77] *Ibid.,* p. 61.

[78] Between May and July, 1952, the People's Bank granted 0.3 billion yuan in loans to private firms, representing a twofold increase over the amount extended in the corresponding period of the preceding year. Starlight, *Fiscal and Monetary Policies in Communist China,* pp. 236–37.

[79] For detailed measures of this type of credit see The Ministry of Trade, The Chinese National Federation of Cooperatives, and PB, "Directive on the Extension of Credit to Public-Private Stores, Cooperative Stores and Mutual-Aid Teams," *FKHP,* IV, 292–95.

[80] Po I-po, "Report on the Results . . .," *FKHP,* VI, 152.

[81] Ko, "On the Inter-Connection . . .," *CCYC,* no. 1, 1958, p. 13. The still private handi-

total bank credit, two approaches appear logical and feasible. One is to determine the aggregate on the basis of the component loans; the other is to estimate it through its relationship with working capital. For either approach, only very limited data are available; they are worth examining nevertheless.

AN APPROXIMATION OF TOTAL BANK LOANS

Using the first approach, total credit can be estimated on the basis of data of agricultural loans. Since the 1956 agricultural loans constituted 45.9 percent of all bank loans,[82] the latter could be derived by applying this percentage to the corresponding amount of agricultural loans given in Table V-3. However, there is one complication. Table V-3 presents the realized agricultural loans in two forms: (1) total loans granted during the year and (2) loans outstanding at the end of the year; and there is no clear indication as to which series the above percentage refers to. This problem can be overcome by utilizing both series and thus having two possible estimates of total bank credit. Thus a tentative estimate is that either total loans granted by the People's Bank in 1956 amounted to 7.4 billion yuan or the aggregate outstanding bank loans at the end of 1956 was 6.6 billion.[83]

Data for other years are less precise. For the years preceding 1956, the percentage share of agricultural loans was "around ten percent," while for 1957 certain changes in various components are known. By combining this information with Table V-3, it can be deduced that, during the period of the First Five Year Plan, the magnitude of total credit from the People's Bank is represented by one of the following two alternatives:[84]

(1) annual total of loans granted fluctuated between 7.4 and 10 billion yuan;

---

craft industry and the small joint enterprises were major targets of urban socialization in 1956.

[82] *Supra,* p. 114.

[83] 3.408 ÷ 45.9% = 7.42 billion yuan; 3.029 ÷ 45.9% = 6.60 billion yuan.

[84] For percentage share of agricultural loans, *supra,* p. 116. For 1953–1955, this percentage is applied to figures in Table V-3 to estimate total loans. The 1957 estimates are derived from the 1956 total loans by adjustments for the changes between 1956 and 1957 in agricultural loans (Table V-3) and in commercial and industrial loans (*supra,* pp. 104–105.)

(2) total loans outstanding at year-end fluctuated between 6.6 and 10 billion yuan.

AN ALTERNATIVE APPROXIMATION

The second approach, via working capital, is equally ambiguous. Except for a few instances, data on working capital are either unavailable or vague, especially in the case of commerce that is known to have relied heavily on bank loans. However, a broad measurement of total working capital can be achieved indirectly.

TOTAL WORKING CAPITAL IN THE STATE SECTOR

The clue to the size of total working capital is contained in a verbal official statement. It has been said that, at the end of 1957, total working capital of enterprises in various economic departments, including industrial, transportation, and commercial departments, "almost equalled" aggregate investment in basic construction during the period of the First Five Year Plan.[85] According to the State Statistical Bureau, the nation's aggregate investment in basic construction during the period was 55 billion yuan, of which 49.3 billion was state investment for economic and cultural department.[86] Of the two investment figures, the second one is more meaningful here because it denotes investment in the sate sector. On the basis of this, a conservative estimate of total working capital in the state sector in the end of 1957 would be about 45 billion yuan.[87]

This rough estimate of total working capital in the state sector in 1957 is consistent with other evidence relating to working capital. This evidence includes the following. (1) The estimated industrial working capital in state enterprises in 1957 was 7.9 billion yuan.[88] (2) By 1956

[85] Editorial, *CHCC,* no. 12, 1957, p. 2. *CHCC* is the joint official organ of the State Planning Commission and the State Economic Commission.

[86] SSB, "Report on the Results of Implementation of the First Five Year Plan (1953–1957) of National Economic Development," *FKHP,* IX, 288–30. Reference on p. 290. In the 1958 Budget Report, the amount of basic investment during the FFYP from budgetary expenditures was given as ￥48.8 billion. *FKHP,* VII, 122.

[87] This means that total working capital in the state sector in 1957 is assumed to be approximately 90 percent of aggregate basic investment in the state sector during the FFYP period.

[88] Appendix C.

the inventory and reserves held by state commercial departments were between 20 and 30 billion yuan;[89] this was reduced by 2 billion yuan during 1956,[90] and replenished by 3.8 billion yuan in 1957.[91] (3) The commodity turnover expenditures of commercial departments in 1957 was expected to be over 7 billion yuan.[92] While there may be omission or overlap in these components, their sum total, which broadly represents the working capital in state industry as well as commodity and non-commodity working capital in the state trading network, falls in a range compatible with the above estimate of 45 billion yuan. The latter may therefore be accepted as a reasonable first approximation.

TOTAL BANK LOANS

In 1957, 54.7 percent of all working capital of the state sector was financed by bank credit;[93] thus total bank loans to the state sector can be derived. Added to this the sum of loans to the non-state sector, the approximation for total bank credit in 1957 would emerge. These steps are summarized in the following:

(1) Estimated total working capital, state sector, end of 1957		¥45.0 billion
(2) Proportion of (1) financed by bank loans		54.7 percent
(3) Total bank loans to the state sector, end of 1957		¥24.6 billion
(4) Add: Loans to non-state sector, end of 1957 (billion):		
Outstanding agricultural loans (Table V-3)	¥2.76	
Outstanding loans to private and semiprivate enterprises*	1.35	4.1 billion
(5) Total bank loans, end of 1957		¥28.7 billion

*Loans to private and semiprivate enterprises for 1956 (¥1.5 billion) are derived by applying their percentage share (*supra*, p. 122) to the 1956 aggregate outstanding bank loans (*supra*, p. 123.) The 1957 figure is then estimated on the assumption that the change in these enterprise loans between 1956 and 1957 was proportioned to the change in outstanding agricultural loans.

[89] Li Hsien-nien, the 1957 Budget Report, *FKHP*, VI, 115. This sum is probably inclusive of the state commodity reserve.

[90] *Ibid.*

[91] "Commodity Turnover in the Domestic Market in 1957," *Stat. Res.*, no. 4, 1958, p. 24.

[92] Li Hsien-nien, 1957 Budget Report, *FKJP*, VI, 134. Commodity turnover expenditures refer to expenses involved in distribution, such as packaging, freights, advertising, wages, etc. *CHCC*, no. 9, 1956, p. 29.

[93] Huang Ta, "The Principle of Bank Credit and the Circulation of Money," *CCYC*, no. 9, 1962, pp. 1–7. Reference on p. 5.

RECONCILIATION

The results of the two approaches to estimate total credit are widely different. The difference is so great that, at first glance, the two sets of data used appear contradictory. However, a review of the overall situation and the way in which the Chinese credit data were presented indicates that the two estimates may be reconciled; in fact, they even tend to be mutually affirming. If we chose alternative one from the results of the first approach, discarding alternative two, then used the estimate from the second approach to represent loans outstanding at year-end (the title of the discarded series), then the two sets of estimates become complementary. In other words, when put together, the information presented in this section leads to the conclusion that while annual total loans granted in 1953–1957 fluctuated between 7.4 and 10 billion yuan, the amount of bank credit outstanding at the end of 1957 was about 28.7 billion yuan.

This conclusion is quite appropriate because it harmonizes with other knowledge on bank loans. First, the presentation of agricultural loans earlier in this chapter demonstrates the tendency toward divergent movement in the two series in which Chinese credit data were presented. That is to say, it shows that, in agriculture and for the period under study, the rate of growth of outstanding loans was steeper than the growth rate in the amount of loans extended each year. There was less justification for this to take place in agriculture than in other areas because agriculture belonged to the non-state sector, which normally was subject to stricter credit control; besides, no inventory was involved here and the rate of growth of the loans-extended series itself was already very steep. Thus, if the disparate rates of growth of the two series occurred in agriculture, there are logical reasons to expect it to take place in other areas also.

Second, the frequent remonstrances in the economic literature against inventory accumulations and the excessive growth of borrowed working capital, the Bank's unsuccessful efforts to liquidate old debts in 1953, the necessity to create a special type of industrial loans for accumulated inventory in 1956, the reiteration that bank loans should not be used for basic construction, and the repeated emphases given to the principle of repaying loans when due all lend support to the hypothesis that a tendency existed for outstanding bank credit to climb. Finally, it is generally known that commercial working capital was much larger than industrial working capital, and that the former primarily depended on bank loans. It has also been said that the nation's working capital increased by several billion yuan each year and that this was a weakness in the country's finance.[94] In this context, the conclusion that much of the annually growing working capital came from increased outstanding bank loans does not appear out of place.

WORKING CAPITAL AND WORKING ASSETS

To avoid a possible confusion of terminology, it should be noted that working capital, on the basis of which bank credit was estimated above, differed from working assets.[95] Working capital was used from the viewpoint of an individual enterprise; it included goods in the circulation process as well as monetary assets such as cash, bank deposits, and accounts receivable held by the enterprise. On the other hand, working assets, being a term of national income accounting, was used from the viewpoint of the economy; it therefore excluded monetary assets and liabilities.

Table V-4 shows the estimated working assets in the state sector. These assets included the state commodity reserve. The total of these assets of 1952–1957 was about 29 billion yuan. This differed considerably from the estimated total working capital in the state sector at the end of 1957, which amounted to 45 billion yuan. Part of the discrepancy might be a result of the exclusion from the above table of the years 1950–1951, for which no data are available. However, the accumulation of working assets in the state sector during these transitional years could not be sufficient to account for the large difference. A part of the

---

[94] Li Hsien-nien, the 1958 Budget Report, *FKHP,* VII, 133.
[95] Ishikawa, *National Income and Capital Formation in Mainland China,* pp. 105–106.

Table V-4
Accumulation of Working Assets in the State Sector at 1952 Prices,
1952–1957
(million yuan)

1952	5,528		1955	5,468
1953	5,825		1956	1,581
1954	6,130		1957	4,519

Total   29,051

Source: Appendix D.

discrepancy, therefore, represents purely monetary assets held by various state units.

The Rate of Interest

The role and structure of the rate of interest underwent a complete transformation during the period under study. As a result, the rate became fixed and lost its allocating function. This section briefly reviews the changes that had occurred.

THE DEVELOPMENT AND POLICY OF THE INTEREST RATE

At the beginning of the Communist era, interest rates in China were high and continued to rise under the hyperinflation. The peak was reached around November, 1949, when the commercial loan rate quoted by the People's Bank was 100 percent per month.[96] As the People's Bank gained control of the banking system, it played an active role in gradually reducing the official rates and eliminating black market activities. Especially large reductions were effected after the price stabilization in the spring of 1950, and again at mid-1952, when private business was depressed. By the later part of 1952, the monthly com-

[96] Starlight, *Fiscal and Monetary Policies in Communist China*, p. 243.

mercial rate was below 2 percent.[97] The policy of the People's Bank during these transitional years was to lower and to stabilize the interest rate.

By 1953 the supremacy of the People's Bank in the money market was established; the emphasis was then shifted toward using a complex system of differentiated rates to promote certain larger national objectives—the objectives of socialization and industrialization. The structure of loan rates announced in August, 1953, along with those of 1955 and 1958, is presented in Table V-5. A glance at this table reveals that the discrepancies in rates did not reflect the varying degrees of risks involved. Nor could they be accounted for entirely by differences in terms. Instead, the rates mirrored priorities assigned to the several segments of the economy. The outstanding feature of the structure was that the interest rate moved inversely with the degree of socialization of the credit recipients, state enterprises being subject to the lowest rate and private enterprises to the highest.

In 1955, the structure was overhauled. Rates as a whole were lowered and in certain respects simplified, but the discrimination became more elaborate. Two developments were current in that year, and both affected the interest rates. One was the banking reform; the tightening of the Bank's control over credit was evidenced in the penalty interest rate imposed on state enterprises for overdue loans and in the introduction of an especially low interest rate for settlement loans. Elements of the second development, that involving an acceleration of the socialization process, were also woven into the 1955 system of interest rates. These included the new low rate for poor peasants' cooperation fund loans and the more finely differentiated scale of interest rates applicable to urban industrial and commercial units at various stages along the road to socialization.

Because of the more intensive application of the discriminative principle, the complexity of interest rates reached a climax in 1955. Thereafter several readjustments took place and the trend turned toward simplification and unification. Beginning in 1958, costs of industrial credit and commercial credit were equalized. This was done by

---

[97] For detailed information and lists of various interest rates for the period before 1953, *ibid.,* pp. 238–49.

Table V-5
Monthly Interest Rates on Loans from the People's Bank, 1953–1959
(in percent)

	1953*	1955†	1958‡	1959
I. Industrial loans				0. 60
State enterprises		0.48	0.60	
Quota loans	0.45			
Nonquota and temporary loans	0.48			
Other loans	0.465			
Industrial cooperatives (handicrafts)	0.42	0.48	0.60	
Industrial mutual-aid teams		0.60		
Public-Private joint enterprise	0.48–1.40§			
Fixed dividend system adopted		0.69	0.60	
Fixed dividend system not adopted		0.72	0.72	
Individual handicraft workers		0.90	0.72	
One-month term	0.90			
Two-month term	1.05			
Three-month term	1.20			
Four-month term	1.35			
Private enterprises		0.99		
One-month term	0.90–1.29			
Two-month term	1.08–1.47			
Three-month term	1.26–1.65			
II. Commercial loans				0.60
State enterprises	0.69	0.60	0.60	
Supply and marketing cooperatives	0.63	0.60	0.60	
Public-private joint enterprises	0.48–1.40§	0.81		
Fixed dividend system adopted			0.60	
Fixed dividend system not adopted			0.72	
Small trader		0.90	0.72	
Private enterprises		1.35	0.72	
One-month term	1.35–1.59			
Two-month term	1.50–1.74			
Three-month term	1.71–1.95			
Pawnshops	1.95			

Bank Loans and the Rate of Interest

	1953*	1955†	1958‡	1959
III. Agricultural loans				
Poor Peasants' Cooperative Fund loans		0.40	0.40	0.40
Collectives and state farms	0.75	0.60	0.48	0.60
Mutual-aid teams	0.75	0.75		
Individual peasants (production loans and loans for subsidiary occupations)	1.00	0.90	0.72	0.60
IV. Loans to credit cooperatives	1.20	0.90	0.51	
V. Settlement loans (for state enterprises and supply and marketing cooperatives)		0.30	0.30	Abolished settlement loans
VI. Penalty rate for overdue loans		10% surcharge on interest	Same as in 1955	

*Rates for state enterprises and cooperatives effective on August 1, 1953, those for joint enterprises and private enterprises effective on January 1, 1954.

†Rates for state enterprises and cooperatives effective on January 1, 1956, all other rates effective on October 1, 1955.

‡Effective January 1, 1958.

§Local financial authorities may fix interest rates within this range according to the degree of state control imposed, the nature of business, the share held by the state and the terms of loans.

Sources:

1953: Industrial and commercial loans—Starlight, *Fiscal and Monetary Policies in Communist China*, pp. 247–48. Agricultural loans—*CJFKHP*, 1955, p. 40.

1955: *Ibid.*

1958: *CJFKHP*, 1957, p. 57.

1959: PB, "Supplementary Regulations on the Reduction of Interest Rates for Savings Deposits and the Unification of Interest Rates on Bank Loans," *JMST*, 1959, p. 379.

raising the rates on industrial loans. However, rates for agricultural credit remained on a lower level. Since by this time the country was by and large socialized, only two differentiated rates were important in each of the three functional areas of commerce, industry, and agriculture. One applied to loans for state and semisocialized units, while another higher one applied to credit for individuals and the remainder of the nonsocialized units.

The communization and the Great Leap led to a further unification of interest rates. In January, 1959, all loans, whether industrial, commercial, or agricultural, whether for socialized units, individual handicraft workers, or commune members, were charged a uniform rate of 0.60 percent per month. This single-rate system was reversed somewhat in 1961 when the charge for agricultural loans (to communes and state farms as well as individual members) was lowered to 0.48 percent, reflecting a shift of the nation's policy in favor of agriculture production.[98]

The above discussion centers on interest for bank credit. The rates for bank deposits were also complex. In general, private enterprises and individuals were favored with higher rates on their deposits; joint enterprises ranked second with rates varying according to local conditions, while state enterprises and the supply and marketing cooperatives received the lowest deposit rates. Thus the deposit rates changed directly with the degree of freedom possessed by the depositors. Since state enterprises were required under the cash control program to deposit their funds, they received the minimum rates, while higher ones were offered to the private sector as inducements for voluntary deposits. The general level of deposit interest rates, like the loan rates, was steadily decreased. Table V-6 outlines the development of interest rates on deposits since 1953.

In conclusion, it can be said that the People's Bank followed two basic principles in the determination of the rates of interest. The first was to enforce a downward trend, which was stabilized eventually at a level of about 7.2 percent per annum for loans and 2 percent for demand deposits. The second was to adjust the system of rates according to the needs of socialization, employing an increasingly discriminative approach as the tempo of that movement rose, then slowly unifying the rates after the transformation was completed.

THE FUNCTIONS OF THE INTEREST RATE

While retaining the rate of interest and claiming the credit for lowering it, the People's Bank has in fact drastically altered the basic economic role played by this rate. By 1953, the system of interest rates was to a large extent arbitrarily determined and was held constant for prolonged intervals of time; it was therefore divorced from economic forces af-

[98] "The People's Bank Lowers the Interest Rate for Agricultural Loans," *JMST*, 1961, p. 226.

Table V-6
Monthly Interest Rates for Deposits
in the People's Bank, 1953–1959
(in percent)

Deposits from	August 1953	October 1955	January 1958	January 1959
State enterprises and cooperatives	0.21	0.18	0.18	0.18
Public-private joint enterprises	0.27–0.60*	0.24	0.18	0.18
Private enterprises				
Demand deposits		0.24	0.24	0.18
Check deposits	0.42			
Passbook deposits	0.45			
Time deposits			0.24	
One-month term	0.60			
Three-month term	0.65	0.42		
Six-month term	0.75			
Personal deposits				
Demand deposits		0.24	0.24	0.18
Check deposits	0.42			
Passbook deposits	0.45			
Time deposits				
One-month term	0.75	0.24	0.24	
Three-month term	0.80	0.42	0.42	
Six-month term	0.90	0.51	0.51	
One-year term	1.20	0.66	0.66	0.40
Three-year term†		0.71	0.71	0.425
Five-year term†		0.75	0.75	0.45
Credit cooperatives		0.90	0.51	

*Local financial authorities may fix interest rates within this range according to local conditions.

†For overseas Chinese only.

Sources:
1953: Starlight, *Fiscal and Monetary Policies* . . . , p. 246.
1955: *CJFKHP*, 1955, p. 40.
1958: *CJFKHP*, 1957, p. 57.
1959: PB, "Supplementary Regulations . . . ," *JMST*, 1959, p. 379.

fecting the supply and demand of money. Moreover, even this system of controlled and differentiated rates was not allowed to function freely in directing and allocating credit for various capital uses according to their relative marginal efficiencies. Instead, credit was apportioned according to centrally-determined priorities so that in the less favored sectors of the economy loans were subject to severe quantitative restrictions over and above the discriminatory interest rates. In other words, in these sectors, credit might not be available even when borrowers were willing to pay the higher rates. On the other hand, certain sectors might be apportioned a larger quantity of credit than could be absorbed at the prevailing rates, as was the case in agriculture, where loans were occasionally extended through persuasion and semicoercion.[99]

Thus, the rate of interest was deprived of its most important function. However, according to Communist authors, the interest rate had several parts to play in the Chinese economy.[100] First, it encouraged deposits from both enterprises and households. Second, it imposed a charge on bank credit, thereby inducing the enterprises to economize on the use of borrowed funds. Third, the margin between interests paid to depositors and those earned from loans provided the Bank with an income.

With regard to the first function, it should be pointed out that the interest rate was not the crucial determinant of the total amount of deposits. In the case of state enterprises, deposits were required by law, whereas in the case of personal savings, nonpecuniary pressures and persuasion were at least as important as the "material incentive" of interest payments. The second function was apparently ineffective in view of the fact that throughout the 1950s the Bank struggled without success to tighten bank credit to state enterprises. The third function was minor from the economic viewpoint. It can therefore be concluded that the rate of interest in Communist China had a relatively insignificant influence on the money flow.

Concluding Remarks

Despite the severe limitation of data, a general picture of bank loans emerges from this chapter. The direction of the credit flow was largely centrally determined, with more than one objective in view. First of all, bank credit served as a regular source of supply of working capital to the state sector; then, in the non-state sector, it also helped to increase

---

[99] For example, see PB, "Directive on Rural Financial Works in the Second Quarter of 1953," *CJFKHP,* 1953, pp. 90–91.

[100] Yang P'ei-hsin, "On Interest Rates in Our Country," *JMST,* 1956, pp. 537–39.

investment, to bring about socialization and to stabilize the economy. To pursue the first objective, bank loans provided most of the capital for state trading, which controlled the distribution of essential goods. Simultaneously, they gave a degree of financial flexibility to state industry by satisfying its marginal requirements of capital. To the non-state sector, the Bank offered moderate amounts of fixed and circulating capital, created financial stimuli to the socialization movement, and when necessary used rural loans as a disinflationary device. The net result of these various objectives and priorities was that commercial loans became the preeminent type of credit; agricultural loans acquired importance in 1956, serving as a shock absorber to the collectivization drive.

The description of bank credit in this chapter substantiates several generalizations concerning the management of bank credit, some of which have been mentioned earlier. First, the frequent divergences of planned and realized figures for bank credit indicate that financial planning in China was still insufficient to provide a guide for the actual granting of bank credit. Second, the structure of loans clearly reveals a desire on the part of the Bank to rely on the real bills policy to restrict the supply of credit to the state sector, particularly since 1955. Third, the available evidence suggests that the increase in the year-end outstanding balance of bank loans was much steeper than the increase in loans granted annually despite the axiom that bank financing should be confined to short-term purposes. The growth of outstanding loans was not entirely due to increased requirements for working capital resulting from economic growth. Instead, it was to a large extent caused by the accumulation of unmarketable inventories in industry and in commerce, by difficulties involved in the collection of agricultural loans, and by a lack of an effective credit criterion in the earlier years. These phenomena were, in turn, symptoms of inefficient use of borrowed capital.

VI

BANK DEPOSITS

◐ OF THE TWO FORMS of money, deposits and currency, the first
was by far the larger in quantity; for the cash control and monetary control programs kept the use of currency in the state sector to a
minimum. With minor exceptions, deposits became the single legitimate
type of financial assets held by state units.[1] They were also the prescribed means of payment in this sector. However, since deposits circulated primarily in the state sector, in which the production and distribution of goods were more directly supervised, the People's Bank tended
to be less concerned with the growth in their volume than with growth
in the volume of currency. This disparate attitude towards the two forms
of money also derived logical support from the two propositions inherited from Soviet banking theory. As mentioned, the first of these held
that deposits formed the most important source of funds from which
loans were extended. Accordingly, only with a rising volume of deposits
could the credit requirements of the enterprises be met. This reasoning
neglected that loans affected deposits and that in the Chinese structure
the two could grow simultaneously without an automatic ceiling. The
second proposition, which was closely related to the first, was that only
currency constituted money.[2] Since deposits could absorb currency by
replacing it, an increase in deposits became, paradoxically, an instrument to reduce the money supply.

[1] Interfirm debts were forbidden, and there was no other form of financial assets available to the state enterprises.

[2] This was related to the Marxian concept that money must have a gold content. In later
years, it was accepted by Communist Chinese economists, especially in aggregative studies
of the economy, that a broader view of money consisted of both deposits and currency.
For example, Yang P'ei-hsin, "On the Question of the Balancing of the Fiscal Receipts
and Expenditures, the Monetary Receipts and Expenditures, and the Commodity Supply
and Demand," *CCYC,* no. 5, 1957, pp. 50–63. Still later, perhaps as a result of the inflationary experience of the Great Leap, some Chinese economists recognized the influence
of bank loans on the total money supply, which included deposits and currency. Huang

136

Bank Deposits

Like loans, bank deposits in Mainland China could be divided into two broad categories: those belonging to units in the state sector and those in the non-state sector. In the following discussion we first deal with these separately and then proceed to examine the aggregate.

The State Sector and Budgetary Deposits

The paramount position occupied by deposits from the state sector can be seen from a few figures. In September, 1949, deposits from public enterprises and government organs accounted for 69 percent of the total deposits of the People's Bank.[3] This proportion rose to 90 percent during the first half of 1950, when the cash control program established the People's Bank as the repository of funds belonging to public units. From then on, as total deposits climbed, the state sector's share in it remained dominant; for example, 85 percent of the Bank's total deposits came from government organs and from public or cooperative enterprises in 1954.[4]

Under the monetary control program, two kinds of deposit accounts were distinguished in the state sector. First, public entities with functions that involved expenditures but entailed no business income, such as administrative and military establishments or schools, were required to deposit their funds in "current accounts" in the People's Bank. Such accounts were not eligible for bank loans. Second, public units and cooperatives that operated as business enterprises kept their working capital in "settlement accounts." Short-term bank credit might be granted to this type of account when necessary.[5] Thus it was through the second type of account that bank loans affected the money supply.

Ta, "Principles of Bank Credit and the Circulation of Money," *CCYC*, no. 9, 1962, pp. 1–7; *idem, Money and Monetary Circulation in Our Socialist Economy*, pp. 119–30.

[3] Of the remainder, 27 percent were deposits from commercial banks. United Nations, Economic Commission of Asia and the Far East, *Economic Survey of Asia and the Far East, 1949*, p. 126. In 1949 private banks were still important, and the People's Bank was the repository of their reserves.

[4] Starlight, *Fiscal and Monetary Policies in Communist China*, p. 254. The cooperative enterprises here apparently referred to the supply and marketing cooperatives.

[5] GAC, "Directive on Measures for 'the Implementation of Currency Control' and 'Measures for the Compilation of Currency Receipts and Expenditures Plan,'" *Central TCCT*, II, 554–56.

Bank Deposits

Inside the state sector there were, again, two main groups of deposits, one originating from the state budget and including various public administrative organs, and the other originating from state enterprises.[6] The second group mainly consisted of a regular pool of working capital since extra funds held by state enterprises were periodically transferred to the budget as profit and depreciation payments or as excessive working capital. There is little published information on enterprise deposits. Budgetary deposits, on the other hand, were slightly more approachable. They were also the more important of the two groups in terms of size and variability. The following discussion therefore concentrates on this type of deposit.

BUDGETARY DEPOSITS

Budgetary deposits included deposits held by the state treasury and various government administrative organizations. They also contained deposits arising from special funds, such as those for basic construction or government insurance.[7] The relative importance and the growth of this type of deposit are our topics here.

THE PROPORTION OF BUDGETARY DEPOSITS

During the rehabilitation period of 1950–1952, budgetary deposits each year accounted for about one-half of the total credit funds. In 1954, this proportion was above 60 percent.[8] After a temporary decline in 1956,[9] the proportion climbed back to between 60 and 70 percent in

---

[6] This distinction seemed parallel to the classification of accounts just mentioned, for state enterprises were also those entitled to "settlement accounts." However, the two classifications were not identical because the budget, a government organ, could borrow from the Bank.

[7] Jung, "On the Balance of State Budgetary Receipts and Expenditures, State Credit Receipts and Expenditures, and Commodity Supply and Demand," *TC,* no. 6, 1957, p. 1.

[8] Ko, "On the Connection . . .," *TKP,* May 31, 1955. The term credit funds in this context refers to total bank deposits because deposits form the major "source of credit funds" (in the sense that the Bank merely loans out what it receives as deposits). Thus the proportions given in the text represent the share of budgetary deposits in the total bank deposits. After 1955, a specific amount of budgetary allocation was given to the Bank each year as credit fund. The term, therefore, has two meanings.

[9] Ko, "On the Inter-Connection . . .," *CCYC,* no. 1, 1958, p. 12. (In 1957, Ko was the

later years.[10] This information is in accord with a series of data on the share of budgetary deposits for 1951–1956. The series is presented in column (1) of Table VI-1. The series was generally growing until 1955. Its drastic decline in 1956 was primarily due to the use of previously accumulated budget surplus to cover the large deficit incurred in that year.[11] However, there was also a decrease in the share of budgetary deposits in 1955, for which no explanation was given in the source. Since 1955 was the year in which the budgetary allocation of a "credit fund" to the Bank out of accumulated surplus was instituted,[12] this might be the reason for the decline. If so, it would mean that the series presented in column (1) is exclusive of credit funds. In other words, if the credit fund were included, the percentage share of budgetary deposits would be higher than the figure shown. This suspicion is confirmed by another source which states that ". . . at the end of 1955, budgetary deposits accounted for 65 percent of total deposits. . . ."[13] This percentage is close to the one shown in the table for 1954, when the credit fund had not yet been created; thus it must represent the 1955 share of budgetary deposits inclusive of credit fund appropriations. This figure is presented in column (2) of Table VI-1. As mentioned earlier, the proportion of budgetary deposits in post-1956 years ranged between 60 and 70 percent of total deposits, and these figures were explicitly inclusive of the credit funds. The lower limit of this range is therefore taken to be the appropriate percentage for 1957 in column (2).[14] As to 1956, there is no direct information on the proportion inclusive of credit fund. It can only be derived from estimated data on the amounts of budgetary deposits and credit funds.[15] The result is 47.7 percent.

Assistant Chief of Fiscal and Monetary Division, 5th Office, SC, *TKP,* December 10, 1957.) The decline in budgetary deposits, amounting to over one billion yuan, was caused by the 1956 deficit spending.

[10] Ko and Wang, "On Several Relationships in Fiscal and Monetary Works," *JMST,* 1962, p. 201. Beginning in 1955, an annual amount of credit funds was allocated from the budget to the Bank. The percentages mentioned in the text include both budgetary deposits and the accumulated budgetary allocations to the Bank.

[11] Jung, "On the Balance . . .," *TC,* no. 6, 1957.

[12] The credit fund will be discussed presently.

[13] Wang Lan, "Financial Planning in the Past Three Years," *CKCJ,* no. 14, 1956, p. 3.

[14] The lower limit is chosen for 1957 because this was the first year of recovery for budgetary deposits after the 1956 decline.

[15] The estimated amount of budgetary deposits inclusive of credit funds was ¥10.84

Table VI-1
The Proportion of Budgetary Deposits
Relative to Total Bank Deposits, 1951–1957

Year	Exclusive of credit funds (%) (1)	Inclusive of credit funds (%) (2)
1951	55.3	
1952	55.0	
1953	57.7	
1954	65.2	
1955	58.3	65.0
1956	41.5	47.7
1957	—	60.0

Sources:
  Col. (1): Jung, "On the Balance . . . ," *TC,* no. 6, 1957, p. 1.
  Col. (2): See text.

Two broad conclusions can be drawn from Table VI-1. First, budgetary deposits almost consistently formed the largest component of total bank deposits.[16] Second, except for a sudden break in 1956, the share of budgetary deposits rose gradually over time. Since the total of bank deposits itself expanded in these years, the rise in the share of budgetary deposits entailed an even steeper rate of growth in the magnitude of budgetary deposits.[17]

THE GROWTH OF BUDGETARY DEPOSITS

Incremental changes. The absolute growth in budgetary deposits can be seen from a series that shows the annual increase of budgetary deposits between 1951 and 1955. The series, presented in Table VI-2, is inclusive of credit fund appropriations.[18] Originally entitled "amount of

---

billion for 1956 (*infra,* Table VI-3), while the amount of credit funds granted up to 1956 was ¥2.42 billion (*infra,* Table VI-7). Thus budgetary deposits exclusive of credit funds were ¥8.42 billion. Since this constituted 41.5 percent of total bank deposits (Table VI-1, column 1), the latter, excluding credit funds, must have been ¥20.29 billion. When credit funds are added to this amount, the total bank deposits for 1956 would amount to ¥22.71 billion, therefore giving a ratio of 47.7 percent.

[16] Budgetary deposits as a percentage of total deposits from the state sector would thus be even higher.

[17] The share of budgetary deposits = budgetary deposits/total bank deposits. A 10 percent increase in this share, accompanied by a rise in the denominator, requires the numerator to increase by more than 10 percent.

[18] Though not clearly stated, this is implied in a footnote in the source.

Table VI-2
Annual Changes in Budgetary Deposits, 1951–1957

Year	Change from preceding year (billion yuan)	Year	Change from preceding year (billion yuan)
1951	+2.02	1955	+2.77
1952	+1.85	1956	−1.65
1953	+1.11	1957	+1.71
1954	+3.74		

Sources:
 1951–55: Jung, "On the Balance . . . ," *TC*, no. 6, 1957, p. 2.
 1956–57: See text.

increase in budgetary deposits in the Bank compared with the preceding year," the series carried no specification as to the point of time of comparison. However, a logical interpretation is that it refers to the change in the balance of budgetary deposits at the end of the fiscal year, which coincides with the calendar year.[19]

The series ends in 1955. As to later years, it is known that in 1956 a deficit in the state budget caused its deposits to decline by "more than one billion yuan."[20] Since the part of the 1956 deficit which was financed with previous surplus and other budgetary deposits amounted to 1.65 billion yuan,[21] this figure can be taken as an appropriate estimate of the decline in budgetary deposits in 1956. For 1957, budgetary deposits rose again,[22] and the budget surplus plus credit fund allocation was 1.71 billion.[23] The increase in budgetary deposits should be of this order of

[19] This interpretation receives support from the fact that, in the source, the data are presented to indicate the close relationship between each year's budget surplus and the change in budgetary deposits. Since budget surplus relates to the end of the fiscal year, the change in budgetary deposits should also be the change at the end of the year.

[20] Ko, "On the Interconnection . . . ," *CCYC*, no. 1, 1958, p. 12.

[21] Li Hsien-nien, 1957 Budget Report, *FKHP*, VI, 109. This is the sum total of the following items (million yuan):

Cumulated budget surplus	1,011
Deposits in special account	504
Revolving fund of local governments	135
Total	1,650

[22] Wang Lan, "Credit Planning during the Period of the First Five Year Plan," *CKCJ*, no. 1, 1958, p. 10.

[23] Li Hsien-nien, 1958 Budget Report, *FKHP*, VII, 118. This is the sum of credit fund (¥1,553 million) and budget surplus of local governments (¥153 million).

magnitude. It restored the 1957 budgetary deposits back to the 1955 level.

Total budgetary deposits. Given the data for annual changes in budgetary deposits, it would become possible to approximate total budgetary deposits during these years if the level of budgetary deposits at the end of 1950 could be determined. This can best be achieved by examining the general conditions of the time, particularly the factors which might affect budgetary deposits. The year 1950 marked the first full year of existence of the new government in the Chinese mainland. In that spring, the inflation was brought under control and the cash control program was instituted. The latter raised total bank deposits by eighteen times, with a large share stemming from public organizations.[24] Furthermore, public deposits were frozen temporarily at the end of the year because of the Korean War.[25] The fiscal budget was small compared with subsequent years, and the budget surplus reported at the time was also minor, amounting to 834 million yuan.[26] Taking into account all of these developments, it may be assumed that there were certain budgetary deposits at the end of 1950, but that the total was small compared with deposits of later years. Since the increase in budgetary deposits in 1951 was 2.02 billion (Table VI-2), a fair estimate for the total at the end of 1950 should be around one billion yuan. The total budgetary deposits presented in Table VI-3 are estimated on this basis.

The large and increasing budgetary deposits were a natural result of the Communist Chinese economic system. Under this system, fiscal receipts, which included profits and depreciation reserves,[27] expanded with the progress of socialization. Since the People's Bank served as the fiscal agent and the state treasury, these growing receipts flowed

[24] *Infra,* p. 161.

[25] Nan, "Report to the Conference Commemorating the Second Anniversary of the People's Bank of China," *HHYP,* January, 1951, pp. 617–19.

[26] *Infra,* Table VI-4.

[27] Unlike the U.S.S.R., in which state enterprises retain a part of their net income as additional fixed and working capital, the Chinese state enterprises had to submit all their profits (except for a bonus fund based on the fulfillment and overfulfillment of planned profits) and depreciation reserves to the budget, then received grants to cover all their capital needs. This is called the total receipts and total expenditures system, as against the Soviet "offsetting of receipts and expenditures" system. Ko, *The Chinese Budget in the Transitional Period,* pp. 74–75, 111. The Chinese system was modified somewhat in 1958.

Table VI-3
Estimated Total Budgetary Deposits, 1950–1957
(billion yuan)

End of	Budgetary deposits (inclusive of credit fund)	End of	Budgetary deposits (inclusive of credit fund)
1950	1.00	1954	9.72
1951	3.02	1955	12.49
1952	4.87	1956	10.84
1953	5.98	1957	12.55

Sources:
1950: See text.
1951–1957: Based on changes indicated in Table VI-2.

in through the banking network and instantly became budgetary deposits before they were allocated to various public organs as fiscal expenditures. In addition to this basic reason, two developments in the 1950s enhanced the upward trend of the budgetary deposits. First, as state enterprises were put on the basis of business accounting and made subject to more effective financial supervision, there was a relative decline in the amount of working capital held by these units. Thus the share of enterprise deposits fell while that of budgetary deposits rose.[28] A second and more important cause for the continued increase in budgetary deposits has already been mentioned. It was the accumulation of budget surpluses.[29] Since the budget surplus was a major component of budgetary deposits as well as an instrument of deliberate policy, its development deserves closer study.

BUDGET SURPLUS AND CREDIT FUND
APPROPRIATIONS

The development of the budget surplus was rather complex and confusing. It fell into two distinct periods with 1955 as the dividing year.

---

[28] This reason was given for the growth in the percentage share of budgetary deposits between 1952 and 1954. Ko, "On the Connection . . ." *TKP,* May 31, 1955. As mentioned in the text, an increase in the percentage share entailed an even steeper increase in absolute amount in this case.

[29] Jung Tzu-ho, "On the Balance . . .," *TC,* no. 6, 1957, p. 2.

Bank Deposits

BEFORE THE CREDIT REFORM (1950–1954)

In the budget message of 1955,[30] it was announced that the accumulated budget surplus for the period up to the end of 1954 was 6,113 million yuan. This total was consistent with the set of data shown in Table VI-4.

The growing cumulative budget surplus shown in column (3) of that table was partly the result of inexperienced planning. In this period, each of the annual draft budgets had a planned deficit that was intended to be covered with the accumulated surplus.[31] However, both realized receipts and realized expenditures turned out to be consistently above the planned figures and, owing to the inclination of the state units to overestimate their expected financial needs, an *ex post* surplus was reported at the end of each fiscal year.

Logically, the entire budget surplus should assume the form of budgetary deposits in the People's Bank. But there are indications that this has not been the actual case. Two budgetary reporting practices, one involving expenditures and the other receipts, tended to inflate the reported surplus so that an increased surplus might not mean an equal addition to the budgetary deposits, especially in the earlier years. First, the reported budgetary receipts (column 1, Table VI-4) apparently contained not just fiscal payments made to the budget by the population and various economic units. It also contained increases in note issues. This meant that a portion of the reported budget surplus was really composed of additions to currency in circulation.[32]

[30] Li Hsien-nien, 1955 Budget Report, *FKHP*, II, 495.

[31] The planned budgetary figures for this period are as follows (in million yuan):

Year	Planned receipts for current year (1)	Planned expenditures for current year (2)	Planned deficit Col. (1) — Col. (2) (3)
1950	4,361	4,938	577
1951	6,070	6,950	880
1952	13,885	15,886	2,001
1953	20,344	23,350	3,006
1954	23,188	24,946	1,758
1955	28,050	29,737	1,687

Source: Wang Tzu-ying, "The Experience and Lessons from the Compilation and Implementation of the 1956 State Budget," *HHPYK*, no. 5, 1957, p. 93.

Each year since 1952 the planned deficit was smaller than the previously accumulated surplus as shown in column (3) of Table VI-4.

[32] Ko, "On the Inter-Connection . . . ," *CCYC*, no. 1, 1958, pp. 8–9. In this work Ko gave a set of revised budgetary receipts (*infra*, Table VI-6) that was much smaller than the set

144

Table VI-4
Budgetary Receipts and Expenditures, 1950–1954 (I)
(million yuan)

Year	Receipts (Previous surplus included) (1)	Expenditures (2)	Surplus (Cumulative) (3)
1950	7,643	6,808	834
1951	14,432	11,089	3,343
1952	19,974	15,994	3,980
1953	25,997	21,488	4,509
1954	30,746	24,632	6,113

Source: Ko, "The Nature of the National Budget in Our Country and Its Function in the Transitional Period," *CCYC,* no. 3, 1956, p. 72.

Second, although the People's Bank had been designated as the government's fiscal agent since early 1950, it functioned mainly as a controller of receipts. All fiscal income that entered the banking system was remitted to the Bank's main office and reported as budgetary receipts. But during this period the Bank exercised little supervision over budgetary expenditures. Funds were transferred by the Bank's Main Office from the budgetary account to accounts of different ministries when fiscal appropriations were made. The ministries in turn distributed them to subordinate public organs and enterprises within their respective systems. Budgetary expenditures were not reported by the Bank but by various public units that adopted heterogeneous reporting standards. The procedure most commonly used by the reporting public units, called the "actual expenditures" method, excluded from budgetary expenditures materials that had been purchased but not yet consumed. The net result was that the budget surplus, so determined, reflected

---

he presented earlier (*supra,* Table VI-4). In the revised table he explained in footnotes that the data excluded budgetary receipts originating from currency issues (amounting to 699 million yuan in 1950 and 1,037 million yuan in 1951) and from previously accumulated budget surplus. Obviously, his earlier table (from which the 1954 accumulated budget surplus of 6,113 million yuan was derived) included currency issues as receipts. Similar footnotes excluding from budgetary receipts funds overdrawn from the state bank in 1950 and 1951 also appear in Feng Hsi-hsi, "The Rise of Our National Economy as Seen Through the State Budget," *TCKT,* no. 12, 1957, p. 28. Strictly speaking, only the People's Bank could issue currency; the budget could only borrow from the Bank and then withdraw currency.

three ingredients: the residual budgetary deposits in the Bank, budget funds held by the public units, and material inventories of these units.[33]

The consequent discrepancy between the reported budget surplus and the actual addition to budgetary deposits in the Bank was perhaps one of the many factors that required adjustment. In any case, during 1955, when attempts were made to strengthen the position of the People's Bank and to improve the soundness of money and credit, a general alignment of the budget and the Bank took place.[34] The Finance Minister's budget message of that year revealed that the accumulated budget surplus for 1950–1954 was apportioned in the manner shown in Table VI-5.[35] In effect, this allocation immobilized about 43 percent of the

Table VI-5
The Allocation of the Cumulative Budget Surplus of 1950–1954
(in million yuan)

A. Repayment of funds overdrawn by the government from the People's Bank during the revolutionary war* and the early years of the People's Republic	2,159
B. Deposit in a special account with the People's Bank	504
C. Transfer to the budgetary revolving fund for local governments†	307
D. Balance of budgetary surplus to be carried forward to 1955	3,143
Total accumulated surplus, 1950–1954	6,113

*This refers to the period between December, 1948, when the People's Bank was established, and October, 1949, when the Republic began.

†At the time of the allocation this amount had already been advanced to local governments to cover needs arising from the difference in timing between their budget receipts and their expenditures.

Source: Li Hsien-nien, 1955 Budget Report, *FKHP*, II, 495.

[33] Jung (Vice-Minister of Finance), "A Lecture Delivered at the Training Class for the Administration of State Budgetary Receipts and Expenditures (Excerpts)," *CKCJ*, no. 22, 1955, pp. 1–2. A similar lecture was given by Huang Ya-kung, District Director of the People's Bank, in the same issue, pp. 2–3. Also Yang Li-hsiao, "On the Meaning and Function of the Administration by the People's Bank of State Budgetary Receipts and Expenditures," same issue, pp. 3–5.

[34] Beginning in 1956 the Bank was put in charge of reporting both fiscal receipts and fiscal expenditures under the system of "Administration [by the Bank] of State Budgetary Receipts and Expenditures." Public units drew budgetary funds from local banks, subject to the limits of their respective quotas. All funds thus paid out by the Bank were considered actual budgetary expenditures, while funds not yet withdrawn by the public units remained budgetary deposits. However, the problem had not been entirely solved even in 1957. Ch'i and Liu, "On Bank Expenditures and Actual Expenditures," *TC*, no. 8, 1957, pp. 17–18.

[35] Li Hsien-nien, 1955 Budget Report.

total reported budget surplus as repayments of old debts and as ear-marked funds for a special account.[36] This step must have helped to disentangle the budget-bank relationship and to prepare the ground for their future coordination in the management of money.

In 1957 a revised set of budgetary data was released; this is shown in Table VI-6. While expenditures remained similar to those in Table VI-4 above, the revised receipts were much lower,[37] leaving smaller annual surpluses. The total amount of budget surplus for 1950–1954 became 3,427 million yuan instead of the 6,113 million reported in the 1955 budget message and in Table VI-4. No information was given as to how the smaller aggregate was spent or how the difference between the two total surplus figures could be bridged. Although available data do not permit a reconciliation of the two sets of figures, it is interesting to note that the revised total surplus is quite close to the sum of item C (the ¥307 million budgetary revolving fund for local governments) plus item D (surplus carried forward, amounting to ¥3,143 million) from Table VI-5. These two items constituted the portion of the original reported budget surplus that was not immobilized in the 1955 allocation.[38]

AFTER THE CREDIT REFORM

From 1955 on, budgetary data became more consistent. The surplus grew smaller relative to the growing budget as planning improved; its

---

[36] The special account apparently was intended as a contingency fund or budgetary reserves. This sum was used in 1956 when a large budget deficit occurred.

[37] The difference can partially be explained by the exclusion from receipts of (a) currency issues of 1950 and 1951 and (b) previous budget surplus. But these factors are not adequate to account for the entire discrepancy.

[38] Thus the surplus given in Table VI-6 was exclusive of the earmarked funds to the Bank (i.e., items A and B of Table VI-5). Another set of data on budgetary surplus that includes credit funds to the bank is as follows:

1951	¥1.06 billion
1952	1.78
1953	.27
1954	2.59
1955	2.50

Jung, "On the Balance of State Budgetary Receipts and Expenditures . . . ," *TC*, no. 6, 1957, p. 2.

147

Table VI-6
Budgetary Receipts and Expenditures, 1950–1954 (II)
(million yuan)

Year	Receipts (Previous surplus excluded) (1)	Expenditures (2)	Surplus or deficit (Noncumulative) (3)
1950	6,519	6,808	−289
1951	12,967	11,902	1,065
1952	17,560	16,787	773
1953	21,762	21,488	275
1954	26,237	24,632	1,604
	85,045	81,617	3,427

Note: Slight discrepancies due to rounding.
Sources: Ko, "On the Inter-Connection and Equilibrium of Budget, Credit and Material Goods," *CCYC*, no. 1, 1958, pp. 8–9. Identical data appeared in the following: Feng Hsi-hsi, "The Rise of Our National Economy as Seen Through the State Budget," *TCKT*, no. 12, 1957, p. 33; Wang Tzu-ying, "The Experience and Lessons from the Compilation and Implementation of the 1956 State Budget," *HHPYK*, no. 5, 1957, p. 93; SSB, *The Ten Great Years*, pp. 19 and 21.

use and allocations were also less ambiguous. The most significant development, however, was the institution of the credit fund. This fund represented an attempt at coordination between the budget and the Bank in the management of money; it was thus an important turning point in Chinese monetary policy. Beginning in 1955, a sum was earmarked from the budget surplus annually as credit fund for the Bank. While this fund might still be considered a part of budgetary deposits, it was nevertheless immobilized and thus was not subject to further appropriations. The development of the credit fund is shown in Table VI-7.

The procedure through which the credit fund was assigned to the Bank underwent a gradual change. Before 1955 there was no specific allocation of the credit fund to the Bank. Early in 1955, as described above, a portion of the accumulated budget surplus was used as repayment of prior debts. It was in the final budget of 1955 that the first formal appropriation of the credit fund to the Bank was listed. This amount (¥2,418 million) was partially financed through the past sur-

Table VI-7
Annual Budgetary Appropriations of Credit
Fund to the People's Bank, 1955–1960
(million yuan)

Year	Credit fund, planned	Credit fund, actual
Early 1955	nil	$2,159*
1955	nil	2,418
1956	nil	nil
1957	600	1,553
1958	800	1,650
1959	3,170	4,430
1960	5,800	—

* This represents the repayment of old bank loans. *Supra,* Table VI-5.
Sources: Li Hsien-nien, Minister of Finance, annual budget reports from 1955 through 1960, *FKHP*, II, 496; III, 214; VI, 109 and 125; VII, 117 and 127; IX, 64 and 72; XI, 34 and 41.

plus.[39] Because 1956 witnessed a large budget deficit resulting in government overdraft on the Bank,[40] no credit fund was granted in that year. From 1957 on, a planned amount of credit fund appeared in the annual draft budget along with other planned expenditures. But the

[39] The 1955 final accounting of budget surplus was as follows (million yuan):

Surplus carried forward from 1954		¥3,155
(This amount should have been ¥3,143 according to the planned allocation in Table VI-5. The cause of the discrepancy is not clear.)		
Surplus of 1955	476	¥3,631
Less:		
Transfer of credit fund to the bank	2,418	
Budgetary revolving fund for local governments	201	2,620
Balance of surplus to be carried forward to 1956		¥1,011

Li Hsien-nien, 1956 budget message, *FKHP*, III, 214.

[40] The 1956 budget deficit was ¥1,831 million, financed by the following:

Cumulative surplus carried forward from 1955	¥1,011
Previous deposit in special account (Table VI-5)	504
Decrease in budgetary revolving fund for local governments	135
Overdraft on the People's Bank	180
Total	¥1,830

(The discrepancy between 1,830 and 1,831 was due to rounding.) Li Hsien-nien, 1957 budget message, *FKHP*, VI, 109.

actual amount of credit fund was determined by each year's realized budget surplus of the central government. For example, the 1957 planned credit fund was ¥600 million, while the implementation of that year's budget resulted in a central government surplus of ¥953 million.[41] The actual credit fund granted was the sum total of these two items, or ¥1,553 million.

Since 1957, then, all realized central government surplus was immobilized as credit fund.[42] The sudden increase of this fund, both planned and actual, in 1959 was due to the introduction of the 100% credit system.[43]

The Non-State Sector

Deposits of the non-state sector included those held by the private or semiprivate firms, agricultural cooperatives, and individuals. Since business deposits had never been large, and agricultural cooperatives did not spread until 1956, personal deposits became the major type of deposits in this sector. These deposits from individuals were often referred to as savings deposits, or simply savings.[44]

Unlike other banking activities, information about savings deposits was frequently publicized even though it was not always consistent or clearly defined. There were several institutional changes in 1955 that affected the classification and presentation of personal deposits. An

---

[41] Before 1957, all budget surplus belonged to the central government. Since then local governments were allowed to retain their budget surplus, in part or as a whole, for future use. Ko, "On the Inter-Connection . . . ," *CCYC,* no. 1, 1958, p. 11. The surplus retained by local governments in 1957 amounted to ¥153 million. Li Hsien-nien, the 1958 Budget Report, *FKHP,* VII, 118.

[42] As a result, the reported budget surpluses for 1958 and 1959 were ¥900 million and ¥1,390 million respectively, both being surplus of local governments. The central government had no surplus after granting the credit fund.

[43] *Supra,* Table IV-1. Under this system, the Bank supplied the entire working capital needed by state enterprises. Therefore, beginning in 1959, all quota working capital, which was previously provided by the budget (at first as a whole and 70% in 1958), came from the Bank. The large amount of credit fund transferred to the Bank in 1959 contained budget appropriations for increases in quota working capital.

[44] Personal deposits or savings deposits refer to all deposits held by individuals. There are various types of accounts; some are time deposits, others are demand deposits.

awareness of these developments would help to clear up some of the apparent confusions in data on savings. The first development was the change in the monetary unit in 1955. The second was a new official definition of "urban" and "rural" areas.[45] The third was an adjustment in the responsibility of the People's Bank with respect to rural deposits. Beginning in 1955, the People's Bank no longer maintained direct contact with the rural population, and personal deposits from the peasants were handled primarily by the credit cooperatives. Finally, there was the establishment of the Agricultural Bank in that year. Because of some of these changes, the growth of deposits in the non-state sector can best be discussed by separating it into two areas—urban and rural.

URBAN DEPOSITS

Urban deposits consisted of personal deposits from the urban population, and the term was synonymous with urban savings.

In the early years, the promotion of personal deposits was an instrument of price stabilization and took place mainly in large cities. In order to make bank deposits, especially time deposits, attractive to the public so as to remove a portion of currency from circulation, various innovations were resorted to by the People's Bank. To forestall the public's fear of loss from currency depreciation under the inflation, a system of "parity deposit" was introduced in 1949. This type of deposit was held in terms of a commodity unit equivalent to a given combination of daily necessities. The money value of the commodity unit in each larger city fluctuated with local prices of the constituent goods. Thus in effect the value of bank deposits was tied to the local cost of living.

When the inflation was arrested in March, 1950, and prices began to decline, the system was adjusted accordingly. The "value-preserving deposit," allowed the owner an option to withdraw, upon maturity, principal and interest in terms of either the commodity unit or the monetary unit, whichever commanded a higher value. Other new devices for the promotion of bank deposits included the substitution of

---

[45] It was announced in November, 1955, that urban areas included not only various cities, but also market towns *(chen)* and certain mining areas. SC, "Regulation on the Standard of Classification of Urban and Rural Areas," *FKHP,* II, 411-17.

lottery rights for interest payments (the lottery deposit)[46] and the introduction of a flexible type of deposit that combined the features of both time and demand deposits. The variety of accounts accommodating different preferences, together with the expanding banking network and improved services, helped to revive and expand personal deposits after their virtual extinction during the prolonged inflation. In June, 1952, the parity system was discontinued, and all accounts were converted into monetary units.

Efforts to absorb urban deposits continued when the nation embarked on economic development under the First Five Year Plan. From that time on the aim was to reduce the purchasing power released through the wage payments that accompanied rising investments. The urban deposit drive was therefore directed toward the wage earners. To raise personal deposits, savings units and volunteer workers were diffused throughout industrial plants, public buildings, institutions, and neighborhoods. These facilities were combined with educational campaigns plus political and social pressures exerted through labor unions and local communities. The result of these tactics was demonstrated by the sustained growth in urban deposits shown in Table VI-8.

Table VI-8 presents data on personal deposits in the People's Bank. During the early years, when few banking facilities existed in the farm areas, personal deposits were mainly urban deposits. The Bank began to move into the countryside in 1951, and rural personal deposits gradually started. They were accelerated in 1953 by a special effort to promote peasants' savings. But during 1955, the rural responsibility was delegated to the credit cooperatives and the Agricultural Bank. Thus personal deposits in the People's Bank after 1955 were once again urban deposits, and the two terms were often used interchangeably.

Since the goal of the urban savings drive was to immobilize a portion of the money income of the city population, the effectiveness of the campaign would be more meaningfully revealed by comparing the growth in urban deposits with that in urban money income.[47] This is

[46] This type of depositor received no interest. Instead, each periodically had a chance to win a large sum of money.

[47] Both series of data—urban deposits and urban money income—are taken from the article published in *CKCJ*, (Table VI-9). They were intended for comparison and may therefore be assumed to be comparable.

Table VI-8
Personal Deposits in the People's Bank, 1949–1959
(million yuan)

End of year	Total (1)	Urban* (2)	Rural (3)
1949	10	—	—
1950	132	—	—
1951	543	—	—
1952	861	842	19
1953	1,319	1,206	113
1954	1,640	1,405	235
1955	—	1,692	—
1956	—	2,236	—
1957	—	2,790	—
1958	—	4,000	—
1959	—	4,720	—

* This series of urban deposits included those in rural market towns, indicating that the term "urban" was that of the post-1955 definition. The change in the official definition of "urban areas" in 1955 could have been the reason for a relatively large and upward revision in urban deposit data for 1952–1955. For an earlier series of urban deposits for 1952–1955, see Perkins, *Market Control and Planning in Communist China,* p. 170.

Sources:

Col. (1): 1949–1954: Wang Wei-ts'ai, "To Further Develop People's Deposits," *HHYP,* no. 3, 1955, p. 147.

Col. (2): 1952–1957: "A Brief Summary of Works on Savings . . . ," *CKCJ,* no. 5, 1958, p. 24. 1958: "Put Temporarily Unused Fund into Savings," *HHPYK,* no. 18, 1959, p. 129. The same figure appears in SC, "Directive on Strengthening the Bank's Leadership in Savings and Positively Developing Personal Deposits," *FKHP,* IX, 137. (In the first of these two sources the figure refers to urban deposits, in the second source it refers to total personal deposits). 1959: "Increase in Urban Savings in the Past Two Years Equals That of Previous Five Years," *JMST,* 1960, p. 373.

Col. (3): Col. (1) − col. (2).

done in Table VI-9. It can be seen from this table that the "average propensity to save" (via saving deposits) climbed steadily during the five-year period as money income rose. Thus an increasing proportion of each year's higher income was deposited in the Bank as savings from individuals, and the growth of this ratio (from 6.5 percent in 1953 to 10.9 percent in 1957) was quite smooth. It appears, then, that in this period urban savings was closely dependent on urban income. However, the behavior of the corresponding marginal propensity was very different; it fluctuated widely from year to year. The low point was reached in 1956 (13.3 percent) when a sudden acceleration in the coun-

Table VI-9
Saving Propensities in Urban Areas, 1953–1957

End of year	Urban residents' income (million yuan)		Urban personal deposits (million yuan)		Propensity to save* (percent)	
	Total (1)	Annual change (2)	Total (3)	Annual change (4)	Average (5)	Marginal (6)
1953	18,680	—	1,206	—	6.5	—
1954	19,660	980	1,405	199	7.1	20.3
1955	20,620	960	1,692	287	8.2	29.9
1956	24,700	4,080	2,236	544	9.1	13.3
1957	25,510	810	2,790	554	10.9	68.4

*The term is used here to refer to the propensity to save through increasing personal deposits.
Sources:
    Col. (1): "A Brief Summary of Works on Savings . . . ," *CKCJ,* no. 5, 1958, p. 24.
    Col. (2): Based on col. (1).
    Col. (3): Table VI-8.
    Col. (4): Based on col. (3).
    Col. (5): Col. 3 ÷ col. (1).
    Col. (6): Col. 4 ÷ col. (2).

try's investment program plus an increase in the wage rate led to a swelling of urban money income. Despite a substantial increase in personal deposits, the resulting marginal ratio was the smallest of the period. In other words, the change in urban savings lagged behind the change in urban income in 1956. The inflationary pressures created in that year compelled a slower pace of development in 1957, with a corresponding lower rate of growth in money income. Meanwhile, the Bank stepped up the savings drive in order to contract currency; this led to a jump of the marginal ratio in 1957 to 68.4 percent. The large oscillation in the marginal ratio indicates that urban savings were directly and automatically dependent not so much on urban income as on the intensity of the savings campaigns conducted by the People's Bank. Thus personal deposits, or, more correctly, the savings drive, served as an important medium through which the Bank attempted to influence the amount of currency in circulation.

To carry out a contractionary policy, the Bank not only raised the quantity of personal deposits but also tried to solidify them by expanding the proportion of time deposits and by lengthening their term. The relative importance of the four types of urban deposits—demand, time, lottery and fixed amount[48]—is shown in Table VI-10. The share of time deposits grew from approximately one-third of the total urban deposits in 1952 to two-thirds in 1955; this proportion then fell somewhat in 1956 and 1957 due to large increases in the total urban deposits, but the absolute magnitude of time deposits continued to climb in these years.[49] Meanwhile the average duration of personal deposits held by the Bank lengthened. The average number of days each deposit yuan was left with the Bank nearly doubled between 1952 and 1957, as shown in Table VI-11.

Table VI-10
Proportions of Four Types of Urban Deposits, 1952–1957
(percent)

| End of year | Deposits | | | | |
	Time (1)	Demand (2)	Lottery (3)	Fixed amount* (4)	Total (5)
1952	34.5	—	—	—	—
1953	47.6	14.3	8.2	29.9	100.0
1954	61.2	16.3	7.4	15.1	100.0
1955	71.6	19.1	5.2	2.1	100.0
1956	63.7	29.8	5.8	0.7	100.0
1957 (October)	64.2	27.2	6.8	1.8	100.0

*This type of deposit was discontinued in 1954, and its shares dwindled for this reason. It was revived again in some cities in 1957.
Sources:
1952: Hu Ching-yün, "Report to the National Conference . . .," *CKCJ*, no. 8, 1956, p. 7.
1953–1957: "A Brief Summary of Works on Savings . . . ," *CKCJ*, no. 5, 1958, p. 24.

[48] "Fixed amount deposit" required the deposit and withdrawal of a fixed sum of money (¥1, 5, 10, 50, or 100). It could be withdrawn on demand, but the rate of interest escalated with the duration of deposit. PB, Shanghai Branch, "Regulations on Fixed Amount Deposit," *East China TCCT*, 1951, pp. 496–97.

[49] The absolute magnitudes of time deposits can be approximated by multiplying the proportions of time deposits (Column 1, Table VI-10) by total urban deposits (Column 2, Table VI-8).

155

Bank Deposits

Table VI-11
Duration of Urban Deposits Held by the People's Bank, 1952–1956

Year	Average number of days held (per deposit yuan)
1952	67 days*
1953	83 days
1954	87 days
1955	116 days
1956	128 days

*The 1952 figure covered the seven largest cities only.
Source: "A Brief Summary of Works on Savings . . . ," *CKCJ*, no. 5, 1958, p. 24.

RURAL DEPOSITS

Rural deposits in the People's Bank were more complex than urban deposits. Before 1955 they consisted mainly of personal deposits held by the rural population, but since then they were predominantly deposits from the credit cooperatives. Rural personal deposits did not gain momentum until the introduction, in November, 1953, of the planned purchase and planned supply program. In order to divert a part of the large and concentrated liquidity that flowed into the countryside as a result of this program, the Bank took two actions at that time. First, as was discussed earlier, it accelerated the formation of credit cooperatives. In addition, it also instituted the "preferential deposit." This was a kind of time deposit maturing in one to six months, and bearing a higher rate of interest than that of the regular savings deposit of equal duration.[50] Only proceeds from peasants' sales of planned purchase and planned supply commodities were eligible for preferential deposits. The objectives of this type of deposit were twofold. On the one hand, preferential deposits helped to delay the realization of rural purchasing power so that the amount of currency in circulation at a given time was mini-

[50] The preferential interest rate was at first (November 6, 1953) 1 percent per month for deposits of one month or more and 1.5 percent per month for deposits of three months or more. The maximum duration allowed was six months. Bureau of Rural Finance, PB, "Positively Develop Preferential Savings for Grain Sales," *CKCJ*, no. 23, 1953, p. 4. These rates were raised to 1.5 percent and 2 percent respectively on December 3, 1953. "Explanations of Several Questions on Preferential Savings for Grain Sales," *CKCJ*, no. 1, 1954, p. 3.

mized. On the other hand, they also stimulated savings and ensured the availability of a certain amount of productive capital to cover expenditures for seeds, fertilizer, etc. during the following spring. Despite the pecuniary incentive of a higher rate of return, however, intensive persuasion and quasi-compulsion were often resorted to by banking personnel[51] in order to overcome the farmers' traditional preference for cash and to reach the high targets set for rural savings.[52]

In 1953–1954, the rural savings drive paralleled the spread of the credit cooperatives. As the latter grew, their deposits in the People's Bank supplemented the preferential deposits. By the fall of 1955, when an extensive network of credit cooperatives was already in existence, the Bank had abolished the preferential deposit and delegated the entire function of promoting rural savings to this network under the leadership of the new Agricultural Bank.[53] The credit cooperative was to accept rural deposits, lend out as rural loans a portion of the cash thus absorbed, and redeposit the balance with the People's Bank through the Agricultural Bank. Thus after the latter part of 1955 the People's Bank no longer received deposits directly from the rural population.[54]

Statistics on rural deposits are more difficult to determine; they are

[51] In some localities, the peasants received preferential deposits as partial payment for their sales to the state according to a fixed and arbitrarily-determined ratio. In other areas pledges for deposits were extracted from the peasants at the time of registration for grain sales. A third method was to allow the peasants to deposit voluntarily after receiving their full payments for grain sales, but results from this method were poor. Bureau of Rural Finance, PB, "Opinions on the Several Procedures for the Development of Preferential Deposit from Grain Sales," *CKCJ,* no. 2, 1954, p. 6.

[52] In November, 1953, the target for absorbing preferential deposit was 10–20 percent of the purchase price for grains. Bureau of Rural Finance, PB, "Positively Develop . . . ," *CKCJ,* no. 23, 1953. By January, 1954, it was raised to 30–40 percent of the purchase price for grains and oil. Shen Ch'ün, "To Exert Leadership in Rural Deposit Work," *CKCJ,* no. 1, 1954, p. 1.

[53] "State Bank Personnel Should Endeavor to Complete the Central Tasks of the Second Half Year," *CJCK,* no. 86, in *TKP,* September 22, 1955.

[54] Statistics published in *TKP,* March 19, 1958, p. 2, give the following figures of total personal deposits in the People's Bank: 1949–1954, same as the total deposits shown in col. (1) of Table VI-8 above; 1956–1957, same as the urban deposits given in col. (2) of the same table. However, the figure for 1955, ¥1,560 million, differs from that in the table. This can perhaps be explained by the fact that 1955 was a transitional year as regards the coverage of total personal deposits in the People's Bank. Before 1955, personal deposits in the People's Bank included urban deposits and rural (preferential) deposits; after 1955 personal deposits in the Bank contained only urban deposits. In 1955 the coverage was not clear.

complicated by the credit cooperatives that accepted personal deposits while redepositing only a portion of these with the Agricultural Bank or the People's Bank. Furthermore, after 1956, the agricultural collectives became important depositors at the credit cooperatives alongside the member-farmers. Thus without detailed specification, the term rural deposits is ambiguous, denoting several possible combinations of different categories of deposits, some of which might involve double countings. This perhaps explains the fact that available data on rural deposits often seem contradictory. However, when the sources of data are carefully examined and the frequent institutional changes are kept in mind, certain scattered data tend to fall into a coherent picture. For example, while newspapers might use the terms "rural deposits" or "rural savings" indiscriminately, in the banking circle (such as in a banking conference report or a specialized journal), "rural deposits" normally referred to the deposits of credit cooperatives at the People's Bank, while "rural savings" or "rural personal deposits" meant (after 1955) individuals' deposits in the credit cooperatives.

Table VI-12 traces the growth of rural deposits in the People's Bank by combining the Bank's personal deposits with credit cooperatives deposits. Data for the former component are taken from Table VI-8. They represent the difference between the nation's total personal deposits and urban deposits. The sudden fivefold increase of this series in 1953 was the result of the drive for preferential deposits in the farm areas. In mid-January of 1955, the sum of preferential deposits and credit cooperative deposits was reported to be 470 million yuan, with the second component accounting for about 50 percent.[55] This information lends support to our data for personal deposits (235 million yuan) in the end of 1954; it also provides an estimate for credit cooperative deposits (again, 235 million yuan).

The reasonableness and the internal consistency of the series of total rural deposits in Table VI-12 are affirmed by two sets of information. First, a pair of official figures quoted by T'an Chen-lin shows that rural deposits were 121 million yuan in 1952 and 799 million in 1956.[56] The

---

[55] Ch'ü, "Work on the Payments of This Year's Grain and Cotton Preferential Deposits Must Be Performed Well," *CJCK,* no. 67, in *TKP,* February 28, 1955.

[56] T'an, "A Preliminary Study of the Income and the Standard of Living of the Chinese Peasant," *HHPYK,* no. 11, 1957, p. 106. Figures were said to be from the SSB.

Bank Deposits

Table VI-12
Rural Deposits in the People's Bank, 1952–1957
(in million yuan)

End of year	Personal deposits (1)	Deposits of credit cooperatives (2)	Total (3)
1952	19	–	19
1953	113	–	113
1954	235	235	470
1955	–	594	594
1956	–	800*	800
1957	–	1,790†	1,790

* The minimum balance in the end of June was 300 million yuan.

† Of this total, ¥400 million was from individuals, the rest was from collectives that postponed the distribution of income to their members until early 1958. Li Shao-yü, "Tasks of Rural Finance in 1958," *CKCJ*, no. 2, 1958, pp. 7–8; "Excerpts of Discussions on This Year's Bank Tasks in the National Conference of Branch Bank Managers," *CKCJ*, no. 2, 1958, p. 2.
Sources:
Col. (1): Table VI-8, col. 3.
Col. (2): 1954: see text.
1955: *NTCJ*, no. 3, 1956, p. 16. This source gives the average deposits per credit cooperative (¥3,817) and the number of credit cooperatives used to arrive at this average (155,559).
1956: Li Shao-yü, Director of Agricultural Bank, "Speech Delivered at the National Conference of Branch Bank Managers," *CKCJ*, no. 6, 1957, p. 7; also Ts'ao, "Summary Report at the Conference of Branch Managers," *CKCJ*, no. 7, 1957, p. 2.
1957: "The Task of Credit Withdrawal Has Been Completed; Works during the Brisk Season Require Further Efforts," *CKCJ*, no. 2, 1958, p. 14; also Ts'ao, "Concluding Report Delivered at the Conference of Branch Bank Managers," *CKCJ*, no. 1, 1958, p. 3. In the second source, the figure was reported to be one billion higher than the figure for 1956, or 1.8 billion yuan.

latter is sufficiently close to our figure for 1956 to be considered as being equal after rounding. The former figure, however, is very different from our 1952 rural deposits. This can be accounted for by the fact that the series of urban deposits (Table VI-8, column 2) that we used to derive the rural deposits had been revised. As suggested above, this revision was made to accommodate the new urban-rural definitions. Should we use an earlier series of data instead of the revised one, urban deposits for 1952 would be 740 million yuan,[57] and the corresponding rural deposits would be 121 million, which is exactly the same figure referred to by T'an. In sum, the large discrepancy for 1952 was caused by the reclassification of the rural areas, while the 1956 figure, which consisted of deposits from credit cooperatives rather than from the

[57] *TKP*, August 9, 1957. Quoted by Perkins, *Market Control and Planning in Communist China*, p. 170.

159

populace, was not affected by this change. The pair of quoted figures, therefore, are consistent with our series of rural deposits.

As a second check, the trend of growth in rural deposits in the People's Bank can be compared with the general development in the assets and liabilities of the credit cooperatives, from which rural deposits originate. The amounts of capital, deposits, and loans of the credit cooperatives have already been shown in Table III-3. These three series do not include all assets and liabilities, nor are they strictly comparable, because the deposit and loan balances were those held at two unspecified and probably different points of time in the year. Nevertheless, they can be combined in order to indicate roughly the change, as well as the order of magnitude, of the credit cooperatives' operations. Column 1 of Table VI-13 gives the sum total of capital and deposits of the cooperatives for 1953–1958, minus the amount of loans granted. This series broadly reflects the amount of cooperative funds available for redeposit in the Bank. When it is compared with data for rural deposits in the table, the two series tend to move closer together, as would be expected from the gradual improvement in the management of the credit cooperatives. In terms of order of magnitude, the two series appear compatible.

Table VI-13
The Scale of Operations of the Credit Cooperatives and Rural Deposits in the People's Bank, 1953–1958
(in million yuan)

Year	The scale of operations (1)	Rural deposits (2)
1953	15	—
1954	190	235* (470)
1955	530	594
1956	858	800
1957	1,810	1,790
1958	2,743	—

*This figure excludes direct rural personal deposits in the People's Bank; it is more appropriate for the comparison here.
Sources:
Col. (1): Capital plus deposits balance minus loans outstanding of the credit cooperatives. Computed from Table III-3.
Col. (2): Table VI-12, col. 3.

Aggregate Deposits in the People's Bank

Detailed statistics on aggregate deposits in the People's Bank have never been published; the most recent absolute numerative data available to the public on total bank deposits were those for the Shanghai area in 1949–1950,[58] which are shown in Appendix E. In addition there are a few comparative figures. From March, 1950, to the end of that year, total deposits in the People's Bank rose by eighteen times.[59] This rise was partly the result of a shift from cash to deposit in the public sector under the cash control program; it was also partly the result of a renewed threat of inflation caused by the Korean conflict near the end of 1950.[60] Between January and August, 1951, total deposits in the People's Bank doubled;[61] at the end of 1954, they had increased by more than five times over the level of 1950.[62] No information is available for the period of 1955–1957, when the Bank's position was strengthened and bank loans were more stringent. However, there was another spurt of growth in deposits during the Great Leap. In 1958, the increase in total deposits equaled that of the entire First Five Year Plan period,[63] and the first half of 1959 witnessed an additional rise of approximately one-fifth of that amount.[64] These large increases were made possible by bank credit granted to state enterprises and communes and were reflected by comparable increases in bank loans during the same periods.[65]

[58] In addition, the United Nations reported that total deposits of the People's Bank in China in September, 1949, amounted to ¥6.97 million (new currency). This was said to be equivalent to U.S. $22.8 million at the average official rate of exchange for the month. United Nations. Economic Commission of Asia and the Far East, *Economic Survey of Asia and the Far East,* 1949, p. 126.

[59] Main Office, PB, "The Task of the State Bank in 1950," *Central TCCT,* III, 183–84.

[60] Because of the Korean War, public deposits were temporarily frozen. Nan, "Report to the Conference Commemorating . . . ," *HHYP,* January, 1951.

[61] Tseng, "A Year's Planning Begins in the Winter," *CKCJ,* no. 11, 1951, p. 3.

[62] Starlight, *Fiscal and Monetary Policies in Communist China,* p. 254.

[63] Ch'en Hsi-yü, "The 1958 Banking Work and the 1959 Tasks," *CKCJ,* May 25, 1959. (translated version; *ECMM* #178, p. 28.)

[64] Ts'ao, "Monetary Affairs in the Past Ten Years," *JMST,* 1960, p. 89. The percentage increase in deposits during the one and one-half years beginning early 1958 was given as 119.4 per cent of the total increase in deposits during the First Five Year Plan.

[65] In 1958, the increase in bank loans was 80 percent of the total loans extended during the First Five Year Plan. Ch'en Hsi-yü, "The 1958 Banking Work . . . ," *CKCJ,* May 25,

In order to arrive at a broad measurement of total deposits in the People's Bank, it is necessary, as in the case of total loans, to rely on indirect estimation. This can be done by utilizing the data on budgetary deposits and their percentage shares discussed above. The estimation of aggregate deposits for 1951–1957 is shown in Table VI-14. The figure for aggregate deposits for 1950, however, is found by combining this estimated series with the relative data mentioned in the last paragraph. The 1950 figure serves as an independent check of the internal consistency of the estimated series, for it must agree with two sets of information—that total bank deposits doubled in the first eight months of 1951,[66] and that by the end of 1954 they had increased by more than five times over the level of 1950. The 1950 datum in column 3 of Table VI-14 satisfies both conditions, indicating that our estimated series is in accord with the published comparative information.

It is now possible to summarize all the data on bank deposits and

Table VI-14
Estimated Aggregate Deposits in the People's Bank, 1950–1957

End of year	Budgetary deposits (billion yuan) (1)	Budgetary deposits as percent of bank deposits (2)	Aggregate bank deposits (billion yuan) (3)
1950	1.00	—	2.40
1951	3.02	55.3	5.46
1952	4.87	55.0	8.85
1953	5.98	57.7	10.36
1954	9.72	65.2	14.91
1955	12.49	65.0	19.22
1956	10.84	47.7	22.73
1957	12.55	60.0	20.92

Sources:
Col. (1): Table VI-3.
Col. (2): Table VI-1. Figures are inclusive of credit fund.
Col. (3): 1950: see text. 1951–1957: col. (1) ÷ col. (2).

1959, *ECMM* translation. For the one and one-half years beginning in 1958, the increase in bank loans was 129.4 percent of the total increase in loans during the First Five Year Plan. Ts'ao, "Monetary Affairs in the Past Ten Years," *JMST,* 1960, p. 89.

[66] Therefore total deposits at the end of 1951 more than doubled the total at the end of 1950.

roughly sketch their relationships. Table VI-15 combines various series derived in this chapter; these include urban and rural deposits (the main constituents of the non-state sector), and budgetary deposits (the major item in the state sector), as well as aggregate bank deposits. The difference between the three component series and the aggregate series represents the unlisted components of bank deposits. These residual bank deposits are shown in column (5) of Table VI-15. Logically, they contain enterprise deposits from the state sector and business deposits from private or semiprivate firms. Since the latter of these two categories could not be significant, the series should roughly reflect enterprise deposits. A note of caution is in order here: it should be remembered that this series is derived from several estimated series and therefore contains whatever residual errors of approximation have not been canceled out. But even though for this reason the absolute values of column (5) are not very meaningful measurements of enterprise deposits, they are nevertheless useful for broad comparisons, especially in terms of changes over time. In this respect, it is interesting to note that the fluctuations of data in column (5) tend to agree with the general

Table VI-15
Deposits in the People's Bank, by Major Components, 1950–1957
(in billion yuan)

End of year	Deposits				
	Aggregate (1)	Budgetary* (2)	Urban (3)	Rural (4)	Enterprise and others (5)
1950	2.40	1.00	0.13	—	1.27
1951	5.46	3.02	0.54	—	1.90
1952	8.85	4.87	0.84	0.02	3.12
1953	10.36	5.98	1.21	0.11	3.06
1954	14.91	9.72	1.40	0.47	3.32
1955	19.22	12.49	1.69	0.59	4.45
1956	22.73	10.84	2.24	0.80	8.85
1957	20.92	12.55	2.79	1.79	3.79

*Budgetary deposits are inclusive of credit fund.
Sources:
  Cols. (1) and (2): Table VI-14.
  Col. (3): Table VI-8.
  Col. (4): Table VI-12.
  Col. (5): Col. (1) − cols. (2), (3), and (4).

information on the development of enterprise deposits. This is true with respect to the overall growth of the series as well as to specific changes. Regarding overall growth, column (5), taken as a whole, is the most stable of the columns of bank deposits presented in the table.[67] This relative stability is consistent with the knowledge that, under the Chinese system at the time, the year-end deposits of enterprise consisted of a pool of regular monetary working capital in the state sector[68] and therefore were not subject to drastic fluctuations.

Specific changes within the series also tend to harmonize with known institutional developments. The large increase in enterprise deposits in 1952 coincided with the institution of the business accounting system, under which state enterprises began to operate as separate economic units and each was given a sum of working capital. Between 1952 and 1954, enterprise deposits were relatively stable. This may have been the result of two conflicting forces: on the one hand, the socialized sector was expanding; on the other hand, the amount of working capital held by each enterprise declined as the People's Bank participated in supplying a portion of quota working capital for industry. In addition, it is known that between 1952 and 1954 the share of enterprise deposits relative to total deposits declined.[69] This too is consistent with a stable level of enterprise deposits during these three years, since total deposits themselves were growing. The increase in 1955 can be explained by a special budgetary appropriation for working capital[70] and the withdrawal of the People's Bank from participation in the provision of industrial quota working capital. The 1956 increase and 1957 decrease in the series were very sudden, so sudden that the 1956 figure appears especially dubious. However, the directions of movement were consonant with reports that enterprise deposits increased by "a large sum" in 1956 and decreased by "a large sum" in 1957.[71] The 1956 rise in

[67] This is especially true if an exception is made of 1956, which was an unusual year. But even including 1956, the relative changes over time are the smallest in column (5).

[68] Unlike the Soviet System, all profit and depreciation reserve as well as excessive working capital were periodically removed from the enterprise by the budget.

[69] Ko, "On the Connection . . . ," *TKP,* May 31, 1955.

[70] A sum of 1.69 billion yuan was taken from the 1954 budget surplus to be used as enterprise working capital. Li Hsien-nien, 1955 Budget Report, *JMST,* 1956, p. 156.

[71] Wang Lan, "Credit Planning during the Period of the First Five Year Plan," *CKCJ,*

enterprise deposits was due to a large-scale reduction of commercial inventory,[72] while its fall in 1957 was caused by economic contraction and inventory replenishments.

Concluding Remarks

Information on bank deposits, though less meager than data on loans, remains inadequate. Fortunately, the available pieces fall into a legible pattern and permit a certain amount of generalization on the composition and development of deposits. The state budget holds the larger share of bank deposits, and the year-end balance of this type of deposit grew rapidly with time. The main cause of this growth was the annual budget surplus, which in turn depended to a large extent on profit and depreciation payments from the public enterprises. Since 1955, credit funds to the Bank were allocated from the budget surplus; in effect they neutralized a portion of the demand deposits held in the state sector. A second group of public depositors was the state enterprises. Their deposits were the most stable and increased gradually except for 1956 and 1957, when violent changes occurred.

Personal deposits from the non-state sector, urban and rural combined, were, until 1957, the smallest in size. However, they assumed the fastest rate of growth. Beginning with a ratio of around 5 percent of aggregate bank deposits in 1950, they reached a magnitude that accounted for one-fifth of the growing aggregate by 1957. This performance could be attributed to two factors: the savings drive, which attracted personal deposits, and the extension of collectives, which were more inclined to hold their operational funds in the form of rural deposits.

The conclusions reached in the preceding chapter on the growth of outstanding loans—that it was much steeper than the rise of total loans granted annually, and that it amounted to an estimated 28.7 billion

---

no. 1, 1958. The changes were mentioned as examples of deficient and unrealistic credit planning, which was particularly serious in the case of enterprise deposits.

[72] Deposits from private and semiprivate business may have also increased because bank loans to these units suddenly grew in 1956 during the socialization movement.

yuan by the end of 1957—appear consistent with the data of aggregate deposits presented in this chapter. As mentioned earlier, the major items of liability in the People's Bank were deposits and currency, while the assets were essentially loans. Thus the two sides, loans versus deposits plus currency, should be roughly equal, or at least of similar orders of magnitude. Judging from the estimated data this seems to be the case. The year-end balance of aggregate deposits had been growing, and it was approximately 20.9 billion yuan by the end of 1957. The gap between loans and deposits logically represents currency in circulation. We shall now turn to this last form of money.

VII

CURRENCY

⚉ THE QUANTITY of currency in circulation, though not the most fundamental determinant of the total supply of money, is nonetheless of cardinal importance because it constitutes the bulk of the purchasing power held in the hands of the population. The use of currency is at once beyond the Bank's direct supervision and immediately relevant to the welfare of the individual. Generally, Communist Chinese bankers tend to take a narrow view and consider only currency as money, neglecting bank deposits, which primarily circulate in the state sector and are more apparently subject to the Bank's control. However, other Chinese writers dealing with aggregative studies of the economy think differently; they include both currency and deposits as money.

Banknotes issued by the People's Bank, called *jen min pi,* or people's currency, is the only currency permitted to circulate in the Mainland.[1] Although it is frequently asserted that the yuan has a gold content or that it is based on gold, this merely means that the government has a centralized holding of gold in an undisclosed amount.[2] There is in reality no proportional relationship between the amount of gold holding and the domestic supply of money and there is no direct attachment of the yuan to a specific amount of gold.[3] The yuan is therefore fiat money.

[1] The circulation of gold, silver, or foreign currencies has been prohibited since 1949. Foreign currencies must be kept in the People's Bank. The holding of gold and silver by the public is allowed but, with minor exceptions, they cannot be traded freely. They can be sold only to the People's Bank at fixed prices.

[2] The assertion that the Chinese currency has a gold content is necessary in order to conform with the Marxian theory of money. In 1957 an economist declared that the Marxist concept of money was obsolete and that the Chinese currency, being purely a paper currency, was actually a more advanced form of money. Shih Wu, "A Discussion on the Foundation of the People's Currency and the Marxian Theory of Money," *CCYC,* no. 2, 1957, pp. 36–50. This view was immediately criticized and contradicted. Huang Ta, "The People's Currency Is a Symbol of a Commodity Currency with Intrinsic Value," *CCYC,* no. 4, 1957, pp. 64–73.

[3] It is also claimed that the Chinese currency is supported by commodities. By this is

For convenience in presentation, this chapter first examines the factors that affect the currency flow, with special attention to the rural areas, then discusses various monetary measures undertaken by the Bank to stabilize this flow and certain specific monetary events; finally it attempts to arrive at a reasonable estimate of the volume of currency.

The Currency Flow and Its Determinants[4]

THE CREATION OF THE CURRENCY SECTOR

In China the basic shift toward a Soviet-type monetary system began with the creation of a distinct and limited area of currency circulation. When, under the cash control program, it was required that all currency held by the public units above a certain minimum be deposited with the People's Bank and that little of it be used for transactions among these units, the large and growing state sector was in fact being excluded from the currency sphere. The use of currency was thereby confined to making payments to, from, and within the private sector.

One major area in the private sector was agriculture. In this area, barter had become prevalent during the prolonged inflation. After prices were stabilized in 1950, the People's Bank, cooperating with the state trading network, attempted to restore this area to a monetary economy. The expanding commercial network, which included the infant supply and marketing cooperatives, began to buy agricultural products from the farmers and paid for them with money furnished by the Bank as commercial loans. At the same time, the network also supplied the farmers with manufactured goods made in urban areas. As exchange and market were revived, the rural areas gradually absorbed

---

meant that the government controls a huge quantity of the nation's essential products that could be used to stabilize prices and therefore also the value of money. Ma Yin-ch'u, "The Superiority and Characteristics of the New Chinese Currency System," *JMJP,* March 9, 1955.

[4] This section is based on materials from Tseng and Han, *The Circulation of Money . . .* (translated version, *JPRS* #3317), chaps. II and III; Tseng Ling, *The Superiority of the Currency System of the People's Republic of China; idem,* "The Effects of Agricultural Collectivization . . . ," *CCYC,* no. 6, 1956, pp. 39–58.

and used more money, which normally took the form of currency. Thus, in the early years, the Bank was preoccupied with the extension of the currency flow into the countryside.

The institution of the cash control program and the restoration of the rural market were two fundamental steps which established and enlarged the currency sector. After these steps were taken, emphasis was shifted to the "channels of circulation" in an attempt to understand, and thus to regulate, the currency flow.

THE CHANNELS OF CIRCULATION

The channels of circulation refer to the routes through which currency flows into and out of the state sector, and thence into and out of the People's Bank. They are, of course, the same routes through which currency is put into circulation or withdrawn from circulation. The size and structure of these channels basically determine the currency flow and the volume of currency held in the private sector. To the People's Bank, information on these channels must be a prerequisite for currency planning and control; in addition, such information also conveniently registers a large part of aggregate economic activities of the private sector. Thus a certain amount of data relating to these channels are available in the Chinese economic literature. They fall into two categories, those relating to the economy as a whole, and those relating to rural areas alone.

THE CHANNELS OF CIRCULATION IN THE ECONOMY

For the economy as a whole during the 1950s, the main channels through which currency could enter circulation (that is, flow out of the People's Bank) were payments made by the state enterprises for the following purposes: (1) purchases of agricultural products, (2) wages, and (3) purchases from private or semiprivate firms. In addition, the granting of loans, including agricultural credit, to the private sector was also an important channel. On the other hand, the basic routes of the reverse flow of cash were (1) receipts of the state trading network, either from retail sales to households or wholesale sales to private and semiprivate firms; (2) public bond sales and tax payments from the

169

private sector; and (3) savings deposits and loan repayments from the private sector. These three return flows reached the state sector through the three basic units of this sector, namely, the state enterprises, the budget, and the Bank; these flows then came together in the People's Bank as deposits.

The relative importance of the different items involved in the currency flow can be seen from Table VII-1. While figures in this table cover only "several regions," they are said to be typical of the country as a whole in 1952. This table reflects the fact that on a national scale the most important category of currency payments to the private sector was the one for agricultural purchases. Naturally, in industrial cities, wages constituted the largest single category; for example, the Port Arthur-Dairen District Bank found that, early in 1954, wages accounted for 70 percent of all currency payments in its area.[5] On the side of the

Table VII-1
The Channels of Currency Circulation
for Several Regions in 1952
(in percent)

Currency paid out (by the state sector):	
Agricultural purchases (including foodgrains, industrial crops and subsidiary products)	35.5
Wages	33.6
Purchases of industrial products from private firms	2.2
Administrative expenditures	5.5
Bank credit (mainly to agriculture)	5.4
Others*	17.8
Total	100.0
Currency received (by the state sector):	
Retail trade by state enterprises and cooperatives	43.6
Wholesale sales to private enterprise	18.4
Taxes, including the agricultural tax	5.0
Repayments of bank loans	7.0
Others*	26.0
Total	100.0

*Not specified.

Sources: Tseng and Han, *The Circulation of Money in the People's Republic of China* (translated version; *JPRS* #3317), pp. 69–70; Tseng Ling, *The Superiority of the Currency System of the People's Republic of China,* p. 39.

[5] Tseng and Han *The Circulation of Money . . . (JPRS* #3317), pp. 103–104.

return currency flow, state retail sales formed the main channel while the channel of direct taxes was the least significant.

Despite the lack of statistical information for the country as a whole for the mid-1950s, it is possible to deduce certain changes regarding the major items contained in Table VII-1 on the basis of broad developments in the country. During the years of the First Five Year Plan, the basic pattern of currency circulation probably remained similar to that in 1952.[6] However, agricultural purchases must have risen under the planned purchase system of 1953, while the role of the private enterprise must have been gradually reduced to oblivion by 1956. On the other hand, the part played by personal deposits in causing a return flow of currency to the Bank might have gained importance after 1954 in view of the growth of the savings drives and the credit cooperatives.[7] Moreover, the share of cash payments springing from agricultural loans must have grown sharply in 1956.

THE CHANNELS OF CIRCULATION IN RURAL AREAS

Within the currency sphere, rural areas were particularly important because they contained eighty percent of the population and were relatively removed from the centralized banking system. The channels of currency circulation in these areas were therefore subject to close scrutiny by the People's Bank. Table VII-2 lists the major items affecting the rural currency flow and their percentage shares in the first halves of 1955 and 1956.

This table complements the preceding one in that it reaffirms the dominance of state agricultural purchases and socialistic retail sales in the circuit of the currency flow. Actually, the percentage shares for state agricultural purchases shown in Table VII-2 represent less than their true proportions. This proposition is based on two arguments.

[6] The large and unspecified "others" item among currency receipts in Table VII-1 could have been caused by receipts from fines imposed on private business during the three-anti and five-anti movements in 1952. If so, such receipts would be nonrecurrent in later years.

[7] By 1960, retail sale receipts of the state commercial network (including commodities and urban services) plus personal deposits accounted for 85 percent of the return flow of currency. Tsiang, "Money and Banking in Communist China," *An Economic Profile of Mainland China,* Studies prepared for the Joint Economic Committee, U.S. Congress, I, 336. Receipts from retail sales of commodities alone accounted for over 60 percent of currency inflow. Tsi, *The Cash Plan of the People's Bank,* p. 26.

Table VII-2
Principal Channels of Currency Circulation in Rural Areas,* 1955–1956
(in percent)

	First half year	
	of 1955	of 1956
Currency paid (by the state sector):		
Agricultural purchases	65.0	45.8
Rural wages	20.7	18.5
Rural bank credit (including agricultural loans, withdrawal of personal deposits and advance payments for agricultural purchases)	14.3	35.7
Total	100.0	100.0
Currency received (by the state sector):		
Retail sales of foodgrains	29.7	23.6
Retail sale of consumer's good other than foodgrains	57.8	60.5
Retail sale of producer's goods (including chemical fertilizers and modern farm equipments)	12.5	15.9
Total	100.0	100.0

*Although channels listed in this table were not exhaustive, they included major currency transactions between the state sector and the farms, and they accounted for a predominant proportion of the rural cash flow.
Source: Tseng Ling, "The Effects of Agricultural Collectivization . . . ," *CCYC*, no. 6, 1956, pp. 40–41.

First, the percentages shown in the table were based on semiannual data. Arithmetically, if there were no pronounced seasonal fluctuations, then the percentage share derived from semiannual data would be close to that derived from annual data. According to available information, this was in fact the case with respect to rural retail sales, but not for state agricultural purchases. The latter bore a distinct seasonal pattern, with over two-thirds of the annual purchases concentrated in the second half year.[8] Thus the percentages for agricultural purchases given in Table VII-2, being those for the first half year alone, underestimated the relative importance of this channel. If seasonal adjustments had been made, the share of state agricultural purchases would, in all likeli-

[8] *Infra,* Table VII-3.

hood, have been much higher than 65.0 and 45.8 percent respectively for 1955 and 1956.[9]

A second argument relates to the lower percentage share for 1956 compared with that for 1955. This decline was not a normal phenomenon. It was caused not so much by an absolute decrease in state agricultural purchases as by the rash of agricultural loans designed to stimulate collectivization early in 1956.[10] These loans temporarily raised the relative importance of rural bank credit as a channel of currency outflow. As a result the 1956 percentage share of state agricultural purchases as well as that of rural wages was correspondingly lowered.[11]

Thus when all circumstances are taken into account, it would be correct to say that, during the First Five Year Plan period, state agricultural purchases normally accounted for at least 70 percent of the volume of currency that flowed from the state sector into rural areas. This information, coupled with the recollection that there was no limit to the amount of commercial loans granted to state enterprises for agricultural purchases, reveals the precarious position of the People's Bank in the management of rural currency. The Bank's discretion over the outflow of currency into the farm areas during the period of study was at best weak. Nor was currency planning easy to achieve, since the currency outflow was affected by the amount of agricultural purchases and therefore by each year's harvest, which was not as predictable as industrial outputs. The power of the People's Bank to limit rural currency, hence currency in general, was circumscribed. In this

[9] Unless seasonal patterns of the other items causing currency to flow into rural areas (i.e., rural wages and rural bank credit) were similar to those of state agricultural purchases. This was not the case. In fact, a portion of the rural bank credit consisted of advance payments for agricultural purchases, and this was a device to counter the seasonal effects of agricultural purchases, thereby to smooth the currency flow; this will be discussed later on in this chapter.

[10] State agricultural purchases in the first half of 1956 were 98 percent of those in the first half of 1955, a decline of 2 percent. Tseng Ling, "The Effects of Agricultural Collectivization . . . ," *CCYC,* no. 6, 1956, p. 40. Computations based on data given in this source show that these purchases amounted to 4.04 and 3.97 billion yuan in the first halves of 1955 and 1956 respectively. On the other hand, rural bank credit grew from 0.89 to 3.09 billion yuan in the same periods, representing an increase of 246 percent. *Ibid.,* p. 57.

[11] Although the percentage shares of wages shown on Table VII-2 declined, the absolute amount of rural wages actually increased by 25 percent from the first half of 1955 to the first half of 1956. *Ibid.,* p. 40.

situation, what actions could the Bank take in order to avoid an excessive currency supply? What policy should it follow so as to exert a measure of control? The next section attempts to pursue these questions further.

The Management of Currency

PLANNING

Like bank credit, the currency circuit was theoretically directed by planning. The total amount of currency in circulation was subject to a limit set by the central government and determined as a component part of the national economic plan.[12] Subject to this limit, the People's Bank compiled a cash plan by coordinating the individual financial plans of various currency-using units in the state sector, which in turn were reflections of these units' physical plans. The cash plan showed the planned figures for various items of receipts and expenditures (in other words, the channels of circulation) and, supposedly, guided the currency operations of the network of banking offices.[13]

In terms of accuracy, cash planning had certain advantages over credit planning. First, the credit plan was more comprehensive, and its components were subject to larger changes. Second, the credit plan, once formulated, circumscribed the freedom of the enterprises; therefore the enterprises were inclined to inflate their credit requirements more than their cash requirements.[14] However, these considerations might have reduced the margin of error of the cash plan in absolute terms, but not necessarily in percentage terms; for the total amount of currency was also smaller than the amount of credit. In any case, there are grounds to suspect the adequacy of cash planning in the period under study. In the first place, physical plans were as yet rudimentary, and the financial plans of individual enterprises, on which

[12] Tseng and Han, *The Circulation of Money* . . . (*JPRS* #3317), pp. 122–26.
[13] *Supra,* Chapter I, pp. 12–13.
[14] Hu Hou-jen, "The Relationship between the Cash Plan and the Credit Plan," *CKCJ,* no. 1, 1957, pp. 12–14.

the cash plan rested, would reflect a composite of estimation errors involved in a complex procedure through an intricate hierarchy. In the second place, the main constituent of the cash plan, the agricultural purchase, was difficult to forecast. This was especially true in the case of subsidiary rural products, neither the prices nor the quantities of which were controlled. In addition, because of the ready availability of bank credit to state enterprises, wage payments made by these enterprises were flexible, and there was no effective control of the total wage fund.

With these difficulties, it is not surprising that the Bank appeared to rely on specific actions and maneuvers to keep the amount of currency from becoming too large. Evidently, the cash plan could not provide the necessary direction,[15] therefore, the Bank could not remain passive. It had to struggle to reduce the quantity of currency in order to stay within the limit set by the central government and, more specifically, to maintain equilibrium in the private sector. At times, however, the Bank failed to achieve these objectives, as was the case in 1956.

CURRENCY MEASURES

Several measures that had the common effect of reducing the amount of currency outstanding were adopted by the People's Bank. These measures achieved the currency-reducing effect in different ways. One type changed the boundaries of the sphere of circulation, a second type smoothed and narrowed the currency circuit, and a third directly removed currency from circulation. The different measures are reviewed below. In their implementations, the growing network of rural credit cooperatives and urban savings organs played an active part.

THE CONTRACTION OF THE CURRENCY SECTOR

Certain structural changes were effected by the People's Bank that tended to restrict the sphere in which currency was used. The first of

---

[15] This can be seen from the following quotation: "During the First Five-Year Plan period . . . because our understanding of the [cash] plan was inadequate and because the plan was inaccurate, it did not receive sufficient emphasis, nor did it perform its appropriate function." PB, "Report on the Need to Further Strengthen Planning in Cash Receipts and Expenditures," *FKHP*, X, 275.

these was the abolition of the gold treasury or capital supply system. Under this system funds were controlled by central ministries and currency was transferred up and down the various pyramids of state agencies. As previously stated, efforts were made in 1953 and 1955 to abolish this system.[16] These developments enabled the Bank to create a direct credit relationship with local units of the state enterprises, particularly with the retail outlets of the commercial hierarchy where transactions were carried out in currency.[17] The more immediate banking contact in turn made it possible for cash to flow into local bank offices as soon as such cash entered the lower echelon of the state sector, thereby reducing the quantity of currency held within the state trading system as a whole. In short, the abolition of the gold treasury system improved the precision with which cash was supplied to and withdrawn from various enterprises according to actual transactional requirements, thereby reducing the amount of currency that was necessary to satisfy these requirements.

A second structural change was the extension of non-cash settlements. Since, among other things, the People's Bank was to be the center of settlements, the use of bank account transfers as a method of making payments, known as non-cash settlement, was encouraged wherever practicable. In the state sector, its use was stipulated by law as early as 1950 although in reality public units did not always comply with this law. In the private sector, however, currency was generally used. The People's Bank therefore tried to reduce the quantity of currency in circulation by promoting the use of non-cash settlements through two courses of action: (1) enforcement of the cash control program in the state sector and (2) extension of non-cash settlements into the private sector.[18] As a result of the rural collectivization drive, the Bank was able to make some progress in the private sector. This drive, under which the collectives replaced the farming households as the basic rural economic units, had two effects. First, it enabled the state to pay

[16] *Supra,* Chapter IV, pp. 81–82 and Chapter V, pp. 96–97.

[17] The rural supply and marketing cooperatives were particularly important because they managed agricultural purchases as well as rural retail sales, both of which were major channels of currency circulation.

[18] Li Hsien-nien, 1958 Budget Report, *FKHP,* VII, 120; Tseng Ling, "The Effects of Agricultural Collectivization . . . ," *CCYC,* no. 6, 1956, pp. 50–51.

for agricultural purchases in a more centralized fashion (to the collectives instead of the individuals). Second, the larger economic units tended to be less reluctant than the individual peasants to deposit their funds with the Bank or the credit cooperatives. It therefore became possible, after the collectivization, for the state to conduct at least a part of its agricultural purchases without the immediate use of currency. Furthermore, a portion of the income thus received by the collectives was retained as accumulation funds or reserves for productive expenditures; both of these, when spent, returned to the state sector in the form of payments for equipment or supplies purchased from the state commercial network. Since these activities could be carried out through non-cash settlements, the use of currency in the rural area was reduced to cover primarily the distribution of income among member peasants after all deductions were made by the collectives.

SHORT-TERM STABILIZATION OF THE CURRENCY FLOW

This type of measure tended to smooth the uneven requirements of currency within a given payment period so as to avoid short-term fluctuations in the quantity of currency outstanding. To a certain extent, the promotion of urban personal deposits served this purpose by lowering the peak demand for currency to cover wage payments. If cash wages were deposited by workers on a given payday and gradually withdrawn before the next payday, the amount of currency required to finance wage payments would be smaller even though total income and spending of the workers remained the same. The need of short-term stabilization of the currency flow was the greatest in agriculture where, broadly, the payment period was one year. The importance of agriculture in the currency sector plus its long payment period led to extreme fluctuations in currency. The largest payment made by the state sector to the private sector was for agricultural purchases, and these tended to concentrate in the period after the fall harvest thereby causing a pronounced pattern of seasonal variations in the demand for currency of the country as a whole. Averaging out these recurrent ups and downs would lessen the maximum amount of currency outstanding and narrow the cash flow. Thus the Bank attempted to stabilize the seasonal demand for currency in farm areas.

177

For the analysis of rural currency fluctuations, the People's Bank divided the calendar year into halves. In the first six months, termed the "slack season," payments to the farm area for agricultural purchase generally fell behind receipts from state sales to this area, resulting in a return currency flow to the Bank. In the second six months of the year, the "brisk season," the opposite was true and currency was injected into the countryside. The seasonal changes of the two basic channels, one for outflow and the other for inflow, and their combined influence on the rural currency flow are shown in Table VII-3.

It can be seen from this table that, because state agricultural purchases concentrated in the second half year (section I of Table VII-3) while state sales were more evenly distributed during the year (section II), the currency flow showed a marked seasonal pattern (section III). The currency changes during the two seasons were originally expressed in the Chinese source as percentages of two different denominators. This procedure resulted in much higher relative figures for currency withdrawals (IIIA3 in the table) than those for currency increase (IIIB3). To facilitate comparisons, these two sets of figures are reduced to a common base in section IIIC of the table. After this adjustment, the inflow and outflow of rural currency during the two seasons of each year becomes much closer, but the seasonal pattern remains.[19]

To reduce this seasonality, the Bank used credit operations as a balancing device. Three types of operations were relied on by the Bank: (1) rural deposits, (2) agricultural loans, and (3) advance payments for agricultural purchases. The last of these was instituted in 1954 when the government began to contract in advance with individual peasants or agricultural cooperatives for the purchase of basic crops. As was mentioned in Chapter V, these advance payments formed a part of commercial credit.

During the first six months of each year, the Bank raised the quantity of outstanding currency through payments made to depositors, the granting of agricultural loans, and the extension of advance payments.

---

[19] Figures in IIIC of the table show that, except for 1953, the increase in currency during the second half year was outweighed by the withdrawal in the first half year. In interpreting these figures, it should be borne in mind that this table covers only the two basic channels relating to commodity flows, i.e., state purchase and state sales. Other channels of the currency flow, such as rural bank credit, might shift the balance.

Table VII-3
Seasonal Patterns of State Agricultural Purchases, State Sales,
and Their Effects on Rural Currency, 1953–1956
(in percent)

	1953	1954	1955	1956†
I. State agricultural purchases:				
A. First half year	30	36	31	27
B. Second half year	70	64	69	73
C. Entire year	100	100	100	100
II. State sales in the rural area:*				
A. First half year	47.6	43.0	47.5	47.0
B. Second half year	52.4	57.0	52.5	53.0
C. Entire year	100.0	100.0	100.0	100.0
III. Rural currency circulation:				
A. First half year:	*(State Agricultural Purchase of the First Half Year = 100)*			
1. State agricultural purchase	100	100	100	100
2. State sales	164	132	200	224
3. Resulting withdrawal of currency from circulation	−64	−32	−100	−124
B. Second half year:	*(State Agricultural Purchase of the Second Half Year = 100)*			
1. State agricultural purchase	100	100	100	100
2. State sales	67.2	83.7	82.0	−
3. Resulting increase in currency	+32.8	+16.3	+18.0	−
C. Entire year:	*(State Agricultural Purchase of the Entire Year = 100)*			
1. Currency withdrawn in first half year (IIIA3 × IA)	−19.2	−11.5	−31.0	−33.5
2. Currency increase in second half year (IIIB3 × IB)	+23.0	+10.4	+12.4	−

* Includes sales of producer's goods and consumer's goods.
† Estimates.
Source: Tseng Ling, "The Effects of Agricultural Collectivization . . . ," *CCYC*, no. 6, 1956, pp. 55–56.

These operations were reversed in the last six months of the year when the Bank absorbed savings deposits, recalled loans and canceled advance payments, thereby depressing the quantity of currency. Together, the three methods constituted the "credit channel" through which the seasonal stabilization of rural currency was effected. This channel was distinct from the "commodity channel" of state purchases and sales which caused the seasonal variations in the first place. Available data for the Bank's rural credit operations in the two seasons are presented in Table VII-4. They show an upward trend for these operations. In addition, the effect of agricultural loans in 1956 stands out boldly.

Table VII-4
Credit Operations for the Stabilization of Seasonal Fluctuations in Rural Currency,* 1953–1956
(million yuan)

I. To Increase Currency during the "Slack Season"

First half year (1)	Agricultural loans granted† (2)	Rural deposits paid out (3)	Advance payments (4)	Total (5)	Index of total 1953=100 (6)
1953	390	40	nil	430	100
1954	250	60	180	490	114
1955	410	320	160	890	206
1956	1,840	350	900	3,090	718

II. To Decrease Currency during the "Brisk Season"

Second half year (1)	Agricultural loans recalled† (2)	Increase in rural deposits (3)	Repayments of advances (4)	Total (5)	Index of total 1953=100 (6)
1953	160	160	nil	320	100
1954	150	380	180	710	221
1955	170	490	140	800	250

*This table illustrates the seasonal changes. However, it is not clear whether the loan and deposit figures are those of the People's Bank alone or include the credit cooperatives. They do not agree in all respects with other data on total loans.

†Figures in this column broadly agree with data given by the same author in another context (Appendix B). However, a large discrepancy exists between the two sets of figures in agricultural loans granted for 1954 (¥363 million instead of ¥250 million). But a discrepancy of similar magnitude exists in agricultural loans recalled for late 1953 (¥264 million instead of ¥160 million). It can therefore be assumed that the discrepancies canceled each other. These differences could be related to the cancellations of some agricultural loans in 1953.

Source: Tseng Ling, "The Effects of Agricultural Collectivization . . . ," *CCYC*, no. 6, 1956, pp. 57–58.

Table VII-5 represents a rearrangement of the same data. It can be seen here that although the withdrawal of savings deposits during the first season of each year was balanced by an increase of this type of deposit during the second season, the former was smaller than the latter, leaving a net increase of savings deposits from year to year. Agricultural loans granted in the first half of each year were also offset by agricultural loans recalled in the second half, but the extension of loans was much larger than their recall, resulting in a growth of agricultural loans outstanding from year to year. For the three-year period of 1953–1955 as a whole, the amount of currency issued in the rural areas through the net increase of agricultural loans (570 million yuan) was broadly balanced by currency withdrawn through the growth in savings deposits (610 million yuan). However, these net figures were not balanced for individual years.

Table VII-6 compares the total changes of rural currency during the two seasons as a result of the three types of banking operations. This table indicates that these operations not only smoothed out seasonal fluctuations but also contributed toward a net increase in rural currency in 1953, a severe contraction in 1954 (the year of growth for the credit cooperatives), a re-expansion in 1955, and a very large increase in currency in early 1956.

Table VII-5
The Seasonal Changes of Agricultural Loans
and Rural Deposits, 1953–1956
(million yuan)

Year	Agricultural loans			Rural deposits		
	Granted 1st half year (1)	Recalled 2nd half year (2)	Net in-crease (3)	Paid out 1st half year (4)	Increased 2nd half year (5)	Net in-crease (6)
1953	390	160	230	40	160	120
1954	250	150	100	60	380	320
1955	410	170	240	320	490	170
1956	1,840	—	—	350	—	—
			570			610

Source: Table VII-4.

181

Table VII-6
**Combined Effects of Agricultural Loans, Rural Deposits, and Advance
Payments on Rural Currency, 1953–1956**
(in million yuan)

Year	Increase in rural currency first half year (1)	Decrease in rural currency second half year (2)	Net change (3)
1953	430	320	+100
1954	490	710	−220
1955	890	800	+ 90
1956	3,090	—	—

Source: Table VII-4.

THE ABSORPTION OF OUTSTANDING CURRENCY

Given the channels of currency circulation described previously, the
quantity of cash outstanding varied with the size of the different inflows
and outflows. As a result, the Bank's influence on the total supply of
currency depended on its ability to affect these flows. On the one hand,
the emission of currency hinged on the two dominant magnitudes of
agricultural purchase and total wage bill, neither of which could be
determined by the Bank. Besides, the magnitude of bank credit extended to the non-state sector was not completely within the discretion
of the Bank.[20] On the other hand, the withdrawal of currency from
circulation was dependent upon three factors: (1) the amount of goods
and services available for sale by state enterprises; (2) the fiscal measures involving direct taxes, which were relatively unimportant and
fixed, and periodic bond sales; and (3) the Bank's ability to attract personal deposits and to recall loans from individuals. Among all these
channels in both directions, the only one on which the Bank had any
appreciable degree of freedom to act was the last. Thus the promotion
of personal deposits, occasionally coupled with a drive to recall agricultural loans, became the main vehicle through which the Bank attempted to contract outstanding currency.

[20] Loans to the non-state sector were more flexible, but they were basically limited either
by plan or by other considerations such as the need for socialization and the availability
of rural producer's goods.

Analytically, the existence of a large amount of personal deposits, which in China comprised both demand and time deposits, would not necessarily affect the pool of outstanding currency. If the sum of withdrawals equaled that of new deposits, there would be no change in the quantity of currency in circulation. Only when total deposits continuously climbed or progressively solidified over time would there be a lasting currency contraction effect. This accounted for the emphasis placed by the People's Bank on the growth of personal deposits, the rise in the proportion of time deposits, and the lengthening of the duration for each deposit yuan held by the Bank. If these conditions were fulfilled, the savings drive would not only remove a part of the currency in circulation, but would also inactivate temporarily some of the excessive purchasing powers.

It should be borne in mind that this discussion is applicable over time or from period to period. Within a given payment period, however, the existence of personal deposits per se could serve to minimize the amount of currency outstanding by stabilizing the flow. Besides, personal deposits also make possible the extension of non-cash settlement to the private sector and therefore indirectly lowered the amount of currency required. Thus, in the Chinese schema, the savings drive was a multifaceted measure. It had a double capacity in contracting the quantity of currency, one with and the other without a concurrent effect in controlling the volume of purchasing powers and therefore in alleviating inflationary pressures.

OBJECTIVES AND POLICY

A careful examination of the various currency measures undertaken by the People's Bank indicates that, while they shared a common goal of minimizing the volume of currency, they also had other objectives that were dissimilar. The two measures affecting the currency sphere were necessary to strengthen and extend the Bank's supervision over local units of state enterprises and rural collectives; thus their long-run objective was to enable the Bank to perform its microfinancial function over these entities. During the transition period, however, these measures led to the replacement of cash holding with deposits; they therefore had a temporary currency-reducing effect. And the Bank utilized them whenever possible in order to keep the quantity of outstanding currency within the prescribed limit.

The stabilization of short-term fluctuations of the currency flow, on the other hand, lessened the cash balance required to finance a given amount of personal income.[21] In other words, its objective was to raise the velocity of currency circulation, thereby enabling each unit of currency to finance annually a larger amount of income or transactions, especially in the rural area. In addition, the methods employed in the stabilization also could influence the distribution of rural income between investment and consumption; for by granting loans and advance payments for productive purposes the Bank was inducing and ensuring a certain amount of agricultural investment. Despite the fact that the stabilization of short-term fluctuations required continued and repetitive banking operations, its currency-reducing effect was nonrecurrent; it would end when the variations were eliminated and the velocity reached a certain level. Therefore this measure was also a transitory device from the viewpoint of currency contraction.

The Bank was thus left with only one type of action that could be employed repeatedly and with a continuous currency-reducing effect. It could remove cash from circulation either by recalling agricultural loans or increasing personal deposits. The collection of rural loans, however, was beset with its own problems;[22] hence the savings drive became the sole major regular instrument for controlling the volume of currency. But even this one method would be effective only under certain conditions. It required either an ever-growing total amount of deposits or an ever-decreasing rate of turnover of these deposits. Both of these have in fact been the objectives of various savings drives conducted in the Mainland.

It may be concluded from the methods employed that the currency policy of the People's Bank, like its credit policy, was negative in nature. The Bank could not effectively control the flow of currency into circulation; therefore it had to rely on measures that influenced the out-

---

[21] The term cash balance is here used in the narrow sense to denote currency balance.
[22] *Supra,* Chapter V, pp. 119–21.

flow. Of these measures, the most important one appeared to be the promotion of personal deposits through the savings drive.

Specific Currency Developments

During the period of the First Five Year Plan, two specific events in the field of currency are worthy of attention, both of which affected the quantity of currency in circulation. The first of these is the currency conversion of 1955, and the second, the currency hoarding of 1956.

THE CURRENCY CONVERSION

In March, 1955, a general change in the currency unit took place at the uniform exchange rate of 10,000 yuan of the old people's currency to 1 yuan of the new people's currency. Several reasons were given by the Chinese for this action, which was completed in two months.[23] First, since prices were stabilized at the end-of-inflation level, they were very high. The currency conversion would restore them to a normal scale by eliminating four digits, thereby facilitating accounting and computation. Second, a completely new issue of banknotes made it possible (1) to improve their quality, thereby preventing counterfeiting, (2) to standardize their designs and colors, thereby making them conveniently recognizable to illiterate peasants, and (3) to include minority languages, thereby expediting their circulation in the border regions such as Tibet and Inner Mongolia.[24]

In addition to these announced reasons, it was also mentioned that the

[23] The order for currency conversion was issued by the state council on February 21, 1955. The conversion began on March 1, 1955. From March 1 to March 31 old notes were allowed to circulate alongside the new notes. After March 31, old notes could only be exchanged for new notes in the Bank. The conversion terminated on April 30. However, old notes of small denominations (5,000 yuan and below) were allowed to circulate until June 10. SC, "Order on the Issuance of the New People's Currency and the Withdrawal of Existing People's Currency," *JMST,* 1956, pp. 531–32; "The Work of Currency Conversion Was Successfully Accomplished," *JMST,* 1956, p. 536.

[24] Tseng and Han, *The Circulation of Money . . . (JPRS* #3317), pp. 111–12; Han Lei, "The Meaning and Functions of the Currency Conversion," *HH,* February, 1955, pp. 23–24.

nationwide currency conversion would have other effects. It would "strengthen the currency circulation" making it a "better instrument of supervision," and would affect the development of savings and the stabilization of the market.[25] Although these statements are vague, they lend support to two a priori propositions. First, a general conversion would enable the People's Bank to gain complete and accurate information regarding the volume and distribution of currency which, in turn, would facilitate the Bank's control over the money flow. Viewed from this perspective, the conversion could be considered a logical ingredient of the banking reform. Second, it is conceivable that the conversion was used as a means to uncover and remove currency hoards. Although, according to regulations, accumulated holdings of cash could be used to purchase goods from the state commercial network, the relatively short length of time (one month) in which this was allowed imposed a limit on such purchases. Possessors of old currency who might be either reluctant to disclose their wealth or unable to spend it all in the specified period would be forced to exchange it for the new currency in the Bank. To the extent that they failed to do so, their hoarded currency ceased to be money. Theoretically, the public could exchange its cash holdings for the new currency at the Bank freely and without limit; but the fact that personal deposits increased steeply during the conversion period[26] casts doubts on the reality of the professed principle of complete freedom of conversion. In any event, the actual increase in personal deposits means that the conversion did have some currency-contracting effect regardless of whether or not this was originally intended.[27]

---

[25] *Ibid.,* p. 24.

[26] In the four days following the announcement of the currency conversion (February 21–24), personal deposits in the seven large cities rose by 10 million (new) yuan, some having terms of more than one year. "Do Well in the Work of Currency Conversion," *JMJP,* March 1, 1955. In the ten days following the announcement, deposits climbed by over 24 million yuan, and the rate of increase of deposits in March, 1955, was the highest of any month since the beginning of the Communist regime. "The Work of Currency Conversion . . . ," *JMST,* 1956, p. 536. Personal deposits during the conversion period were 22 percent above those for the corresponding period in 1954. Starlight, *Fiscal and Monetary Policies in Communist China,* p. 190. The rise in personal deposits was publicized in China as evidence of the population's increased confidence in the new currency.

[27] Chinese bankers argued that, since the conversion took place at a time of stable prices, it was not needed for the purpose of contracting the amount of currency. This argument was advanced as an explanation for adopting one uniform rate of exchange instead of

CURRENCY SHORTAGE AND THE PROBLEM
OF HOARDING

Because the availability of currency to various branches of the People's Bank was strictly controlled, while the granting of credit to the commercial network for agricultural purchases (which required the use of cash) was unlimited, a shortage of currency developed periodically in the rural banks during the brisk season. Local banks often could not supply sufficient amounts of cash to pay the peasants for their sales to the supply and marketing cooperatives. A form of I.O.U., referred to as "white slips," was sometimes used. This phenomenon was considered undesirable by the Bank, and local offices were regularly urged to absorb currency (through savings drives, cash control, etc.) as fast as possible in order to prevent a shortage of cash and the use of white slips. In other words, the Bank attempted to meet the demand for cash by accelerating the velocity of currency circulation.

The problem of currency shortage was especially acute in 1956 when, paradoxically, more cash was released into the rural areas as a result of the sudden surge in agricultural credit. At the end of March, 1956, currency held in the rural area rose to 70 percent of the total currency in the nation, as compared with 50 percent in the corresponding period in 1955; and the total currency was itself growing.[28] In spite of this increase in cash in the farm sector, however, the newly formed collectives and many poor peasants as well as the banks experienced money difficulties. A general tightness of cash accompanied a sluggish market around March and April of that year.

Several factors were said to be responsible for this condition, the most important one being an increase in currency hoarding by the better-off farmers. While hoarding was made possible by an unequal distribution of currency in the rural areas,[29] the immediate cause was

differentiated rates. Yang P'ei-hsin, "The Meaning and Functions of the Currency Conversion," *JMST,* 1956, pp. 533–35.

[28] Tseng Ling, "Effects of Agricultural Collectivization . . . ," *CCYC,* no. 6, 1956, pp. 45–47. Lu, "Conditions of Rural Currency Circulation during the First Half Year," *CKCJ,* no. 14, 1956, pp. 10–11. Total currency in circulation increased by 30 percent at the end of March, 1956, over the total at the end of March, 1955.

[29] The rural currency was unequally distributed, concentrating in areas of industrial

the uncertainties created by the collectivization drive. The peasants, fearing that their assets might be appropriated by the collectives as investments, were unwilling either to spend their money or to deposit it in the credit cooperatives; they secretly hoarded cash.[30] Thus, despite the enlarged amount of currency outstanding, the People's Bank granted further consumption and productive loans and advance payments of over one billion yuan in order to relieve the rural shortage of money.[31] This decision perhaps contributed to the inflationary pressures that alarmed the authorities at the end of 1956.

A related development in 1956 during the period of currency shortage was the issuance of "circulation notes" by the agricultural collectives. These were used as substitutes for cash. Originating as coupons with small fixed face values intended for circulation within the collectives to facilitate the internal exchange of goods,[32] these notes grew into denominations of five or more new yuan and were gradually used as a medium of exchange between the collectives and outsiders. In effect, they became quasi-currency issued by various collectives and were later condemned by the People's Bank.[33]

The Quantity of Currency

While certain banking statistics involving the private sector, such as agricultural loans and savings deposits, are relatively more abundant than those involving the state sector, this is not the case with currency. Statistics on currency in absolute terms are not published in the Main-

---

crops. Tseng Ling, "Effects of Agricultural Collectivization . . . ," *CCYC,* no. 6, 1956. It was said that 20 percent of the farming households held 70 percent of the rural currency. Li Ch'ang-Ch'in, "The 'Circulation Notes' Should Not Be Legalized," *CKCJ,* no. 23, 1956, pp. 19–20.

[30] Early in 1957, it was estimated that approximately one-third of the rural currency was being hoarded. "Does the People's Currency Serve as Store of Value?," *CKCJ,* no. 4, 1957, pp. 4–5.

[31] Tseng Ling, "Effects of Agricultural Collectivization . . . ," *CCYC,* no. 6, 1956, p. 48.

[32] For example, a member might sell manure to the collective in return for vegetable coupons that entitled him to purchase vegetables from the collective.

[33] Tseng Lin, *The Circulation of Money . . . , (JPRS* #3317), p. 92; "Circulation Notes in Rural China," *Far Eastern Economic Review,* April 11, 1957, pp. 466–67. Li Ch'ang-Ch'in, "The 'Circulation Notes' Should Not Be Legalized," *CKCJ,* no. 23, 1956.

land. But, like credit data of the state sector, some comparative information has been given in scattered sources.

The absolute volume of currency for the period between 1949 and 1957, however, has been estimated by Professor Choh-ming Li. The estimation has been made on the basis of consumers' money income.[34] When his method is examined in the context of the general economic conditions in Communist China, there are reasons to believe that it is subject to bias. An attempt is therefore made to construct an alternative series. In the following, Li's method is presented and analyzed, an alternative estimation is made, and, finally, the new series is evaluated.

LI'S ESTIMATES

Li's series on the volume of currency is reproduced in column (1) of Table VII-7. His procedure of estimation can be summarized as follows: (1) Consumers' money income for 1955 and 1956 is approximated on the basis of available data for the "social purchasing power." (2) The increase in consumers' money income from 1955 to 1956 (5,060 million yuan) is then compared with the currency increase between the end of 1955 and the end of 1956 (1,690 million yuan); from these two changes the income velocity of currency circulation is computed. (3) The resulting income velocity (2.99 or 3) is then applied to the total consumers' money income for 1956 (38,320 million yuan) to derive the average volume of currency in circulation for that year (12,770 million yuan). (4) Estimates for other years are extrapolated from the 1956 figure on the basis of available comparative information.

Given the lack of data, this method of estimation is ingenious. However, one crucial determinant of the outcome is the accuracy of the income velocity estimate; it is in this area that certain doubts may be raised. The income velocity derived by taking the ratio of two increments (i.e., change in consumers' money income/change in currency) would be a good approximation of the overall average income velocity (i.e., total consumers' money income/total currency) if the latter were fairly stable over the relevant time span. In a period of shifting average

---

[34] Choh-ming Li, *Economic Development of Communist China,* pp. 154–61.

Table VII-7
Two Series of Estimated Quantity of Currency, 1949–1957
(billion yuan)

Year	Li's series	Our series	
	End of year (1)	End of year (2)	End of June (3)
1949	1.0	0.5	—
1950	2.5*	1.2	1.2
1951	—	2.2	1.9
1952	7.4	3.6	2.1
1953	9.7	5.0	—
1954	—	below 5.0	—
1955	11.1	5.4	below 4.0
1956	12.8	7.1	5.2
1957	11.7 (June)	6.7	6.0
1958	—	—	6.0†

* Average for the year.
† Expected.
Sources:
Col. (1): Choh-ming Li, *Economic Development of Communist China* (Berkeley; University of California Press, 1959; reprinted by permission of The Regents of the University of California), p. 160.
Cols. (2) and (3): See text.

velocity, however, the two measurements would diverge. If income velocity were generally slowing down, then logically, one would expect the velocity calculated on the basis of increments alone to be lower than the overall average velocity. On the other hand, if income velocity were increasing, then the velocity for the marginal portion of currency would be too high an approximation of the average velocity.

Li's method, then, implicitly assumes that the income velocity of currency remained constant between the end of 1955 and the end of 1956. As has been seen in the discussion in the last section, this was not in fact the case. In 1956 there was a rise in the quantity of currency outstanding and a concurrent shift of the currency distribution in favor of the rural area. This phenomenon alone would have depressed the nation's average income velocity, since the rural income velocity is likely to be lower than that in urban centers. But, on top of this phenomenon, there was the problem of increased hoarding of currency by the peasants, and the condition was serious enough to warrant special discussions and actions from the People's Bank. There can therefore be little doubt that the overall income velocity in China declined in 1956 compared with the velocity in 1955.

Thus it can be deduced from the 1956 development that the income velocity computed by Li is probably lower than the true overall average velocity for that year. The resulting estimate for the 1956 volume of currency, on which all other annual currency figures are based, is therefore correspondingly too high. For example, if the true average income velocity were 4, instead of the 3 that Li obtained from the marginal increments, then the entire estimated series of currency would be reduced by one-fourth.

While this evaluation of Li's methodology leads to the conclusion that his series tends to have an upward bias, precise information is lacking on the degree of the bias. Hence an adjustment for the bias is not feasible. However, because of the bias, it can be assumed that Li's series represents a maximum approximation that sets the upper limit to the volume of currency.

AN ALTERNATIVE SERIES

The nature and extent of available materials on Chinese currency are such that it is difficult to estimate the quantity of currency in a single independent series with an appreciable degree of reliability. However, there are sufficient data to support an approximation of the minimum amounts of currency in circulation. Such a series can be useful because, first, when combined with Li's, it provides an estimated range within which the actual data are very likely to fall. Second, as will be seen in the evaluation, this minimum series proves to be closer to the actual data than Li's. Therefore, when the nature of its bias is borne in mind, the minimum series may be considered the better of the two estimations if both are used individually.

Columns (2) and (3) of Table VII-7 show the minimum estimates of the volume of currency for 1949–1957. These estimates are based on scanty evidence, as quantitative approximations of Chinese currency necessarily have to be. But they are made in a direct manner, with little manipulation of the available data, and the basic information originated from banking officials and authors in the Mainland who were familiar with the actual conditions of the time. Since our immediate objective here is to find the minimum quantity of currency, this procedure may be permissible.

The 1949 figure in column (2) is derived from the following information.[35] (a) Early in January, 1950, when the first issue of public bonds began, it was said that the planned sale of 200 million units of bonds could retire "more than half" the currency in circulation.[36] (b) Previously, it had been estimated that the total value of the entire bond issue was approximately 300 million yuan.[37] Combining the two statements, it appears unlikely that the actual currency in circulation at the end of 1949 could have fallen below 500 million yuan.[38] Since it is known that, in 1950 and 1951, currency issued to cover budget deficit amounted to 0.7 billion and 1.0 billion yuan respectively,[39] these are added to the 1949 figure to derive the minimum quantities for the end of 1950 and 1951.

Estimates for 1952 through 1955 in column (2) of Table VII-7 are based on the same relative information as that used by Li. This includes the following. (a) The quantity of currency in 1952 was about three times that of 1950.[40] (b) The quantity at the end of 1953 was ten times

---

[35] The author is indebted to Mr. John Y. H. Liu, Research Fellow of the Hoover Institution and the Union Research Institute of Hong Kong for pointing out this information.

[36] Yang P'ei-hsin, "Prices, Money and Public Bonds," *HCS,* I, no. 11 (January 29, 1950), 8–11.

[37] T'ao, "The Sale of Public Bonds and Economic Development," *HCS,* I, no. 7, (December 4, 1949), 4–6. Like the case of bank deposits in that period, public bonds were issued in 1950 in commodity units, each containing a given combination of daily necessities. The money price of the unit fluctuated with the average of the wholesale prices of these commodities in six large cities. T'ao estimated just prior to the sale that each unit of bond was worth about ￥1.50.

[38] According to what seems to be the common usage in Communist China, "more than half" is generally quite close to half, or else a larger proportion would be stated. Thus it is possible that the actual amount of currency at the end of 1949 was closer to 0.6 billion than to 0.5 billion. The latter amount is used here in order to ascertain the minimum.

[39] Ko, "On the Inter-Connection . . . .," *CCYC,* no. 1, 1958, p. 9. The figures given were 699.15 million and 1,037.13 million yuan.

[40] Tseng Ling, "Is There Inflation in China at the Present?," *CCYC,* no. 5, 1957, p. 41. This ratio relates the average amounts of currency for the two years; however, assuming the seasonal pattern unchanged, it should be applicable also to the totals at the end of the two years.

that at the end of 1949.[41] (c) At the end of the period of 1953–1955 the volume of currency was 50 percent higher than that in 1952.[42] Although the currency figure for 1954 cannot be derived, it is known from data presented above that currency in the rural sector was severely contracted through both the credit channel and the commodity channel.[43] Therefore the figure for 1954 is not likely to be higher than that for 1953.

The increase in currency at the end of 1956 as compared with the end of 1955 (¥1.69 billion) was widely publicized.[44] Actually, the increase just before the close of the year was even higher than the announced figure since between October and December the Bank had taken emergency action to contract currency and, through the recall of agricultural loans and the absorption of rural deposits, it had already managed to force a return flow to the Bank in the amount of 1.17 billion yuan.[45]

The contraction policy was continued in 1957 so that, by the end of that year, total currency in circulation was less than it was at the end of 1956 by 0.45 billion yuan.[46] However, part of the decrease was illusory, caused by a postponement to early 1958 of the distribution of net income by the collectives to their members. Since before the distribution these funds were often held in the form of bank deposits, whereas when distributions took place cash would be required, currency at the end of 1957 became smaller because of the postponement.[47]

Column (3) of Table VII-7 gives some rough estimates for mid-year, when the currency flow is at a seasonal low. These figures are approximated indirectly on the basis of column (2), and are therefore subject

[41] Ho Wei, "The Real Nature of the Rightist Opposition to the Policy of State Monopoly in Purchases and Sales," *HH*, no. 14, 1957, pp. 14–16.

[42] Tseng Ling, "Is There Inflation . . . ," *CCYC*, no. 5, 1957.

[43] *Supra,* Tables VII-3 and VII-6.

[44] Li Hsien-nien, 1957 Budget Report, *FKHP*, VI, 114.

[45] Ch'en Hsi-yü, "Report to the Conference of Branch Bank Managers . . . ," *CKCJ*, no. 6, 1957, pp. 1–2. The unusually large increase in currency was partially a consequence of the spread in hoarding.

[46] Li Hsien-nien, 1958 Budget Report, *FKHP*, VII, 120.

[47] "Excerpts of Discussions . . . ," *CKCJ*, no. 2, 1958, pp. 1–6. It was estimated that, as a result of the postponement of distribution, over one billion yuan of the rural deposits would be withdrawn early in 1958. Ts'ao, "Concluding Report Delivered at the Conference of Branch Bank Managers." *CKCJ*, no. 1, 1958, p. 5.

to a larger margin of error than those in column (2). The mid-year estimates for 1950–1952 are computed from a published index.[48] Those for 1955–1957 are based on the following data. (a) Between the end of 1956 and the end of June, 1957, over 1.1 billion yuan was withdrawn from circulation.[49] (b) The amount of currency withdrawn in the first half of 1957 was more than five times higher than the amount withdrawn in the first half of 1956.[50] (c) Currency withdrawal in the rural sector (where seasonal changes in currency originate) during the first half of 1956 was about 13 percent of that in the corresponding period of the previous year.[51] Finally, the mid-1958 figure was the banker's own estimate given in late 1957.[52] As it turned out, the Great Leap began in 1958, and the actual volume of currency was, in all likelihood, higher than was expected.

EVALUATION

Although the preceding estimation began as an attempt to determine the minimum quantity of currency in circulation, a careful study of the results leads to the conclusion that this series is a reasonable approxima-

---

[48] The index shows the amount of currency in circulation in the second quarter of each year, with the fourth quarter of the previous year as base. The index is as follows:

4th quarter of	*2nd quarter of*
1949 = 100	1950 = 233.7
1950 = 100	1951 = 161.0
1951 = 100	1952 = 93.3

Tseng and Han, *The Circulation of Money . . .,* (*JPRS* #3317), p. 67. The second quarter index is applied to the end of year figure (column (2) of Table VII-7) to derive the mid-year estimates in column (3).

[49] Tseng Ling, "Is There Inflation . . .," *CCYC,* no. 5, 1957, p. 42.

[50] "Conditions in the Past Half Year, Requirements . . .," *CKCJ,* no. 14, 1958, pp. 1–2.

[51] Tseng Ling, "The Effect of Agricultural Collectivization . . .," *CCYC,* no. 6, 1956, p. 41. In a later article by the same author, this percentage was given as 20; Tseng Ling, "Is There Inflation . . .," *CCYC,* no. 5, 1957, p. 14. Since the earlier article was an objective analysis of money, while the later one was a rebuke against the rightist elements, 13 percent is perhaps a more reliable figure. In any case, currency withdrawal in the first half of 1955 was comparable in magnitude to that in the first half of 1957, and the latter was quite large because of the 1956 inflation. The large 1955 withdrawal is consistent with our discussions on the functions of currency conversion that took place early in 1955 (*Supra,* section on The Currency Conversion), and with data presented in Table VII-3.

[52] "Excerpts of Discussions . . .," *CKCJ,* no. 2, 1958, p. 1. It was estimated that the volume of currency in mid-1958 would be close to the mid-1957 level.

tion of the true values. This conclusion is based on several indications, all of which tend to substantiate the validity of the lower series.

SUPPORTING DATUM

There is one piece of information that, while not utilized in the above process of approximation, offers support to the consistency of these estimates.[53] The value of currency in circulation at the end of 1949 was one-twelfth of that in June, 1957.[54] This relationship holds true between the estimated figures for these two dates in columns (2) and (3) of Table VII-7.

THE VELOCITY OF CIRCULATION

Unlike Li's series, the new series is estimated directly, without the use of the income velocity of currency circulation. The behavior of this velocity, when computed from the new estimates, could therefore be used an an independent test to see whether or not the series contradicts the actual monetary conditions in the Mainland at the time. In Table VII-8, the new estimates of the quantity of currency for 1955 and 1956 are divided into Li's data on total consumers' money income for the corresponding years in order to measure the change in the income velocity between the two years via Li's method. It can be seen that, as expected from previous discussions, the velocity declined between the end of 1955 and the end of 1956. The behavior of the income velocity derived from the new estimated figures, then, is consistent with the shift of currency distribution and the development of rural hoarding that took place in 1956.

Table VII-8 further illustrates the arithmetic relationship between the falling overall income velocity (from 6.2 in 1955 to 5.4 in 1956) and the much lower marginal velocity for 1956 computed from increments (3.0). The latter, lower magnitude is the one used by Li as an approximation of the former, thereby resulting in a large bias in his estimation of the volume of currency.[55]

---

[53] This information was taken into consideration by Li in deriving his estimates; therefore it could not be used as a separate supporting evidence in his case.

[54] Ho Wei, "The Real Nature of the Rightist Opposition . . .," *HH,* no. 14, 1957.

[55] Li was aware that the income velocity he used tended to be low. Choh-ming Li, *Economic Development of Communist China,* p. 159, footnote 46.

Table VII-8
The Income Velocity of Currency Circulation in 1955 and 1956

	Aggregate consumers' money income (1)	Quantity of currency (our estimate) (2)	Income velocity (3)
End of 1955	￥33,260 million	￥5,400 million	6.2
End of 1956	38,320 million	7,100 million	5.4
Increments, 1955–1956	5,060 million	1,700 million	3.0

Sources:
    Col. (1): Choh-ming Li, *Economic Development of Communist China,* (Berkeley: University of California Press, 1959; reprinted by permission of The Regents of the University of California), p. 159
    Col. (2): Table VII-7, Col. (2).
    Col. (3): Col. 1 ÷ Col. (2).

THE SIZE OF THE ESTIMATES

The validity of the new series may also be tested by examining the general level of the estimates. Since the series represents an estimation of the minimum quantity, there is little likelihood of overestimation. But could it be so underestimated as to be inconsistent with the requirements of currency in the country? To a degree, the reasonable size of the income velocity already tends to reject such a hypothesis. On top of that, the magnitude of the estimates might be checked against historical developments for consistency as was done by Li. The estimates might also be examined on a per capita basis.

Historical comparison. With respect to historical background, it is known that the volume of currency at the end of June, 1937, was 1.4 billion yuan, as compared with our estimate of 5.2 billion in June, 1956. During this interval, the general price level increased about three times, absorbing most of the estimated increase in the supply of currency. In addition, there were other developments that tended to raise the demand for currency; these included such changes as the extension of the use of money into the rural economy through compulsory agricultural purchases, the increased economic activity under the First Five Year Plan, and population growth.[56] But balancing these factors were others that tended to reduce and to minimize the use of currency. There were,

[56] Choh-ming Li, *Economic Development of Communist China,* p. 161.

for example, the restriction of the use of currency under the cash control program, the continued expansion of the socialized sphere and the concomitant contraction of the currency sector, and the various measures that mitigated currency in the private sphere, including the savings drive. When all of these offsetting changes are taken into account, the level of currency in circulation during 1956 does not appear so low as to be incompatible with the historical currency requirement in 1937.

Per capita currency requirment. On a per capita basis, the available evidence also supports the estimated level of currency. In 1956, about 80 percent of the currency in circulation was held by individuals.[57] Thus, on the basis of our estimated quantity of currency, the cash balance in the hands of households would total approximately 4.2 billion yuan in June, 1956. This is equivalent to an estimated cash holding of 6.70 yuan per capita[58] or 32 yuan per household.[59] These averages are consistent with certain urban and rural data for the same year. (1) According to a family budget study, the average urban industrial worker's household had a cash holding of 12.24 yuan at the end of June, 1956.[60] (2) In 1956, currency held in the hands of individual workers in Shanghai amounted to 1.95 percent of their money income, while 91.08 percent of the latter represented wage income.[61] In the same year, the average money wage for industrial workers in the socialized sector as a whole

[57] The other 20 percent was held by various public and private organizations, including agricultural cooperatives, credit cooperatives, and other government and private organs. "Work Hard to Accomplish the Task of Currency Withdrawal during This First Half Year," *CKCJ,* no. 8, 1957, pp. 1–2.

[58] The Mainland population in June, 1956, was assumed to be 621 million. This is an average of the figures for the end of 1955 (615 million) and the end of 1956 (628 million). "Data on China's Population, 1949–1956," *TCKT,* no. 11, 1957, p. 24.

[59] Based on an average of 4.8 persons per household. This was the average given for rural households. The size differed in different areas, varying from 4.2 to 6.2. "Data from a Survey of Rural Family Income and Expenditures in 1954," *TCKT,* no. 10, 1957, pp. 31–32. That the urban family had about the same average size can be seen from a 1956 budget study of workers in Shanghai. This study was based on 534 households containing 2,539 persons, which gives an average of 4.75 per household. "The Change of Workers' Standard of Living in Shanghai during the Past 27 Years," *TCKT,* no. 13, 1957, pp. 6–7.

[60] The study was conducted by the SSB, based on a sample of 6,000 families located in 27 large and medium cities. "Positively Participate in Social Savings," *JMJP* Editorial, March 4, 1957, reprinted in *HHPYK,* no. 7, 1957, pp. 86–87. The average cash holding rose to ¥23.07 per household in the end of September, 1956, probably as a result of the general wage increase.

[61] "The Change in Workers' Standard of Living . . .," *TCKT,* no. 13, 1957.

was 610 yuan.[62] If the Shanghai workers were representative of socialized industrial workers, then the combination of these three figures would give an average cash holding per industrial worker's family of about 13 yuan.[63] (3) Statistical data on the currency holding in the rural areas are more difficult to determine. In certain areas growing special cash crops, such as cotton and apples, the peasants' cash holding was said to be very high.[64] However, two model surveys of foodgrains districts, which are more representative of rural areas in general, gave the following data. First, in an area in Hopei province, idle cash was mainly held by 21 percent of the families that had an average of 50 yuan per household.[65] Second, in a village of Liaoling province, the per capita cash holding was 12 yuan at the end of 1955, with the following distribution.[66]

Income class	% of total households	% of total currency held	Average currency held per household
Rich	7	44	¥350
Middle	73	50	40
Poor	20	5	not stated

When it is borne in mind that the rural income period is longer and therefore the cash balance larger than the urban one and that rural cash balance tends to be seasonally high in December and low in June, the above data on per capita currency holding are not incompatible with our per capita estimates for June, 1956.[67]

[62] This refers to the average wage of workers and employees in socialized industry, communications, and basic constructions. It excludes employees of cooperative organizations. "Statistical Data on the Improvement of Living Conditions of Workers and Employees," *TCKT,* no. 14, 1957, pp. 13–14.

[63] Assuming one industrial worker per family.

[64] For example, the highest figures were given for a certain special crop area in Liaoling province, where in the end of January, 1956, the upper income households had an average cash balance of ¥1,026. But even in this area the low-income households, which accounted for 62 percent of total households, had a cash average of only ¥23 per household. Tseng Ling, "The Effect of Agricultural Collectivization . . .," *CCYC,* no. 6, 1956, p. 47.

[65] *Ibid.,* pp. 46–47. No date is given for this survey.

[66] *Ibid.,* p. 47.

[67] Another family budget study of workers in Peking shows that the average family had 4.28 persons, with a per capita monthly income of ¥21 and a per capita monthly purchasing power of ¥16. "A Review of Market Price in the First Quarter of 1957," *TCKT,*

THE PATTERN AND AMPLITUDES OF FLUCTUATIONS

A fourth indication that testifies favorably to our estimation of the quantity of currency lies in the pattern of fluctuations in this series. To facilitate comparisons of changes in the quantity of currency, the two series of currency estimates are expressed in index form with 1952 as the base year.[68] These are presented in Table VII-9 and in Chart 2. It can be seen from the chart that whereas Li's series shows a comparatively smooth increase from 1952 to the end of 1956, our series indicates a less even but steeper trend. In our series there are abrupt changes for 1953 and 1956, and the peak index in 1956 is almost twice as high as that of the base year. Thus the pattern of fluctuations that is reflected in our series indicates a stronger degree of currency inflation over the five-year period of 1953–1957, with particularly severe peaks occurring in 1953 and 1956. That there were extraordinarily large increases in the quantity of currency during these two years appears to have been confirmed by the Chinese economic literature. In the literature, 1953 has been repeatedly mentioned as a year subject to monetary "tension"; there

Table VII-9
Indexes of the Estimated Quantity of Currency, 1952–1957
(1952 = 100)

End of year (1)	Li's estimates (2)	Our estimates (3)
1952	100	100
1953	131	139
1954	—	Below 139
1955	150	150
1956	173	197
1957	158 (June)	186

Source: Table VII-7.

no. 11, 1957, pp. 26–27. These figures, too, are not out of line with our estimated quantity of currency.

[68] The period 1949–1952 was transitional. After the stabilization of prices in 1950, economic activity was restored and the use of money in rural areas was extended, both leading to large increases in the transactional demand for money. By the end of 1952, however, conditions were considered stabilized and normal; therefore, 1952 was used as the base year.

Chart 2
Two Indexes of Estimated Quantity of Currency, 1952–1957

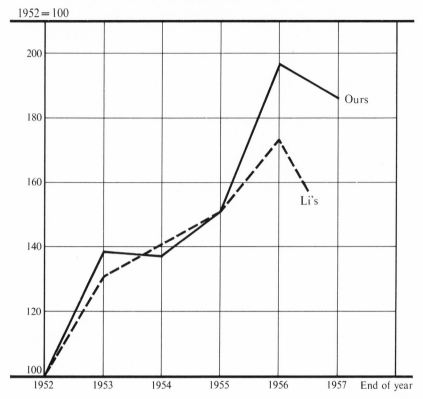

Source: Table VII-9

were also open expressions of concern over the increase in currency supply and the threat of inflation during 1956. Thus the course of growth and the fluctuations in currency depicted by our estimates seem to be more realistic. A corollary to this proposition is that the actual volume of currency in circulation in China was probably closer to our estimates than to Li's estimates.

THE RELATIONSHIP OF LOANS, DEPOSITS AND CURRENCY

Finally, our series of currency data fits in better than Li's with the total deposit and total loan estimates presented in the last two chapters. Ac-

200

cording to these estimates, loans outstanding at the end of 1957 totalled 28.7 billion yuan, while deposits amounted to 20.9 billion. The difference between these two sums primarily constituted currency in circulation, and our estimate for currency at the end of 1957 is 6.7 billion yuan. Considering the fact that the Bank had other items of liability, such as capital, in addition to currency and deposits, and that the three sets of approximations were based on sparse and fragmentary information, the results of these approximations appear to be remarkably consistent with one another.

For all these reasons, then, it could be concluded that our series of currency estimates is likely to have a smaller margin of error than Li's. However, it should be emphasized again that the errors involved in both series are one-sided. That is to say, while Li's series represents an over-estimation, our series, which aims at the minimum, has a margin of error in the opposite direction.

Concluding Remarks

Even though the bulk of the currency came into existence as a consequence of bank credit granted to state enterprises that was used to make wage and agricultural payments (especially the latter), the People's Bank was evidently more concerned with restricting the quantity of currency in circulation than it was with limiting the volume of credit outstanding. This situation is a reflection of two conflicting forces. First, the Bank was unable to control credit quantitatively for fear that such restraints might interfere with the productive activities of the enterprises. Second, currency directly affected consumer prices, especially those not subject to price control, and the Bank was anxious to avoid overt inflation. As a result of this conflict, the Bank could not prevent inflation by regulating the increase in currency issue. Hence it had to influence the cash flow in a negative way, that is, through devices leading to the removal of currency already in circulation.

Various methods had been employed during the period under study that tended to contract the volume of circulating currency. However, while most of these measures had permanent effects in narrowing the currency flow, they could not be used repeatedly as a regular instrument of currency absorption. They were, therefore, temporary stopgaps from the viewpoint of currency absorption. The one measure that could be employed at the Bank's discretion was the savings drive. Hence this could be considered the sole regular instrument for the management of currency.

VIII

MONETARY POLICY

❂ THE FOREGOING SURVEY of institutional and quantitative development provides sufficient background information to reveal the interrelationship of various forces affecting the money supply. It is now possible to distill out of it certain generalizations relating to the monetary policy of Communist China.

One conclusion emerging from the inquiry relates to the role of the People's Bank. During the period covered, the Bank had in general established direct contact with individual productive units, especially those in the state sector, and had therefore laid the foundation for exercising microfinancial control. However, actual financial supervision was at best very limited. For the effectiveness of such supervision hinged on a relatively accurate degree of planning, and this prerequisite had not been fulfilled; attempted enforcements of Bank control merely led to resistance and complaints from enterprises as well as from organizers of the collectives. Thus the primary responsibility of the Bank, and therefore its major contribution to the economy, was macromonetary in character. In other words, the traditional banking function of serving as an intermediary between savings and investment while maintaining a sufficient degree of overall monetary equilibrium remained the more significant role of the People's Bank.

Given this conclusion, the question arises as to how this traditional role was achieved. That is to say, how was the nation's aggregate money supply coordinated to meet the corresponding demand? What did the Bank do to avoid inflation or deflation, overt or concealed? The ideal solution to this problem in a command economy would be, again, complete planning, under which the monetary equivalent to every physical transaction would be planned and balanced in advance. However, our review of the Chinese conditions indicates that this has not been attainable in China. Thus, specific measures must have been unavoidable,

203

and a search for an answer to the above question becomes an inquiry into the nation's monetary policy in a broad sense.

To pursue this topic, we begin with a review of the aggregate money supply, then look at the nature and objective of the nation's monetary policy, and finally discuss the methods by which the policy is carried out.

The Aggregate Money Supply

As stated in the introductory chapter, "money" is used here in a relatively loose sense to include various types of bank deposits as well as currency. Our findings above indicate that Chinese bank credit was granted leniently to the state sector and that the total loan balance tended to cumulate over the years. These loans generated a large volume of deposits, which circulated in the state sector with three possible destinations. They could be (1) retained in the state sector as enterprise deposits, (2) submitted to the government and changed into budgetary deposits, or (3) paid out to the private sector and transformed into currency. The last type could in part become personal deposits. Thus there were four main forms of monetary assets in the economy—budgetary, enterprise, and personal deposits, and currency.

These assets shared, to varying extents, one common characteristic: they could be used as means of payment under specified circumstances. However, none of them was highly liquid in the Western sense. Even the use of currency, the most liquid of the four, was subject to certain limitations since it was not eligible for inter-enterprise transactions. Thus if by money supply is meant only those assets that could be exchanged for any available goods or services at any moment anywhere within the nation, then money did not exist in China; in that case it would be senseless to speak of her monetary policy.

In order to examine the Chinese system, therefore, it is necessary to broaden our definition of money to include various assets that, despite limited liquidity, were nevertheless generally acceptable means of payment within prescribed boundaries and were thus capable of exerting inflationary pressures in the economy in different sectors. Among them, currency had the highest degree of "moneyness" since it could be spent instantly within its sphere of circulation. Personal deposits and enterprise deposits had a lesser degree of "moneyness" and could perhaps be considered near-money.[1] Budgetary deposits were the least liquid; for lack of a better description, they might be termed potential money.[2] Finally, the portion of budgetary deposits earmarked as credit fund had no liquidity at all; it was demonetized. As in the case of the U.S., what should be included as components of the nation's money supply is a matter of convenience, depending on the question being discussed or the use to which the statistics are being put.[3] In a strict and narrow definition of the term, only currency should be included. This was the definition adopted by the Chinese authorities because it was the most crucial one from the viewpoint of maintaining monetary equilibrium in the consumers' market. On the other hand, the total sum of means of payment available to the private sector (including agricultural co-operatives) would include currency plus personal deposits; while the broadest definition of the Chinese money supply would include all four categories (excluding credit fund) and would roughly indicate the total sum of means of payment created by the Bank. Since various definitions are possible, and since we are interested in the overall monetary operation, it seems appropriate to use the term in its broadest sense here and call it aggregate money supply. Table VIII-1 recapitulates the monetary data and presents this broadest concept of money supply.

The Nature and Objective of Monetary Policy

Before embarking on a discussion of the methods by which the money supply and demand were kept in approximate balance, it is necessary

[1] These two types of deposits are grouped together for the following reasons: Although theoretically personal deposits could be freely withdrawn, in fact the depositors were subject to various pressures to increase the deposit balances; besides, personal deposits consisted of some time deposits. Enterprise deposits, on the other hand, were nominally subject to bank supervision and thus less liquid than personal deposits, but such supervision was not very effective. Thus in practice the two types of deposits probably had similar degrees of liquidity.

[2] Even budgetary deposits could be withdrawn rather unexpectedly, as in 1956.

[3] For the intricacy of the definition of the U.S. money supply, see, for example, Kaufman, "More on An Empirical Definition of Money," *American Economic Review,* LIX, no. 1 (March, 1969) 78–87.

Table VIII-1
The Aggregate Money Supply, 1950–1957
(in billion yuan)

End of year	Budgetary deposits* (1)	Enterprise and other deposits (2)	Personal deposits† (3)	Currency (4)	Aggregate money supply* (5)
1950	1.00	1.27	0.13	1.2	3.6
1951	3.02	1.90	0.54	2.2	7.7
1952	4.87	3.12	0.86	3.6	12.5
1953	5.98	3.06	1.32	5.0	15.4
1954	9.72	3.32	1.87	Below 5.0	19.9
1955	10.07	4.45	2.28	5.4	22.2
1956	8.42	8.85	3.04	7.1	27.4
1957	8.58	3.79	4.58	6.7	23.7

*Budgetary deposits and money supply are both exclusive of the cumulative credit fund, which amounted to 2.42 billion yuan in 1955 and 1956, and 3.97 billion in 1957 (Table VI-7)..
†Personal deposits represent the sum of urban and rural deposits, including those of agricultural cooperatives.
Sources:
  Cols. (1) to (3): Table VI-15.
  Col. (4): Table VII-7, col. (2).
  Col. (5): The sum of col. (1) through (4).

and customary to ascertain more precisely the objective of the Chinese monetary policy. That is, to ask what price level did the People's Bank attempt to nurture or sustain? Of the three possible price conditions, rising, falling, and stationary, the last one was obviously chosen by China as an appropriate goal. The reasons for the choice were simple. With the high rate of investment envisioned by the First Five Year Plan, it was clearly not feasible to have a generally falling price level even though, because of the Marxian commitment, the long-run aspiration of the economy was to lower prices so as to raise the population's standard of living. On the other hand, the traditional fear of inflation and the desirability of preventing erosion of the many controlled prices made it necessary for the authorities to avoid rising prices. Thus broadly speaking the objective of the nation's monetary policy in this period was to maintain a stable price level.

Two crucial monetary phenomena, discussed elsewhere in this study, marked the character of the Chinese monetary policy. The first was that the Bank in reality possessed an unlimited capacity to generate credit as long as loans were used to finance payments within the state sector. Thus credit expansion in this sector was possible and convenient. The capacity was dampened, however, by payments made to the private sector. Here currency was used that was subject to a quota. The second phenomenon was that, although credit was confined to the financing of certain types of working capital investment, credit policy toward state enterprises was by and large passive in the sense that the Bank had little quantitative control over loans.[4] Neither could it effectively limit the amount of currency that flowed into circulation as a result of such credit, since loans granted to enterprises could be spent by the latter in cash for certain purposes.[5] The restrictions on both credit and currency were therefore mainly qualitative, defining the uses to which they might be put.

Given these conditions, it may be deduced that the People's Bank could not in fact regulate the money supply through a deliberate loan policy. That is to say, it could not determine the flow of money that entered into circulation. The only alternative open to the Bank, then, was defensive. It could vary the size of the return flow to the Bank, or, to state it differently, it could absorb money already in circulation. Thus the Communist Chinese approach to the money supply was distinct from the Western, positive approach. In this sense, the term monetary policy used here has a broader connotation than that used in the West.

Instruments of Monetary Stabilization

Monetary policy in Communist China was rather one-sided; it primarily aimed at contracting the money supply. With centralized and concerted efforts toward rapid industrialization, there was little danger of prolonged deflation. Rather, the fear was essentially that of inflation caused by a desire to increase investment in the face of low savings potential.

In the Chinese economic framework and under a broad definition of aggregate money supply, there were two ways to carry out a contrac-

---

[4] *Supra,* Chapter V, pp. 86–87, 135.
[5] *Supra,* Chapter IV, p. 72.

tionary policy: quantitative and qualitative. Thus there were two aspects to the Chinese monetary policy. One aimed at decreasing the aggregate quantity of money, while the other attempted to reduce the overall liquidity of the money mix. The latter could be achieved by substituting a less liquid form of money for a more liquid one so that the degree of moneyness became lower even though the aggregate quantity remained unchanged. These two aspects of monetary policy were often intertwined, and the duality derived quite logically from the nation's monetary mechanism and the sectorized economy. All the instruments of monetary policy employed in China affected the aggregate money supply in either one or both ways.

The instruments themselves were developed pragmatically and gradually over the years. In the early period, attempts were sporadic and piecemeal rather than integrated. By 1955, however, a more regular and coordinated pattern appeared. Detailed measures affecting money have already been presented. Here the intention is to take a total view of these measures, observe how they form an overall monetary regulating mechanism, and, insofar as possible, analyze and evaluate these measures. Broadly, several instruments were relied upon in order to control the aggregate money supply. First, there was the real bill principle, the purpose of which was to set an elastic limit to the amount of bank loans created. The second instrument amounted to a budgetary offsetting policy that tried to neutralize a part of the bank deposits already in existence by earmarking it for the credit fund. Finally, there was the minimization of currency that attempted to contract the most liquid form of money. These instruments will be further examined.

THE INVENTORY CRITERION AND THE PRODUCTIVE CREDIT PRINCIPLE

While Bank loans to state enterprises were quite unlimited in the earlier years, during the credit reform of 1955 the People's Bank began to institute a criterion based on inventory. As a result, the Bank in effect accepted the productive credit or real bill principle as a cornerstone for its credit policy. This principle did not impose a numerical control over the total amount of loans granted. But the Chinese, following the

Soviet Union, believed that it would enable the money flow to conform to the commodity flow, thereby avoiding monetary disequilibrium. That the productive credit policy does not necessarily guarantee stability in a market economy has been established;[6] that the same policy had made possible the prewar Soviet inflation has been accepted by Western students.[7] Nonetheless, its adoption in China in 1955 represented a step forward from the previous credit system in which loans were granted to enterprises upon request. How this lending criterion has in fact served the country is difficult to assess, for the situation was soon complicated by many important economic changes.[8]

TWO RELEVANT FACTORS

A logical analysis of the possible monetary effects of the productive credit principle in China brings into focus certain institutional factors that deserve consideration. Two of these factors are notable; one springs from the underdeveloped nature of the economy and the other from the planned system.

The state agricultural purchases. The underdeveloped nature of China was emphasized implicitly by Communist authorities in their discussion of bank loans. These authorities repeatedly stated that loans granted to the state commercial network for the purchase of agricultural and subsidiary products were noninflationary and that therefore the Bank should extend complete and unquestioned credit support to such transactions.[9] This argument amounted to a full endorsement of the productive credit principle in the area of agricultural purchases, an area that was significant by virtue of its size as well as its direct command over the volume of currency in the consumer's market. The explanation given for this position was rather simple. A lion's share

[6] Robertson, "Theories of Banking Policy," *Economica,* VIII (June, 1928), 131–46; *idem, Money,* pp. 82–89 and Appendix B.

[7] Powell, *Soviet Monetary Policy;* Holzman, "Soviet Inflationary Pressure, 1928–1957: Causes and Cures," *The Quarterly Journal of Economics,* LXXIV, no. 2 (May, 1960), 167–88.

[8] Chronologically, the 1955 credit reform was followed by a period of inflation in 1956. However, there were several causes of this inflation. These will be analyzed in the next chapter.

[9] Tseng Ling, "Is There Inflation in China at the Present?" *CCYC,* no. 5, 1957, p. 46; Ko, "On the Inter-Connection . . .," *CCYC,* no. 1, 1958, p. 15.

of consumer's goods in China consisted of rural products in either their original form (such as foodstuffs) or manufactured form (such as cotton yarns).[10] Even in the latter form the production process was by and large direct and uncomplicated, often relying on cottage industries or small factories. Thus whatever agricultural or subsidiary products the commercial network might acquire with bank loans could, within a short period of time, be resold in the urban or rural retail market for cash. Moreover, official retail prices for consumer's goods were much higher than the controlled prices for agricultural purchases; such a pricing policy allowed a wide margin of profit to the commercial enterprises and in turn formed an important source of budgetary receipts. In sum, profits of commercial enterprises and budgetary receipts would vary directly with the amount of agricultural purchases.[11] From this viewpoint, then, financing agricultural purchases actually tended to have a deflationary effect in the currency sector instead of the opposite effect, since it enabled the state sector to absorb more currency through retail sales than it paid out through agricultural purchases.[12]

Although this official monetary analysis in defense of the inventory criterion and the real bill principle was incomplete because it focused on the currency flow alone, it did point out a basic characteristic of the Chinese economy. Unlike an industrial nation with complex production processes, China remained essentially agricultural, with consumer's goods consisting of simple basic necessities, and the period of production of goods was generally very short. The production period in turn had implications concerning the conditions required to main-

---

[10] The agricultural and subsidiary products, some slightly processed, accounted for three quarters of the commodity supply in the domestic market. Wang T'uan, "Fiscal and Monetary Works and the Policy of Emphasizing Agriculture," *JMST,* 1962, pp. 197–98.

[11] Thus the state monopoly of trade in agricultural products was a way to mobilize resources for investment via the budget.

[12] Whether the total receipts from retail sales are higher than the total cost of agricultural purchases depends, of course, on how large a share of agricultural purchases was exported and hence unavailable for domestic sales. But given the prices and the amount of exported agricultural goods, the larger the agricultural purchase, the higher would be the amount available for retail sales and therefore the commercial profits. Thus the Bank should encourage agricultural purchases with full credit support.

tain monetary equilibrium in the economy. Other things being equal, the shorter period of production in China should permit a lower savings ratio,[13] which is compatible with monetary equilibrium in the face of a given investment.[14] In other words, a given savings ratio would, without causing inflationary pressures, support a larger amount of working capital investment financed by the Bank in China than in other, more industrialized countries. The productive credit principle was therefore less likely to be inflationary in China.

The noninflationary or even deflationary effects claimed by Chinese authorities for the productive credit principle when applied to agricultural purchases could be interpreted in yet another way. One reason why this principle might not provide monetary equilibrium is because the final output created by the bank-financed working capital may not equal, without price change, the increased demand for final goods caused by the accompanying growth in money supply.[15] The size of this growth in aggregate demand for final goods following the Banks' financing of working capital depends on the velocity of circulation of money, whereas the increase in aggregate supply of final output from the same investment depends on the gross productivity of the working capital. Should the former ratio be larger than the latter, then the rise in aggregate demand would become larger than the increase in final goods, and the adoption of the productive credit principle might be inflationary. By the same reasoning, were the sizes of the two ratios

[13] By savings ratio is meant the proportion of real national income that the public wishes to save in the form of bank deposits.

[14] This can be seen through the Robertsonian equation of monetary equilibrium, $aK = \frac{1}{2}bD$ in which K represents the proportion of annual real national income which the public wishes to keep command in the form of bank deposits, a is the proportion of bank deposits that the banks lend out, crystallized in the form of working capital, b is the proportion of working capital that has been built up through bank financing, and D is the proportion of a year that is covered by a period of production. Robertson, "Theories of Banking Policy," *Economica*, VIII, no. 23 (June, 1928), p. 136. Under productive credit principle b equals one. D is smaller when the period of production of goods is short. When D is small, as in China, it allows K to be lower, and the latter approximates the savings ratio. Thus, given the investment in working capital a, the shorter period of production on one side of the equation allows a smaller savings ratio on the other side.

[15] Tsiang, "Money and Banking in Communist China," *An Economic Profile of Mainland China*, Studies prepared for the Joint Economic Committee, U.S. Congress, I, 334–35.

reversed, the principle could be deflationary. In the case of China, the productivity of the working capital financed by the Bank was arbitrarily kept high because of the controlled difference between prices for agricultural purchases and those for final goods. On the other hand, the velocity of circulation of money could not be freely and significantly increased because the trading of a predominant share of the nation's products was controlled by the state. Thus the Chinese gross productivity of the bank-financed working capital was likely to be higher than the velocity of money; to this extent, the productive credit principle would have a deflationary effect.

Inventory accumulations. While the backward nature of the economy and the simplicity of its consumption pattern permitted the real bill principle to operate with noninflationary or even deflationary effects, a second feature of the system tended to work toward the opposite result. In China there was a persistent tendency for the nation's inventory to grow rapidly. The causes for this accumulation were varied, some of them intentional, the rest unintended. As a deliberate policy, inventory held by the commercial sector was built up as a contingency commodity reserve or as a stabilizer of economic fluctuations caused by good or bad harvests.[16] The inventory might also have risen in response to the expanding requirements of a growing economy. However, a portion of the large inventory represented involuntary accumulations of producer's or consumer's goods.[17] These accumulations were the consequence of mistakes, delays, changes in plans, or deficiencies committed by producing and distributing units as they strove to overfulfill in quantity at the expense of quality. To the extent that this growing

---

[16] The necessity for such a reserve was emphasized in many articles. For example, Ko, "On the Inter-Connection . . . ," *CCYC*, no. 1, 1958, p. 16. In the draft budgets for 1955 and 1956, an appropriation for the state commodity reserve was mentioned as an item under the category of "expenditures for other economic constructions." However, there was no specific reference to this item in the final budgets. There seems to be no clear-cut separation between the state commodity reserve and commercial inventory, nor is there information on how large a part of the reserve was financed by the budget and how much by the bank.

[17] In a speech, the premier objected to the practice of treating the accumulated unmarketable inventory as a part of commodity reserve. Chou En-lai, "Report on the Proposal for the Second Five Year Plan for Development of the National Economy," *Literature of the Eighth National Congress of the Communist Party of China,* pp. 120–21.

inventory, which was financed by bank loans under the productive credit principle, curtailed the flow of goods available to producers or consumers, the result of the principle would be inflationary.

AN EVALUATION

Thus the impact of the real bill principle in China was conditioned by her overall economic structure. Since the effects were diverse and compensating, it is difficult to determine a priori what the overall influence has been. However, it would be correct to say that in general the principle tended to exert a contractive influence on the currency sector while permitting expansion in the deposit sector. The first half of this proposition involves agricultural purchases and has been stressed by those Chinese authorities who were inclined to identify money with currency. The second half appears to receive support from the association of the growth in state commercial loans with that of inventory during the years studied.[18]

Broadly, then, it might be concluded that while the real bill principle might not have been effective in contracting the aggregate money supply quantitatively, it did tend to contract qualitatively by lowering the overall degree of liquidity.

Besides, the principle provided a flexible limit to bank loans and to the creation of new money. Such a limit was perhaps more appropriate for China than a rigid one for two reasons. First, since China was a predominantly agricultural economy, the size of her national products was strongly influenced by the harvest, and the real bill principle stood ready to finance acquisitions of variable quantities of products, thus allowing her to be more fully mobilized toward investment. Second, in the industrial sector where the production process was more complex and indirect, deviations from plans, and therefore bottlenecks, could develop easily. The financial laxity made possible by the real bill principle would provide the enterprises with funds to overcome such barriers and prevent breakdowns in production.[19]

---

[18] *Supra,* Table V-2 and discussion.
[19] With funds available from the Bank, the enterprises could smooth out the bottlenecks through, for example, substitutions or bidding resources away from other firms.

THE CREDIT FUND AND THE OFFSETTING POLICY

In contrast to the policy of credit creation, which was anchored on an essentially passive criterion, the credit fund was an active and deliberate instrument whereby deposits were removed from circulation. Thus while the Bank created money according to inventory, the fiscal budget periodically neutralized a portion of the money so created. This offsetting policy was developed gradually and was the result of a series of trials and errors.

DEVELOPMENT

In the Chinese monetary framework, much of the credit extended by the Bank would eventually flow into the budget. Perhaps partly because of the ease with which bank loans were provided to the enterprises in the earlier years, unintentional budget surplus, or government savings, was realized in that period despite annual planned deficits.[20] Such unplanned budget surplus cumulated and served as an unintended fiscal offset to the growth in money supply. However, this relationship was not adequately appreciated by the authorities at the time.

In 1953, an especially large amount of the cumulative budget surplus was allocated for current expenditures, leading to a very large planned current deficit for that year. The monetary effect of this rapid reduction in the offsetting fund quickly manifested itself. The inflation was later remedied through various government drives that restored the cumulated budget surplus by the end of the year and even contributed a small current surplus.[21] This episode evoked an awareness on the part of the authorities of the linkage between the budget surplus and Bank credit; the first appropriation from the budget to the Bank was then made. The appropriation did not assume the form of a credit fund; instead it was an allocation taken out of the cumulative budget surplus for 1950–1954 to repay previous government overdrafts. At the same time, the budget data were revised, leaving a smaller total surplus for 1950–1954.[22] The procedure amounted to a simultaneous writing-off

[20] *Supra,* Table VI-4 and Ch. VI note 31.
[21] Kuo, "Views on the State Budgetary Surplus," *CCYC,* no. 8, 1959, p. 60. A fuller discussion of the 1953 inflation follows in the next chapter.
[22] *Supra,* Tables VI-5 and VI-6.

of bank credit and of budget surplus. For better comparison, the different series pertaining to the budget-Bank relationship are presented in Table VIII-2. The surplus figures in column (2) were those after the write-off.

By the end of 1955, a more clear-cut offsetting policy emerged as the first formal grant of credit fund was made to the Bank out of the (revised) cumulative budget surplus. However, even though a large portion of the surplus was so used, it was only a portion and not the whole. The Chinese term credit fund connotes a kind of capital fund that was assigned to the Bank to be loaned. Actually, this function was redundant because the monetary structure already allowed the Bank an unlimited capacity for expanding credit. Hence the credit fund, in effect, merely served to impound some of the budget surplus so that it would

Table VIII-2
A Comparison of Budget Deposits, Budget Surplus,
and Credit Fund, 1950–1959

(in billion yuan)

End of year	Budget deposits (Excl. credit fund) (1)	Budget surplus (Excl. credit fund) (2)	Credit fund, actual (3)	Credit fund, planned (4)
1950	1.00	−0.29	nil	nil
1951	3.02	1.06	nil	nil
1952	4.87	0.77	nil	nil
1953	5.98	0.28	nil	nil
1954	9.72	1.60	nil*	nil
1955	10.07	0.48	2.42	nil
1956	8.42	−1.83	nil	nil
1957	8.58	nil†	1.55	0.60
1958	—	nil†	1.65	0.80
1959	—	nil†	4.43	3.17

* There was a repayment of government overdraft of ¥2.16 billion. This is not included here as credit fund since the repayment was accompanied by a write-off of the budget surplus for 1950–1954.

† The budget surplus of the central government for each of these years was ¥0.95, ¥0.85, and ¥1.26 billion respectively. These were all impounded as credit fund.

Sources:
Col. (1): Table VI-3.
Col. (2): Table VI-6 and Chapter VI, footnotes 39 and 40.
Cols. (3) and (4) Table VI-7.

215

not be spent. In other words, the credit fund absorbed a part of the existing money supply by inactivating it.[23]

The large realized budget deficit of 1956 engulfed the unapportioned share of the cumulative surplus and, in addition, incurred a bank overdraft;[24] therefore no credit fund was assigned that year.[25] However, the inflationary experience of 1956 once again stimulated progress in the monetary policy. Beginning with 1957 two improvements were introduced in the allocation of the credit fund. First, a planned credit fund was allowed for when the annual budget was formulated; second, the entire realized budget surplus was added to the planned amount. The former innovation was tantamount to the deliberate creation of an *ex ante* budget surplus to serve as a monetary offset.[26] The latter meant the entire *ex post* budget surplus automatically became available for use as credit fund. Thus there was a built-in offsetting mechanism.

The offsetting policy, then, went through several stages. Beginning inadvertently and spontaneously, it became a discretionary policy and eventually became institutionalized as an automatic stabilizer. The driving forces behind the changes were the inflationary lessons of 1953 and 1956. Apparently, the historical apprehension of inflation plus experiences in these two years reverberated sufficiently to permit a strengthened position of the Bank and of monetary considerations. Other things being equal, the maturing of the offsetting policy and the impounding of the budget surplus compelled a smaller government expenditure and, indirectly, a lower rate of state investment. In this sense, the development of the offsetting policy could be viewed as the result of a contest between those who were proponents of a faster speed of industrialization at the cost of more severe monetary disequilibria and those who were concerned with maintaining a relative degree of mone-

[23] The fact that data for budget deposits were at times presented as being inclusive of credit fund indicates that the latter was still considered a part of budget deposits, but a part earmarked for a special purpose.

[24] The bank overdraft was 180 million yuan, *Supra,* Ch. VI, note 40.

[25] Logically, the overdraft could be considered a negative credit fund. But it is not clear whether that overdraft was repaid later or, if so, how it was repaid. The amount was relatively small anyway.

[26] In other words, a predetermined amount of budget savings was assigned in order to balance the growth in working capital investment financed by the Bank.

tary stability while developing the nation. Naturally, the People's Bank belonged to the latter camp; hence it exercised a restraining influence on the economy.

SIGNIFICANCE

How significant was the offsetting policy in the maintenance of monetary stability? How important was the credit fund as an instrument of absorption? The answer to these questions can be gauged by the proportion of money neutralized. Owing to the restriction of data, this proportion can be computed for two years only; nevertheless, it provides a quantitative indication of the relative strength of the policy. Table VIII-3 shows the relationship between the credit fund and four different categories of money: the aggregate money supply, aggregate Bank deposits, deposits in the state sector, and budget deposits. Credit fund amounted to a substantial proportion of all categories. Even in its beginning year, credit fund constituted almost one-tenth of the aggregate money supply; and the percentage rose as the category of money became more constricted. Thus nearly one-fifth of the budget deposits was inactivated in the same year. Furthermore, the table indicates that the four proportions were higher in 1957 than in 1955. It may be concluded that the credit fund was of considerable and growing importance as a means of monetary stabilization.[27]

While all the percentages in Table VIII-3 testify to the relative significance of the credit fund, the second pair, which relates credit fund with deposits in the state sector, is perhaps the most meaningful in the present discussion. For, in the framework of the overall monetary policy, the credit fund is primarily an instrument of absorption operating in the deposit flow, particularly that of the state sector. In performing this function, credit fund offset approximately one-seventh of the state sector deposits in 1955 and almost one-fourth of those in 1957.

---

[27] It should be noted that the four categories of money data that served as denominators in computing the percentages are data inclusive of credit fund. If data that are exclusive of credit fund were used, the percentages would be larger. For example, the share of credit fund in total money supply would be 10.9 percent and 16.8 percent respectively for 1955 and 1957.

Table VIII-3
The Proportion of Neutralized Money Supply,*
1955 and 1957
(in percent)

Cumulative credit fund as percent of:	1955	1957
1. Budget deposits	19.4	31.6
2. State sector deposits†	14.3	24.3
3. Aggregate deposits of the People's Bank	12.6	19.0
4. Aggregate money supply	9.8	14.4

*The deposits and money supply data are inclusive of credit fund.

†Deposits for the state sector is the sum total of budget deposits and "enterprise and other deposits."

Source: Computed on the basis of data in Tables VIII-1 and VIII-2. Cumulative credit fund was 2.42 billion yuan in 1955 and 3.97 billion in 1957.

THE MINIMIZATION OF CURRENCY
AND THE SAVINGS DRIVE

Just as credit fund was used to remove existing deposits from circulation, various measures were adopted to contract the currency flow.[28] Some of these measures, such as the extension of non-cash settlement and the seasonal stabilization of rural currency, involved a substitution of the use of deposits for the use of currency, thus leaving the aggregate quantity of money unchanged. Other measures, such as the abolition of the capital supply system, lessened the transactional requirements of currency, and therefore those of money also. But, regardless of their monetary effects, the currency-reducing effect of all three measures mentioned was temporary, since these measures were the result of transitions and could not be used repeatedly.

Another instrument that could be used to contract currency was the savings drive. This method also replaced one form of money with another; therefore, while it was currency reducing, it was not necessarily money reducing. Besides, a partial result of the savings drive was to smooth the short term fluctuations in the demand for currency; here again its impacts were transitory. In part, then, the effects of the savings drive were similar to those of the other measures. However, the

[28] *Supra,* Chapter VII, pp. 175–83.

drive had an additional aspect that was unique: it could be used regularly. To the extent that it succeeded in creating a large and growing amount of time deposits, it acted to make illiquid, at least for a while, some of the money supply. Therefore the savings drive served a dual function: it reduced the amount of currency in circulation and, to a lesser degree, it also temporarily inactivated a fraction of the personal deposits. Both tended to reduce the overall liquidity of the aggregate money supply.

The currency-reducing effect of the drive can be seen directly in the growth of personal deposits. However, this effect is brought to a sharper focus by column (1) of Table VIII-4, in which personal deposits are expressed as a percentage of the sum of personal deposits and currency. The denominator measures, though only roughly, the quantity of money available in the private sector (which includes agricultural cooperatives).[29] Thus in 1950 personal deposits consitituted about 10 percent of the money supply in the private sector. From 1952 on, the proportion

Table VIII-4
A Comparison of Personal Deposits and
Money Supply, 1950–1957

| | Personal deposits as percent of | |
End of year	Money supply of the private sector* (1)	Aggregate money supply (2)
1950	9.8	3.6
1951	19.7	7.0
1952	19.3	6.9
1953	20.9	8.6
1954	27.2	9.4
1955	29.7	10.3
1956	30.0	11.1
1957	40.6	19.3

*Money supply of the private sector is approximated by the sum total of personal deposits and currency. This approximation is subject to two qualifications. (1) It excludes deposits of private enterprises, and (2) it includes currency held in the state sector. Both items were relatively small and their effects cancel each other.

Source: Computed on the basis of data in Table VIII-1.

[29] *Cf.* footnote to Table VIII-4.

grew quite continuously until it reached 30 percent in 1956. In 1957, partly due to the postponement of cash distribution by the agricultural collectives to their members, it jumped to over 40 percent. The significance of the savings drive as a tool to absorb currency can also be seen from a different angle by looking at Chart 3.

Chart 3 compares four series of monetary data: personal deposits, currency, money supply of the private sector (approximated by the sum of personal deposits and currency), and total money supply in the economy. It can be seen that the last two series increased at about the same rate, albeit the trend for money in the private sector was slightly steeper. This means that the quantity of money in the private sector grew just as fast as, if not faster than, that in the state sector. In contrast to this near-parallel growth, the two forms of money inside the private sector grew disparately. Currency climbed at a relatively moderate pace, while personal deposits rose rapidly, indicating a successful retardation of the currency growth by the savings drive.[30]

It is more difficult to evaluate the second function of the savings drive and to measure its impact on the aggregate money supply. These questions hinge upon the size of time deposits for which data are unavailable. However, component shares of personal deposits for urban areas are known.[31] If the proportion of time deposits in urban areas could be taken to represent the proportion for the entire nation, then the total amount of time deposits could be estimated. Since no other information is available and since, in any case, urban deposits were much larger than rural deposits, this procedure may be acceptable. The results are presented in column (3) of Table VIII-5.

The series of estimated time deposits is then compared with the nation's aggregate money supply. Although it accounted for only 2.4 percent of the latter in 1952, the ratio grew steadily and amounted to 9.7 percent in 1957. Thus it may be concluded that, whereas the influence of time deposits on the temporary freezing of money supply

---

[30] As was pointed out earlier, currency grew at about half the rate of budget deposits (*Supra,* Table VIII-1). This was partly due to the increasing dominance of the budget in the economy, but it was also partly due to the rapid rise of personal deposits at the expense of currency.

[31] It may be recalled that personal deposits were also called savings deposits; they included various types of demand deposits as well as time deposits from the population.

Chart 3
**The Growth of Aggregate Money Supply and Selected Components,
1950–1957**

Billion yuan

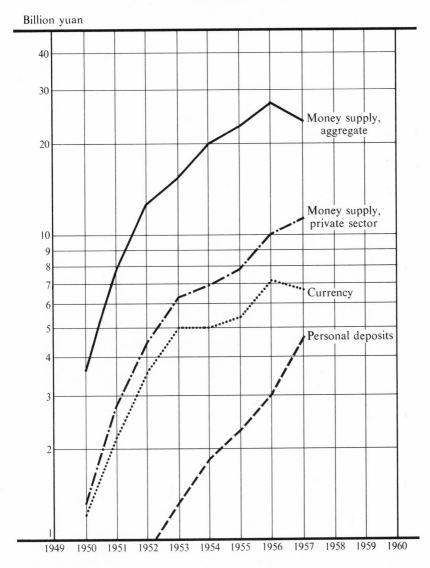

Source: *Table VIII-1*

Table VIII-5
Estimated Time Deposits of the People's Bank,
1952–1957

End of year	Personal deposits (bil. ¥) (1)	Proportion of time deposits (%) (2)	Time deposits (bil. ¥) (3)	Time deposits as proportion of aggregate money supply (%) (4)
1952	0.86	34.5	0.30	2.4
1953	1.32	47.6	0.63	4.1
1954	1.87	61.2	1.14	5.7
1955	2.28	71.6	1.63	7.3
1956	3.04	63.7	1.94	7.1
1957	3.58*	64.2	2.30*	9.7

*Personal deposits for 1957 totalled 4.58 billion yuan. However, rural deposits in 1957 included one billion yuan of deposits from collectives, which would soon be distributed to members. This part is subtracted here in order to derive the amount of time deposits.
Sources:
Col. (1): Table VIII-1, Col. (3).
Col. (2): Table VI-10, Col. (1).
Col. (3): The product of Cols. (1) and (2).
Col. (4): Col. (3) divided by Col. (5) of Table VIII-1.

was less than the demonetizing effect of the credit fund,[32] the former was nevertheless important. Besides, the savings drive had been serving as a monetary stabilizing instrument long before the credit fund was instituted. In fact, ever since 1949 the People's Bank had been occupied with the promotion of personal deposits, and the aggressiveness of the Bank's savings campaigns fluctuated with the degree of inflationary pressures in the economy. The savings drive was a flexible tool, often sternly used, for achieving monetary equilibrium.

Concluding Remarks

Of the three instruments of Communist China's monetary policy—the inventory criteria, the credit fund, and the savings drive—the first

[32] For the two years for which data are available, credit funds amounted to 9.8 percent of total money supply in 1955 and 14.4 percent in 1957. Time deposits, on the other hand, represented 7.3 percent and 9.7 percent of money supply for these two years. Thus the effect of time deposits was about two-thirds the effect of credit fund.

determined the defensive nature of the policy, while the other two were compensatory measures that absorbed money or reduced its liquidity in the two broad sectors, state and private, of the economy. When this kind of monetary policy is compared with its Western counterpart, a basic difference in emphasis stands out boldly.[33] The Western banking system tends to manipulate the quantity of credit available to investors so that total investment can be equated to spontaneous saving by the society, thus avoiding price fluctuations and the resulting forced saving. In contrast to this, the People's Bank would attempt first of all to satisfy the need for certain types of investment, which were qualitatively defined, and then to mobilize sufficient savings to accommodate this investment. Thus even though both types of policy might share the same objective of maintaining monetary equilibrium and price stability, one would achieve it by tailoring investment to the level of voluntary savings, while the other would adjust savings to satisfy the requirement of investment. The Chinese policy was therefore investment oriented. The main type of investment that was provided by the People's Bank was investment in working capital for the distribution of goods. But the nature of the economy plus the state of planning were such that it was not possible to predict accurately the size and/or the composition of the nation's products. Therefore, in order neither to hinder production nor to leave the products in private hands, the Bank satisfied the working capital requirements of commercial enterprises as the need arose. The monetary effects produced by these needs were then compensated for by money savings taken out of the budget and coaxed or coerced from the population.

This fundamental difference in orientation between Communist China and the West is not surprising; it merely mirrors the distinction between the two economic systems, although this distinction has been sharpened by the underdeveloped state of China. The Chinese monetary mechanism and policy for the period under study was thus consonant with her basic economic structure and with the nation's desire to promote rapid economic growth. Furthermore, it can be said that the implementation of her monetary policy was quite rigorous, with considerable contractive effects both in quantitative and in qualitative terms.

---

[33] For simplicity, the condition of full employment is assumed in this discussion.

Monetary Policy

But how successful was the People's Bank in achieving the objective of monetary policy? Was it able to maintain overall equilibrium during the First Five Year Plan? The next chapter explores the monetary performance of the economy and its relationship with monetary policy.

IX

THE MONETARY
PERFORMANCE

AMONG THE MANY important problems confronted by a developing nation, an especially vital one is achieving a high rate of capital formation without generating a disruptive degree of inflationary pressure. In a command economy such as China's, this pressure can manifest itself in various forms. Open inflation involves price movements, but there can be two types of prices. The official prices for items that are controlled can be changed only by the government; this type of open inflation is "decreed." On the other hand, there may be price changes through market adjustments, and this type of inflation is "free." Alternatively, the controlled prices may be frozen by the state, resulting in suppressed inflation, under which a relatively stable price level is accompanied by such familiar symptoms as rationing, waiting lines, and idle cash ready to be spent.

Given their monetary structure and policy, how have the Chinese performed in this respect? What was the consequence of the monetary policy adopted? Were the disequilibrating forces that are commonly associated with accelerated investments kept in check? If not, was the failure a result of defects in the monetary mechanism, defects in planning itself, or unexpected exogenous factors? Or, still further, was inflation itself purposely used as a means of extracting savings? These are all fascinating questions that as yet cannot be fully answered. However, an examination of the degrees and causes of inflation or deflation during the period under study should provide some meaningful clues and tentative conclusions.

225

Monetary Stability and the Segmented Market

Under the Chinese system, there were essentially two distinct markets that were closely linked to the two broad sectors of the economy and the two money flows. Most of the producers' goods and wholesale transactions were handled by units in the state sector in which bank deposits served as the regular means of payment. On the other hand, consumers' goods as well as rural producers' goods were retailed in the non-state sector in which currency was the main form of money used.

The distribution of goods in the state sector was dominated by planned, direct allocation at fixed prices. Consequently, the monetary factor could exert relatively little influence on prices or the supply of goods in this sector; an increased money supply here would either be spilled into the non-state sector or enter the budget as enterprise payments. However, ready availability of bank credit to enterprises in this sector could have indirect or secondary monetary effects. It could make possible such phenomena as inefficient and wasteful management or inferior quality of products and subsequent accumulation of unmarketable inventory of finished goods; it could also support the competitive purchase and stockpiling of extra-plan raw materials by the enterprises. To the extent that all of these could reduce goods available to the retail market, they tended to create a shortage there. Thus any monetary disequilibria in the economy, including those originating in the state sector, would eventually be reflected in the non-state sector. In short, it was essentially in the retail market that the nation's excessive money supply could express itself in various forms of inflation.

The Measurement of Inflationary Pressures

How can the extent of monetary instability in the retail market be determined? In a free economy, the price level can be taken as an indicator; in the U.S.S.R., the suppressed inflationary pressures can be gauged by comparing the official price with the collective farm market price. In China, however, the economic structure and the conditions of data are such that it is difficult to derive a satisfactory method of measurement.

One way to overcome this problem is to estimate the extent of inflation qualitatively and impressionistically, as has been done by Professor Dwight H. Perkins. Perkins estimated the possible bias of the official price index through scattered information on free market prices and rationing, and concluded that inflation was quite mild.[1] The question arises as to whether it is possible to go further to find a more systematic and quantitative measure. In this regard several approaches are possible. Even though the poverty of data prevents a firm quantitative estimate, it would be useful to explore these approaches so as to illustrate the difficulties involved, to indicate the blind alleys and, if possible, to derive a first approximation of some quantitative measure that could then be used to supplement the conclusion arrived at qualitatively. For these reasons, the various possible types of measurement are presented and appraised below.

THE PRICE-MOVEMENT APPROACH

The simplest and most logical index of inflationary pressures is naturally based on the general price movement. Professor T. C. Liu and Dr. K. C. Yeh have computed two indexes of this type in their exhaustive study on the Chinese economy.[2] These are reproduced in columns (1) and (2) of Table IX-1. Each figure in the two series represents a percentage comparison of prices between the indicated year and the preceding year. In other words, the two series are link index numbers. Thus an index of 100 means an absence of price change relative to the preceding year and, therefore, an absence of inflationary or deflationary pressures. By the same token, an index larger than 100 reflects inflationary pressures, and one smaller than 100, deflationary pressures. These indexes have been derived respectively from two series of prices published in the Mainland, one measuring retail prices in eight cities, the other costs of living for workers in twelve leading cities. Hence both indexes essentially mirror price movements in the retail market.

Both the first and second indexes show inflationary pressures for

---

[1] Perkins, *Market Control and Planning in Communist China,* pp. 155–59.

[2] Liu and Yeh, *The Economy of the Chinese Mainland: National Income and Economic Development, 1933–1959,* pp. 105–13.

Table IX-1
The Liu-Yeh Indexes of Inflationary Pressures*, 1952–1957

Year	First index (1)	Second index (2)	Third index (3)	Fourth index (4)
1952	99.0	—	101.4	101.9
1953	104.9	105.6	105.9	109.1
1954	101.9	101.2	102.0	103.0
1955	100.9	100.4	102.0	103.0
1956	99.9	99.8	101.7	102.5
1957	101.2	102.0	101.2	101.8

* Index = 100 when there are neither inflationary nor deflationary pressures.
Source: Liu and Yeh, *The Economy of the Chinese Mainland: National Income and Economic Development, 1933–1959* (Princeton: Princeton University Press; copyright © 1965 Rand Corporation), pp. 106, 112–13.

1953. However, neither registers any pressure in 1956, and this is at variance with many Communist reports on the existence of an inflationary tendency at that time. One possible explanation that can be advanced for this divergence lies in the change in the degree of socialization. By 1956, the socialization process was almost completed in China, and the sphere of controlled prices had been expanded. The retail price series and the costs-of-living series, on which the two inflationary indexes have been based, primarily represented official prices. In other words, whatever inflationary pressures might have existed in China in 1956 might be partly repressed by price control and partly expressed in rising prices unregistered by the government price series.[3] Consequently, unless there was decreed inflation, the pressures would not show up in these two Liu-Yeh inflationary indexes. The plausibility of this explanation is supported by a 1957 development. In that year, there were some upward adjustments of official prices in response to the pressures built up in 1956; these adjustments are reflected in the 1957 figures in both columns (1) and (2) of the table. It may thus be concluded that a measurement of inflationary pressures constructed on the basis of the published Chinese price data is useful in revealing open inflation that was decreed, but it cannot adequately reflect the total inflationary pressures.

[3] For a discussion on the probable bias of the official price indexes in China, see Perkins, *Market Control and Planning in Communist China,* pp. 156–58.

THE INFLATIONARY-GAP APPROACH

Table IX-1 also presents the third and fourth indexes of inflationary pressures constructed by Liu and Yeh. These indexes represent their authors' attempts to utilize macroeconomic relationships to determine the inflationary or deflationary gap in the Chinese economy. This gap has been represented by an "expenditure gap," which is roughly the difference between the nation's total investment expenditures (domestic and foreign) and her total savings. The expenditure gap was then compared with two aggregates—gross domestic expenditures and personal consumption—to derive the two separate indexes of inflationary pressures. Underlying this procedure is the assumption that the expenditure gap computed from observed data is a good approximation of the *ex ante* difference that constitutes the gap causing inflation or deflation in the Keynesian theoretical framework. The major component data that have been used in determining the expenditure gap are the results of the authors' own national income estimation, and the latter is the main topic of their comprehensive inquiry. Since an evaluation of national income statistics and their estimation are both beyond the scope of this study, the two resulting indexes of inflationary pressures cannot be thoroughly examined here. Suffice it to say that the authors of the indexes have expressed the feeling that the expenditure gaps they have computed for 1956 and 1957 are probably underestimated.[4] Accordingly, the two indexes of inflationary pressure for these years must also be underestimated. Thus this pair of Liu-Yeh indexes encounters a problem similar to the one confronted by the first pair.

THE PURCHASING POWER APPROACH

There is another logical way in which a nation's inflationary pressures may be gauged. In an economy subject to price control, stability is achieved when the total effective monetary demand equals the value of goods available in the market. Any discrepancy between the two magnitudes would constitute a disequilibrating force, inflationary or deflationary, and the direction would depend on which magnitude is

[4] Liu and Yeh, *The Economy of the Chinese Mainland . . . ,* pp. 107–108.

the larger. There are two series of Chinese data which appear to correspond to these two aggregates in the retail market. The first, called the social purchasing power, measures the capacity of urban and rural residents and collective units to purchase retail commodities and is expressed in monetary terms.[5] It is therefore close to the concept of effective monetary demand in the retail market. The second, the "social commodity retail sales," represents the total value of goods sold in the retail market.[6] Any excessive purchasing power not balanced by retail sales that can be shown in a comparison of these two series would theoretically create inflationary pressures. An inflationary index based on this concept is computed and presented in Appendix F. A closer examination of this index reveals that the method of construction of the Chinese data renders this approach sterile.[7]

THE CURRENCY SUPPLY APPROACH

One final method for measuring inflationary pressures is possible. This consists of a simple comparison of the change in quantity of currency with the change in commodity supply. The Chinese banking authorities in the Mainland followed this approach in their discussions of monetary stability.[8] This is not surprising since, in the Chinese framework, the macromonetary function of the Bank was to supply the correct amount of money, especially currency, to satisfy the transactional demand at controlled prices; thus a growth in currency supply not commensurable with the growth of commodity supply would be considered disequilibrating.

To the Western economist, it is immediately apparent that this approach is an adaptation of the simple quantity theory of money. It assumes that inflation exists when the quantity of currency grows faster than commodity sales in a full employment economy where prices are

[5] Nai-Ruenn Chen, *Chinese Economic Statistics: A Handbook for Mainland China,* p. 88.

[6] Social commodity retail sales include all retail commodities; the latter in turn include consumers' goods as well as producers' goods purchased by the peasants. *Ibid.,* pp. 75–76.

[7] For details, see Appendix F.

[8] For example, Tseng Ling, "Is There Inflation in China at the Present?" *CCYC,* no. 5, 1957, p. 41.

by and large controlled and therefore relatively stable.[9] The application of this theory in the currency sector of Communist China is perhaps acceptable because the currency flow, and thus the velocity also, was regulated by the state sector. This regulation was possible because wages and agricultural payments from state organs plus socialistic retail sales were the main determinants of the currency circulation. Besides, there was no speculative demand for money in this economy. The holding of money was solely for transactional and precautionary motives that, under normal circumstances, were relatively stable.

INFLATIONARY INDEXES: OPEN,
REPRESSED, AND TOTAL

Table IX-2 presents the inflationary indexes that are based on comparative growths in currency and in commodity supply.[10] Two such indexes can be constructed. The first (column 5) relates the index of currency to the index of social commodity retail sales at current prices. It reflects the part of inflationary pressures that, because of the partial price control, cannot cause retail prices to change; in other words, it measures the latent or suppressed component of inflationary pressures in the consumer's market. The reason for this is that the retail sales series has already incorporated the allowable price changes. Any inflationary pressures that might have caused prices to rise—that is, open inflation—would not be reflected by the inflationary index computed from this series.

In order to record the total disequilibrating force a second inflationary index is derived (column 6). Here the social commodity retail sales series was first deflated by the national average retail price index so

---

[9] Thus the value of commodity supply, represented by the commodity retail sales series, is roughly the PT in Fisher's equation of exchange $MV = PT$. Assuming V to be fairly constant, the change in M (quantity of currency) would drive up P (retail price) in a free market unless T (the volume of commodity) changes to the same extent. Therefore, with price control, the discrepancy between the increase in M and that in PT reflects repressed inflationary or deflationary pressures unless V changes.

[10] The index of currency is based on our estimates in Chapter VII. Even though these estimates aim at the minimum quantities and may therefore be subject to a downward bias, the index used here merely reflects relative changes, rather than the absolute totals; therefore it is not subject to this bias.

Table IX-2
Inflationary Indexes Based on Quantity of Currency Relative to
Commodity Supply, 1952–1957
(1952 = 100)

End of year	Cur-rency index (1)	Retail price index (2)	Index of commodity Retail sales		Inflationary index	
			At current prices (3)	At 1952 prices (4)	Repressed (5)	Total (6)
1952	100	100.0	100.0	100.0	100	100
1953	139	103.2	125.7	121.8	111	114
1954	139*	105.5	137.7	130.5	101*	107*
1955	150	106.3	141.7	133.3	106	113
1956	197	106.3	166.5	156.6	118	126
1957	186	108.6	171.3	157.7	109	118

*Index is below the indicated figure.
Sources:
  Col. (1): Table VII-9, col. (2).
  Cols. (2) and (3): SSB, *The Ten Great Years,* pp. 153 and 146.
  Col. (4): Col. (3) ÷ col. (2).
  Col. (5): Col. (1) ÷ col. (3).
  Col. (6): Col. (1) ÷ col. (4).

as to eliminate the effects of price changes.[11] The resulting index of retail sales at constant prices is then compared with the currency series. In this comparison, an excessive relative growth in currency would roughly reflect the entire inflationary pressure regardless of the form in which it is manifested. As to the degree of open inflation, it can be seen from the retail price index, column (2). Thus there are really three indexes of inflationary pressures in Table IX-2, indicating respectively the degree of open, repressed, and total inflation.

QUALIFICATIONS

It should be borne in mind that underlying the two computed indexes there are certain basic assumptions.

The base year. The year 1952 serves as the base for all series in Table IX-2; this implies that 1952 is considered a relatively normal year. This

---

[11] The retail price index used here refers to the nationwide average retail price index, not the series used by Liu and Yeh.

assumption is justified on the grounds that, for the most part, by the end of 1952 the economy was stabilized, the banking structure was established, and many transitional monetary developments connected with wars and hyperinflation were completed. However, there were also specific developments in this year, such as the five-anti movement and the Korean War; therefore it might or might not be a year of absolute monetary equilibrium. Thus the inflationary indexes merely indicate the changes in inflationary pressures relative to 1952.

Non-commodity expenditures. A second assumption relates to the data on retail sales. This series measures commodity sales, which, although a dominant component, is not the sole constituent of total retail sales. Therefore, the inflationary indexes built on this series assume that the rate of growth in total retail sales can be represented by that in commodity retail sales. To state it differently, the indexes assume parallel changes in commodity and noncommodity sales. If in fact commodity sales increased at a rate faster than non-commodity sales in the years under study, then the inflationary indexes would underestimate the inflationary pressure. On the other hand, if the reverse were true, then the indexes would be an overestimation.

Liquidity preference. A third underlying assumption is a relatively constant liquidity preference schedule. As mentioned, under the Chinese system other forms of financial assets were not available, and demand for cash to hold was primarily for transactional and precautionary purposes. Except in one instance, there is by and large little evidence that sudden sporadic shifts in the liquidity preference have occurred during the five-year period. The one exception was the abrupt increase in currency hoarding in rural areas in the spring of 1956 discussed in Chapter VII. However, this was caused mainly by fears and uncertainties during the collectivization drive and was short lived. To the extent that this episode affected the rural liquidity preference during part of the year, the inflationary indexes for 1956 might be slightly overestimated.

In conclusion, it may be said that the inflationary indexes derived via the currency supply approach are subject to simplifying assumptions and qualifications. Nevertheless when all circumstances and alternatives are taken into consideration, they remain the only useful quantitative indicators of approximate changes in inflationary pressures that can be built on the basis of existing knowledge.

The Extent of Inflation

Judging from the set of indexes based on the currency-supply approach, what can be said about the degree and character of the inflationary or deflationary pressures in Communist China? First, the general direction of the indexes is upward. Between the end of 1952 and the end of 1957, inflationary pressures rose by eighteen percent. Roughly half of this was openly released, causing the retail price index to increase mildly at an average rate of approximately 1.7 percent per annum. The other half represented repressed or concealed inflation, averaging about 1.8 percent annually. The annual rate of growth of total inflationary pressures during the five-year period averaged 3.5 percent a year.[12] Viewed in the context of the nation's economic development, this rate is rather moderate. During the five years, the rate of investment in China was high,[13] and her average annual growth rate was above 6 percent.[14] When this performance is compared with that of India, the difference is notable. During India's Second Five Year Plan the rate of investment was lower, and the rate of growth was about 4 percent;[15]

[12] Here the average annual rate of increase is equal to the increase in the inflationary index between 1952 and 1957 divided by the number of years. If, instead of this method, a least squares linear trend is fitted to the total inflationary index series, then the equation would be $Y = 103.55 + 3.78X$ with 1952 as origin. This gives an annual rate of increase of 3.78 percent.

[13] Liu and Yeh estimated the average proportion of capital formation in domestic products (1952 prices) to be 23.8 percent in gross terms and 19.8 percent in net terms during 1952–1957. Ta-chung Liu, "The Tempo of Economic Development of the Chinese Mainland, 1949–65," *An Economic Profile of Mainland China,* I, 62.

[14] The Liu-Yeh estimates of the annual growth rates of national products during 1952–1957 were 6.2 percent (gross) and 6.9 percent (net). *Ibid.* Eckstein estimated the annual growth rate to be about 6.5 percent for the First Five Year Plan. Eckstein, *Communist China's Economic Growth and Foreign Trade,* p. 46.

[15] The Second Five Year Plan of India began in 1956–1957 and ended in 1960–1961. This period was more comparable to the Chinese First Five Year Plan because industrial development was accelerated. During the Second Plan period, India's total investment, public and private, amounted to Rs. 675 billion (at current prices), whereas her national income totalled Rs. 6,699 (at 1960–1961 prices). National income at constant prices grew from Rs.

but the inflationary pressures incurred were much stronger than those in China since the average annual increase in the Indian price level was about 6 percent.[16] This comparison suggests that although Communist China failed to avoid monetary instability in this era of accelerated development, she nevertheless was able to alleviate it and keep it within tolerable limits during the First Five Year Plan period as a whole.

The above discussion focused on the net change in inflationary pressures during the five-year span. While this is useful in evaluating the total long-run performance, it obscures the underlying short-term fluctuations. It is therefore necessary to supplement the above analysis with an examination of the year-to-year movements in the inflationary indexes. Chart 4 presents the two computed inflationary indexes and the retail price index. It can be seen that, while the retail price series, representing open inflation, rose gradually and smoothly throughout the period, both of the computed indexes fluctuated and formed two cycles. The peaks fell in 1953 and 1956; these were immediately followed by contractions in 1954 and 1957, with 1955 serving as a dividing year that was mildly expansionary. If a linear trend were fitted to the total inflationary series to depict the long-term tendency, then 1953 and 1956 would stand out strikingly as two unusually high years. In each the inflationary pressures rose by more than 10 percent relative to the preceding year—a rate much higher than the long-term average rate of increase.

Thus there were stronger short-run inflationary pressures that the Chinese money and banking system was unable to prevent. What caused these bursts of inflationary pressures? Was it the fault of the monetary policy? Why were they short-term and how were they contained? A closer examination of the situations in 1953 and 1956 will help to answer these questions.

1,213 billion in 1955–1956 to Rs. 1,450 billion in 1960–1961, giving a rate of increase for the five-year period of less than 20 percent. Government of India Planning Commission, *Third Five Year Plan,* pp. 32, 35, 733.

[16] The index of wholesale prices rose from 98.1 to 127.5 (1952–1953 = 100 during the five year period, giving a total rate of increase of 30 percent. The cost of living index rose from 96 to 124 (1949 = 100) in the same period, representing an increase of 29 percent. *Ibid.,* p. 733.

Chart 4
Indexes of Inflationary Pressures: Open, Repressed, and Total,
1952–1957

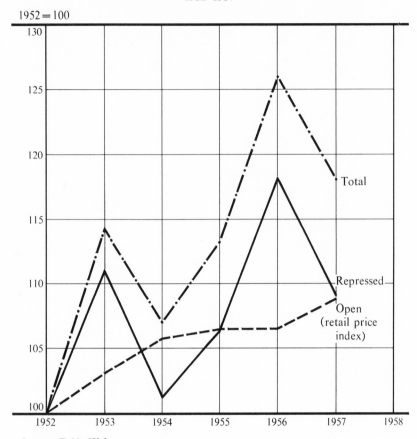

Source: Table IX-2

Inflationary Periods: Causes and Cures

The circumstances under which strong inflationary pressures took place, in 1953 and in 1956, were vastly different. It is therefore more convenient to review the two periods individually.

236

THE 1953 INFLATION

In 1953 the economy was partly socialized, with the state and cooperative trading network handling about 41 percent of the nation's retail sales and 69 percent of wholesale transactions.[17] It was the first year in which formal planning was attempted. In addition, state enterprises had been newly put on the basis of individual accounting and separate responsibilities.

CAUSES

The apparent cause of the inflation was the ambitious budget for that year. The 1953 planned budget not only was large; it also allowed a current deficit of three billion yuan, to be covered by accrued surplus from previous years.[18] As discussed earlier, much of the budget surplus under the Chinese system was made possible by the creation of credit, and the cumulative surplus of the earlier years in turn served as an unintended fiscal offset. The spending of this surplus by the government would thus expand the active money supply. This was obviously what happened, for monetary "tension" existed by the second quarter of 1953,[19] and prices soared.[20]

But what caused the large planned current deficit? Were the planning authorities aware of its expansionary effect? Was it a deliberate attempt to reap forced savings through inflation? The answer to the last two questions is probably negative, for the large deficit was the result of a combination of factors. First, because 1953 marked the end of the

---

[17] Based on data in Nai-Ruenn Chen, *Chinese Economic Statistics,* pp. 393–94. Another source gives the shares as 49 percent (retail) and 69 percent (wholesale). Yang Po, "A Preliminary Analysis of the Process of Socialist Transformation of Private Trade in China," *TCKTTH,* no. 15, 1956, p. 9.

[18] *Supra,* pp. 144.

[19] This was frequently mentioned. For example, Ko, "The Nature of the National Budget . . .," *CCYC,* no. 3, 1956, p. 78; Kuo, "Views on the State Budgetary Surplus," *CCYC,* no. 8, 1959, p. 60; Wang Tzu-ying, "The Experience and Lessons . . .," *HHPYK,* no. 5, 1957, p. 92.

[20] "In the spring of 1953, grain prices in the markets of such important grain regions as Hunan, Kiangsi, Shantung, Hopeh, Anhwei and Shensi provinces were 30 or even 50 per cent higher than state trade company prices. The peasants, especially prosperous, refrained from selling the grain." Tseng and Han, *The Circulation of Money . . .,* JPRS #3317, p. 78.

recovery period and initiated an era of economic development, efforts were made to accelerate the amount of state investment. This can be seen by the large budgetary appropriation for basic construction for this year. This appropriation was more than 60 percent higher than the one for 1952, and the amount of the increase was close to the amount of the planned budget deficit.[21] Second, the conditions of planning at this time were such that much reliance was placed upon past performances. In the two years preceding 1953, both fiscal revenues and expenditures tended to be underestimated in the planned budget; but the discrepancy in revenues was larger than that in expenditures, causing the annual planned deficit to become a realized budget surplus at the end of each fiscal year.[22] This experience rendered the planning authorities less apprehensive of a large planned deficit since there was a good chance that a part or even the whole of it would not be realized. Finally, and perhaps the most importantly, the authorities were not fully conscious of the relationship between bank credit and the budget surplus,[23] nor were they aware of the balance budget multiplier effect of a growing budget. This lack of comprehension caused them to ignore the higher level of the budget and to believe that the planned deficit, even if realized, could be covered by the existing accrued surplus without secondary effects. In other words, the surplus was considered to be

---

[21] The appropriation for basic construction was ￥5.01 billion in 1952 and ￥8.15 billion in 1953. These figures differed from actual investment in basic construction, which was ￥3.71 billion in 1952 and ￥6.51 billion in 1953. Nai-Ruenn Chen, *Chinese Economic Statistics,* p. 158.

[22] The inaccuracy was partly caused by the individual enterprises' conservative estimates on their expected revenues and an upward bias for their estimated expenditures. The following data indicate the degree of inaccuracy in budget planning for the earlier years.

Year	Realized state revenues as percent of planned revenues	Realized state expenditures as percent of planned expenditures
1950	149.5	137.9
1951	213.6	171.3
1952	126.5	105.7
1953	107.0	92.0

Wang Ch'uan-lun, "The Two Fundamentally Different Attitudes on the Question of Budget Deficits," *CHYYC,* no. 5, 1958, pp. 11–18.

[23] Ch'en Ju-lung, "On the Question of Balancing State Budget and Bank Credit," *TC,* no. 4, 1957, p. 4.

merely a contingency reserve, and its offsetting and counter-inflationary role was not sufficiently understood.

Thus, given the basic need to increase investment and the necessarily rudimentary state of planning, one crucial reason for the large planned deficit, and therefore for the 1953 inflation, was an incoherent economic policy. It failed to integrate the fiscal policy with the monetary policy and to take into account the inflationary tendency of a larger budget.

CURES

The cures for the 1953 inflation were similarly more pragmatic than systematic. A variety of actions were undertaken that could have had disinflationary effects. First of all, in response to the planned budget that activated the cumulated surplus, the Bank attempted to counteract the monetary effect by contracting commercial loans.[24] The new regulations effected in March, 1953, enabled the Bank to reduce and to regulate loans to the trading network,[25] which was the most important category of all bank credit. Unfortunately, the enforcement of credit restrictions had other impacts. It forced the state trading network to liquidate its inventory, and it also hampered the network's ability to purchase goods produced by industrial concerns. In turn, these developments encouraged a relative expansion of private trading and prevented the state sector from controlling a growing proportion of the nation's products. The Bank's action was therefore in direct conflict with the goal of socialization; it had to be abrogated in July.[26] This policy reversal marked the failure of the Bank's endeavor to exercise orthodox, active monetary control. It also brought out the basic incompatibility between this type of monetary policy and the economic system the nation wanted to adopt.

As inflationary pressures mounted in the spring, a second response came from the government. The Central Committee of the Communist Party issued an emergency directive to "increase production, increase revenues, practice austerity, tighten expenditures and balance the state

---

[24] *Supra,* pp. 82–83.

[25] Kuan and Tai, "The Great Monetary Achievements . . .," *CJYC,* no. 1, 1958, p. 61.

[26] The decision was made in the Financial and Economic Conference of the Central Government, *ibid.,* p. 62.

budget."[27] Thus an effort was made through public exhortations, rather than formal revision of plans, to contract budget expenditures and to eliminate the fiscal deficit that was the original cause of the inflation. By the end of the year realized budget revenues were above planned revenues, while realized expenditures were lower than planned, resulting again in a budget surplus at a below-plan budget level in 1953.[28] How much of this discrepancy between the planned deficit and the realized surplus was due to inaccuracy in the original plan, how much to the production and austerity drive, and how much to a deliberate scaling down of investment[29] is not possible to assess. But since the effects of all these adjustments were felt via the budget, they can be classified as a group of fiscal measures.

The developments in the spring of 1953, when prices climbed and private trading revived, had further consequences in terms of socialization. The rising price for foodgrains, the basic consumer's product, enabled and encouraged the peasants to refrain from selling grain to government agencies. At the same time, private traders began to be active. There was thus a decline in the share of foodgrains concentrated in the hands of the state.[30] To face this problem, the planned purchase and planned supply system, under which the state monopolized the trading of foodgrains and vegetable oils, was instituted in November. The monetary effect of this program was twofold. On the one hand, by controlling the supply of basic necessities the program eliminated open price inflation in these items. On the other hand, it created repressed inflation, for peasants who formerly held grain and sold it gradually as the need arose were now required to exchange for a lump sum of cash the entire stock of available surplus grain immediately after the harvest. Thus the idle

[27] Ch'en Ju-lung, "On the Question of Balancing . . .," *TC*, no. 4, 1957, p. 4; Ko, "On the Inter-Connection . . .," *CCYC*, no. 1, 1958, p. 11; Jung Tzu-ho, "On the Balance of State Budgetary Receipts and Expenditures, State Credit Receipts and Expenditures, and Commodity Supply and Demand," *TC*, no. 6, 1957, p. 2.

[28] Wang Ch'uan-lun, "The Two Fundamentally Different Attitudes . . .," *CHYYC*, no. 5, 1958.

[29] The final basic construction investment in 1953 was lower than its budgetary appropriation, but this was also true in other years. Nai-Ruenn Chen, *Chinese Economic Statistics*, p. 158.

[30] The share of grain delivered or sold to the state fell from 20.4 percent of the crop for the 1951–1952 agricultural year to 18.1 percent of the crop for the 1952–1953 agricultural year. Tseng and Han, *The Circulation of Money . . .*, p. 78.

currency balance held in the rural area grew sharply. The money came from bank loans to commercial enterprises, since by this time the Bank was again committed to the providing of unlimited credit support for state trading. In effect, then, the expansion of the state monopoly on the distribution of basic agricultural products removed some open inflation but generated repressed inflation.

The People's Bank once again took action to contain the new form of inflationary pressures. This time it relied solely on negative and qualitative measures of monetary contraction, that is, measures that enlarged the return flow of currency. Thus the preferential deposit was instituted alongside the planned purchase and planned supply program so as to recall temporarily a portion of the currency paid out to the peasants under the program.[31] This was supplemented in 1954, and replaced in 1955, by a stronger measure of currency absorption: the countrywide formation of credit cooperatives. The credit cooperatives solicited idle cash as capital and as deposits. Part of these were then directed towards rural investment, while the other part became rural deposits in the People's Bank.

In general, developments during the 1953 inflation reflected a strategy of pragmatic trials and errors. The inflation sprang partly from an inadequate understanding of macroeconomic relationships. A positive monetary policy for its correction proved unpracticable, and emergency fiscal measures were used as the main counteracting force. The open inflation necessitated an extension of the state monopoly over the trading of rural products. In turn, this extension retarded the price rise at the cost of accelerating repressed inflation, which was finally removed through negative monetary measures implemented rather drastically by the Bank in 1954. Thus both the origin of and the remedy for the 1953 inflation involved complex interactions among loosely coordinated policies in three economic sectors: fiscal, monetary and commercial.

Viewed from the standpoint of monetary policy, 1953 was an important transitional year. The experience in this period forced the Bank to abandon the more traditional method of monetary contraction through credit restriction and to turn to negative measures designed for absorp-

---

[31] *Supra,* pp. 156–57.

tion. Moreover, the inflation brought home the linkage between bank credit and budget surplus, leading to the eventual adoption of the off-setting policy.

THE 1956 INFLATION

By 1956, planning had become more comprehensive, the monetary system had been overhauled, and the nation's trade was by and large brought under the state's control. This was the year of accelerated socialization under which the remnants of private trade and industry as well as nearly all of the rural farms were transformed into cooperatives.[32] It was also a year of high investment following a bountiful harvest. Moreover, a general wage reform was implemented at this time.

CAUSES

The origin of the 1956 inflation was more complex than that of the 1953 inflation. During both of these periods there were parallel leaps in state investment and in the total budget,[33] but the resulting planned budget deficits were of dissimilar orders of magnitude.[34] The 1956 planned deficit was much smaller. Hence, in contrast to 1953, the fiscal factor alone could not adequately account for the strong inflationary pressures that occurred in 1956. When the general condition of the nation is examined, it appears that the main thrust of the inflationary force for the later era came from two other autonomous sources—the socialization movement and the wage reform. In addition, the high investment also added to the pressures through its effects on bank credit.

The socialization movement. The higher speed of socialization directly influenced the supply of money, especially currency, through the increased availability of loans to the non-state sector in support of the

[32] State and cooperative trade accounted for two-thirds of the retail volume in 1956; it had already accounted for about 95 percent of the wholesale volume in 1955. Nai-Ruenn Chen, *Chinese Economic Statistics,* pp. 393–94.

[33] State budget appropriation for basic construction increased from ¥9.52 billion in 1955 to ¥14.87 billion in 1956. This was an increase of 56 percent, whereas the rise between 1952 and 1953 was 62 percent. *Ibid.,* p. 158.

[34] Planned budget deficit for 1956 amounted to ¥1.01 billion compared with ¥3.01 billion for 1953. Ch'en Ju-lung, "On the Question of Balancing . . .," *TC,* no. 4, 1957, p. 4.

movement. Part of this credit was extended to traders, handicrafts producers, or individual transportation workers as inducements to join their respective cooperatives; thus their indebtedness grew by 0.94 billion yuan in 1956 against a planned increase of 0.29 billion yuan.[35] However, the proportion of this credit granted to agriculture in order to stimulate the growth in rural collectives was far more significant. Rural loans granted jumped from 1.0 billion yuan in 1955 to 3.4 billion in 1956,[36] whereas the planned amount for the latter year was only 2.2 billion.[37] Thus the actual financial support given to the socialization movement was much greater than originally intended, and the collectivization drive was an especially important contributor to the inflation.

A predominant share of that year's rural loans, including the poor peasants cooperative fund loans went to the collectives for productive purposes.[38] Consequently, rural credit in this period served two purposes: it was a tool to promote socialization and a source of investment funds. In a sense, then, the inflationary pressures brought about through increased loans were, like those caused by the fiscal deficit and the large budget, related to a desire to increase investment. However, the immediate reason for the sudden spurt of agricultural credit in 1956 was to expedite the transformation of private farms into semisocialized units with a minimum of disruption.

The wage reform. A second exogenous force enhancing the currency inflation was the general revision of wages. The wage reform, effected in April, 1956, aimed at unifying the nation's wage system while gearing it more closely to the principle of "to each according to his labor." The then existing wage pattern, being partly a result of historical development, was deemed somewhat irrational and egalitarian; in addition, the general wage level had fallen behind the growth in productivity.[39] The reform, therefore, combined an all-around increase in wages with certain modifications in the wage structure. The wage-point system, which was attached to a commodity unit, was completely abolished so that only money wage was used; the structure of wage differentiation was

[35] *Supra,* p. 122.
[36] *Supra,* Table V-3.
[37] Li Hsien-nien, the 1956 Budget Report, *FKHP,* p. 230.
[38] *Supra,* pp. 112–13.
[39] SC, "Decision on Wage Reform," *HHPYK,* no. 15, 1956, p. 175.

refined and the differentials widened; regular promotions were allowed; the use of the "piece-wage" was encouraged; and finally, the system of bonuses was improved and expanded while allowances were rationalized. All these changes tended to raise the incentive to work, but they also affected the total wage bill.

Since the criterion used to determine the overall rate of increase in wages[40] was the average gross productivity rather than the marginal productivity of labor, the increase was too large in view of the abundant supply of unskilled labor.[41] As a result, there was a sudden influx of labor from the country to the cities,[42] and the number of new workers employed greatly exceeded the planned increase.[43] In addition, promotions, bonuses, and allowances were given rather generously, while lagging revisions in work norms relative to technological changes had the effect of inflating piece-wages.[44] All these developments impinged on the wage bill of 1956, augmenting it by 2.7 billion yuan instead of the planned increase of 1.78 billion.[45]

The fiscal budget. The independent impact of the fiscal budget on the 1956 inflation is more difficult to evaluate, for the budget level and the deficit were reflections of several developments. Logically, the oversize wage bill would affect budgetary revenues through the shift in enterprise costs and profits unless bank credit were used to compensate for the difference. Therefore, the question arises as to how much of the

[40] The average rate of increase for existing workers was 14.5 percent. *Ibid.,* p. 176.

[41] This was pointed out by Perkins. Dwight H. Perkins, *Market Control and Planning in Communist China,* pp. 149–50.

[42] *CHCC* Data Office, "The Situation of Labor Wages in 1956," *HHPYK,* no. 10, 1957, p. 116.

[43] The planned increase in the number of workers was 0.84 million men for 1956. The actual increase was 2.3 million out of a total employment of 21.179 million men. Cheng K'ang-ning, "Improve Labor Wages Planning Works by Summarizing the 1956 Experience," *CHCC,* no. 8, 1957, p. 9. These figures were given by the planning agency and therefore refer to employment within the state plan. Another set of data from the SSB shows that national total employment in 1956 was 22.31 million, and the increase was 3.58 million men. "Statistical Data on the Improvement of Living Conditions of Workers and Employees," *TCKT,* no. 14, 1957, p. 13.

[44] *CHCC* Data Office, "The Situation of Labor Wages in 1956," *HHPYK,* no. 10, 1957, p. 116.

[45] Cheng K'ang-ning, "Improve Labor Wages . . .," *CHCC,* no. 8, 1957, p. 9. Again these figures, released by the planning office, refer to wages within the state plan. The SSB data show an increase in total wages in the nation of ¥3.6 billion in 1956. "Statistical Data on the Improvement . . .," *TCKT,* no. 14, 1957, p. 13.

realized budget deficit of 1.83 billion yuan was an indirect consequence of the wage reform. And the planned current deficit of 1.01 billion yuan could not serve unequivocally as an indicator of the spontaneous inflationary factor coming from the budget deficit, for, unlike the situation in 1953, the credit fund had already been established by 1956. If sufficient offsets to bank credit were provided by this fund at the end of 1955, then the budget surplus carried over and used to finance the 1956 planned current deficit would represent true budget savings.[46] In other words, whether or not the planned current deficit of 1956 was inflationary depends on the adequacy of the fiscal offsets existing at the time, and there is no information to clarify this point. The picture is further clouded by the problem of inexact planning. Was the planned current deficit for 1956, like those of preceding years, an allowance for the inherent bias of enterprise estimation? Such an allowance appears to have played a part in budget planning. For example, in forming the 1956 budget, it was expected that five percent of the planned capital investment would not be realized.[47]

Although it is hard to isolate the fiscal effect on the inflation because of the above-mentioned uncertainties, it may still be correct to say that a portion of the 1956 inflationary pressures did originate from budgetary sources. Several clues tend to point in this direction. First, the actual budget deficit in 1956 was about twice the size of the unplanned increase in the wage bill. Therefore, even though wage reform might have caused some of the deficit, it could not account for the whole of it. Second, many Chinese economists believed in retrospect that the accumulated budget surplus carried over to 1956 should not have been spent.[48] This creates the suspicion that the pre-1956 growth in bank credit had not been fully offset. The subsequent change in policy, which allowed the entire budget surplus of the central government to automatically be-

[46] The credit fund assigned in 1955 immobilized a major part of the accumulated budget surplus, leaving a balance of ￥1.01 billion to be carried over to 1956 and used to cover the planned current deficit of that year. *Supra,* Chapter VI, footnote 39.

[47] This expectation was based on past performances. But in 1956, 99.9 percent of the planned capital investment was realized; this was considered to be a factor contributing to the inflation. Po I-po, "Report on the Results of Implementation . . .," *FKHP,* VI, 151.

[48] For example, Ko, "On the Inter-Connection . . .," *CCYC,* no. 1, 1958, p. 11. Wang Tzu-ying, "The Experience and Lessons . . .," *HHPYK,* no. 5, 1957, p. 91.

come credit fund, reinforces this suspicion. Third, the higher level of the 1956 budget would have had some inflationary impacts even without a deficit because of the balanced-budget multiplier. Finally the Chairman of the State Economic Commission admitted that state capital investment in that year was excessive. The amount of overinvestment was given as between 1.5 and 2.0 billion yuan;[49] this constituted over 10 percent of total investment.[50] As mentioned above, about 5 percent of the investment was not expected to be realized, although in fact it was. This part of the overinvestment and the resulting budget deficit, then, can be attributed to planning errors. However, the remaining part of the overinvestment cannot be so accounted for; it must have augmented the fiscal deficit, which in turn became a source of inflationary pressures.

State investment. Out of the complex picture of the fiscal budget, state investment emerged as an important determinant; it is thus necessary to make some observations on the role of state investment in the 1956 inflation. As stated, the rate of increase in capital investment was unusually high in that year, the only previous period with a comparable rate being 1953. Logically, high state investment per se is not necessarily expansionary; if it is accompanied by an appropriate amount of savings mobilized through the budget, then stability can be maintained. Thus the inflationary effect of a large state investment depends essentially on the budget level and the fiscal deficit it creates. This factor has already been discussed in the last section.

Nevertheless, in the Chinese framework, a large state investment could have had a secondary impact on inflation. For although fixed capital originated from the budget, a part of the concomitant working capital came from the Bank. In fact, a function of bank credit was to provide a flexible source of financing to the enterprises. Thus late in 1956, when raw materials became scarce as a result of increased investment, industrial enterprises began to compete in the purchasing and hoarding of materials and goods with funds borrowed from the Bank.[51] The consequent growth in industrial loans then added to the inflation.

---

[49] Po I-po, "Report on the Results of Implementation . . .," *FKHP*, VI, 151. It is not clear how this figure was arrived at.

[50] Total budget appropriation for basic construction in 1956 was 14.9 billion yuan. Nai-Ruenn Chen, *Chinese Economic Statistics,* p. 158.

[51] *Supra,* p. 109.

In summary, there were three main causes of the 1956 inflation: the desire for rapid yet peaceful socialization, an erroneous wage policy, and the impatience for a faster rate of capital formation. All these tended to raise the volume of money and of aggregate demand. The situation was further aggravated by certain changes on the supply side. For example, the collectivization effectively reduced the peasant's capacity to produce rural subsidiary products and thus depressed the supply of certain consumer's goods.[52]

DEVELOPMENT AND CURES

Even though loans for the socialization movement began to be extended early in 1956, the inflationary effect was not immediately apparent. It was obscured by the upheavals caused by the collectivization of the countryside. In the first place, the reorganization of rural production led to a decline in the peasants' private subsidiary income; in the second place, the anxiety and uncertainty aroused by the sweeping change stimulated rural hoarding of currency. As a result of these developments, there were actually a shortage of money, a decline in the sale of consumer's goods, and a sluggish market in the farm area during the spring.[53] The Bank further extended rural loans in order to correct this situation.

By the third quarter of the year, however, the pressures began to come to the surface. After June, the rural reorganization was nearly completed, the wage increase under the April reform began to be implemented retroactively,[54] and the year's sale of agricultural products to the state began. There was a general upsurge in urban and rural purchasing power, certain consumer's goods became scarce,[55] and prices for selected items rose.[56] Meanwhile, the speed of investment also

---

[52] For a description of the decline in subsidiary output, see Perkins, *Market Control and Planning* . . ., p. 72–74.

[53] TCKTTH Data Office, "The Great Achievement on Socialist Construction and Socialist Transformation during the First Half Year of 1956," *TCKTTH,* no. 5, 1956, p. 6.

[54] "A Brief Summary of Works on Savings during the Period of the First Five Year Plan," *CKCJ,* no. 5, 1958, p. 24.

[55] TCKTTH Data Office, "Rapid Progress Was Made by Various Sectors of the National Economy in the Third Quarter of 1956," *TCKTTH,* no. 21, 1956, p. 2.

[56] TCKTTH Data Office, "The Condition of Domestic Market Prices in 1956," *HHPYK,* no. 10, 1957, pp. 114–15.

caused a shortage in basic producer's goods such as steel, coal, and lumber.[57] As in 1953, a combination of policies was used to combat the situation.

Commercial disinvestment. Pressures arising from the increased demand for both consumer's and producer's goods were first relieved by the state commercial network. Approximately 2 billion yuan in goods was drawn from the state commodity reserve and commercial inventory in 1956. Since the added supply of goods was taken from stock previously purchased and accumulated with bank financing, this procedure amounted to a disinvestment on the part of the trading network and led to the repayment of commercial loans. However, contrary to the situation in 1953, this time the action was initiated by the commercial hierarchy rather than by the Bank and was therefore a part of commercial policy.

Monetary contraction. The Bank's anti-inflationary actions were taken separately in various monetary spheres. They affected the urban and rural flows of currency as well as the credit circuit.

(1) Currency. With regard to urban currency, absorption was the primary tool because loans to non-state enterprises in the cities were relatively small. In these areas, savings drives generally accompanied the implementation of the wage reform and greatly augmented urban personal deposits.[58] However, the rate of growth of urban deposits did not at first keep pace with that of urban income. Compared with previous years, the 1956 marginal propensity to save in the form of urban deposits suffered a sudden decline. It was not until 1957, when an intensified savings campaign was called forth in the nation, that a larger share of the increased income became personal deposits.[59]

---

[57] "The Basic Situation of the Implementation of the 1956 National Economic Plan and an Explanation of the 1957 Draft Plan," *CHCC,* no. 4, 1957, p. 3.

[58] Between July and December, 1956, urban deposits increased by ¥473 million, accounting for 87 percent of the total increase for the year. "A Brief Summary of Works on Savings . . . ," *CKCJ,* no. 5, 1958, p. 24.

[59] *Supra,* Table VI-9. The marginal propensity climbed steeply in 1957 because the growth of personal deposits was relatively larger than that of urban income. However, if we combine the 1956 and 1957 figures and compare the two-year change in deposits with the two-year change in urban income, then the marginal ratio for the two-year period becomes 22.5 percent, which is of a similar order of magnitude as the marginal ratios in 1954 and 1955.

In the farm area the Bank invoked both the positive monetary measure of reducing loans and the negative measure of absorbing deposits. Here the problem of inflation became acute when, instead of realizing a normal post-harvest seasonal decline, outstanding farm credit continued to climb by more than 200 million in September and October.[60] Since this was the season of heavy state agricultural purchases and thus of increased payments to the countryside, the currency flow was greatly swollen. At the end of October the State Council issued a special directive stressing the recall of agricultural loans while the People's Bank took emergency measures to contract rural credit and to expand rural deposits so as to reduce the volume of currency in circulation.[61] This tight money policy was continued in 1957.[62] Even though productive loans were granted once again in the spring and planting season, their volume was limited;[63] and the Bank resumed pressures for repayment of existing indebtedness as soon as harvesting began,[64] albeit the result was unsatisfactory.[65]

The Bank's rural monetary policy was somewhat hindered by the collectivization drive. The recall of loans was circumscribed by the consideration that the Bank should permit the new agricultural cooperatives to distribute higher income to the participating farmers. At the same

[60] Lieh Jung, "Subsidiary Agricultural Loans Should Not Be Granted Blindly," *CKCJ*, no. 24, 1956, p. 6. Normally farm loans began to decline in September.

[61] SC, "Directive on Certain Questions Regarding Rural Financial Works," *FKHP*, IV, 302–304; Chen Hsi-yü, "Report to the Conference of Branch Bank Managers . . . ," *CKCJ*, no. 6, 1957, p. 1. From the end of October to the end of December, 1956, the Bank's emergency measures reduced currency in circulation by ￥1.17 billion. Evidently, this was achieved in the main through increased deposits since outstanding agricultural loans fell only slightly in November. Lieh Jung, "Subsidiary Agricultural Loans . . . ," *CKCJ*, no. 24, 1956.

[62] In mid-January, 1957, outstanding agricultural loans were reduced to ￥2.94 billion from ￥3.03 billion at the end of 1956. Li Shao-yu, "Speech Delivered at the National Conference of Branch Bank Managers (Excerpts)," *CKCJ*, no. 6, 1957, p. 7.

[63] The increase in agricultural loans during the first eight months of 1957 was ￥0.56 billion (Table V-2, col. 1) as compared with 2.13 billion for the same months of 1956. Ch'en Hsi-yü, "Report . . . during the Brisk Season," *CKCJ*, no. 18, 1957, p. 1.

[64] PB, "Directive on the Collection of Loans in 1957," *FKHP*, V, 153–56.

[65] The target for the recall of rural loans during the brisk season (September–December) of 1957 was at first set at 0.8 billion yuan. Ch'en Hsi-yü, "Report . . . during the Brisk Season," *CKCJ*, no. 18, 1957, p. 2. This was later lowered to 0.7 billion. "Conditions in the Past Half Year, Requirements . . . ," *CKCJ*, no. 14, 1958, p. 1. Between the end of August and the end of December, the actual decline of outstanding loans was 0.27 billion (Table V-2, col. 3).

time, the absorption of deposits tended to conflict with the agricultural cooperatives' desire to direct peasant savings toward collective investment. However, the collectives were helpful to the Bank in a roundabout way. They were more willing than the peasants to deposit their centralized holdings of funds, a large share of which consisted of income to be distributed to individual members. The rise in rural deposits in the end of 1957 was mainly a result of the collectives' decision to shift the distribution date to 1958; this move effectively delayed the realization of a part of the rural purchasing power.

(2) Credit. To contract the deposit flow, the Bank relied on neutralization. It did not seriously restrict loans granted to state enterprises;[66] instead, a credit fund of 6 billion yuan was incorporated into the planned budget, thereby creating an *ex ante* offset. As it turned out, the realized budget surplus of the central government was larger, and it was wholly assigned to the credit fund.

Fiscal restraint. Besides commercial and monetary measures, which were relatively prompt and flexible, the inflationary gap was further narrowed by a more basic remedy. There was a downward adjustment of budget expenditures, and the reduction applied mainly to state investment, especially investment for basic construction.[67] Thus a fundamental cause of the inflation was removed. On top of this, other budget expenditures, such as costs of defense and administration, were cut.[68] While the scaling down of investment eased the shortage of producer's goods, the stabilization of wages[69] and the call for austerity that restrained collective consumption[70] lessened pressures in the consumer's market.

[66] The decline in commercial loans in 1956 was a result of commercial policy rather than monetary policy. In 1957, industrial and commercial loans increased despite the monetary contraction.

[67] The planned investment in basic construction for 1957 was ￥11.1 billion or 79.4 percent of that for 1956. Po I-po, "Report on the Results of Implementation . . . ," *FKHP*, VI, p. 160. In 1956, it was 162.2 percent of that of 1955. "The Basic Situation of the Implementation of the 1956 National Economic Plan . . . ," *CHCC*, no. 4, 1957, p. 2.

[68] Li Hsien-nien, the 1957 Budget Report, *FKHP*, VI, 125.

[69] Wages and employment were stabilized. However, the total wage bill was larger in 1957 because the wage reform began in April, 1956, and therefore higher wages were effective only during a part of 1956 whereas they were effective for the entire year of 1957. Po I-po, "Report on the Results of Implementation . . . ," *FKHP*, VI, pp. 171–72.

[70] The purchasing power of collective units in 1957 was reduced by 8.1 percent compared with 1956. *TCYC* Data Office, "A Survey of the Commodity Circulation in the Domestic Market in 1957," *TCYC*, no. 4, 1958, p. 24.

Partial free market and price adjustments. Finally, inflationary pressures of 1956 were in part relieved through price changes in selected areas. Several developments contributed toward these price changes. First, a limited rural free market was reopened in 1956 primarily for the purpose of stimulating the supply of subsidiary products.[71] Second, the state purchase prices for certain major agricultural items were raised in the hope of inducing growth in their output.[72] Finally, official prices for certain consumer's goods were revised in order to absorb the surplus purchasing power.[73] Thus price movements were resorted to in order to restore monetary equilibrium. These movements were designed to encourage a higher quantity of production on the one hand and remove the excessive liquidity on the other. In other words, partial open inflation was allowed to take place.

Broadly, then, a mixture of commercial, monetary, and fiscal policies was used in 1956–1957 to moderate the existing inflationary pressures and to prevent further inflation. However, open inflation could not be avoided entirely; it was merely regulated and confined to specific areas.

Concluding Remarks

Our review and measurement of the Chinese monetary performance indicate that, over the five-year period as a whole, the degree of monetary disequilibrium was mild relative to the nation's rate of economic growth. However, the path leading to this achievement was not smooth. Rather, it was one of fluctuations: of overexpansions and subsequent contractions. Certain questions may be raised with regard to these fluctuations. To begin with, it might be legitimately asked whether the short-run instability was an inherent consequence of the Chinese monetary policy that rested on the real bills principle. The Soviet experience had indicated that such a policy could cause inflation in a command

---

[71] Perkins, *Market Control and Planning . . .* , pp. 74–76; Miyashita, *The Currency and Financial System of Mainland China,* pp. 97–103.

[72] For a discussion of price adjustments, *ibid.,* pp. 97–99; Perkins, *Market Control and Planning . . .* , pp. 70–71.

[73] For example, between January and April, 1957, retail prices of pork, salt, woolens, cigarettes, oil and fat were raised. "Why Were Prices for These Commodities Raised," *HHPYK,* no. 10, 1957, pp. 110–11; "Press Conference Held by Spokesman of the State Council on the Question of Market Price," *HHPYK,* no. 10, 1957, pp. 109–10.

251

economy. In the case of Communist China, despite the permissive aura of her monetary policy, it is difficult to view the real bills principle as a major factor responsible for the inflation. In 1953 this principle had not yet been established, and in 1956 excessive credit arose not so much from inventory borrowing, since there was a decline in commercial loans even though industrial loans rose, as from the socialization movement and the discretionary wage reform. Thus, unlike that of the U.S.S.R., the Chinese inflation can not be explained by an erroneous monetary policy. Instead, it would be more correct to interpret the fluctuations as results of an eclipse of the stability consideration in favor of other competing economic goals, especially the goal of socialization.[74]

This leads to a second question: were the inflations intended? That is to ask, were price changes and the resulting forced savings purposely used as a means of financing priority programs such as socialization and investment? This question cannot be answered with certainty, but the general developments suggest the negative. Both expansions appeared unanticipated, and their origins could be traced to a mixture of inadequate macroeconomic coordinations and inexperienced planning. Furthermore, inflationary pressures were combated rather pragmatically and hastily as they appeared. All this did not signify a pre-calculated procedure. However, once monetary disequilibrium had come into existence, its correction was not allowed to take precedence over the priority programs, at least not in the short run. Under the circumstances, inflation became an expedient, an alternative to be tolerated temporarily until corrective measures could be devised, albeit it was not intended. On the other hand, over a longer period, the objective of monetary stability was not so easily sacrificed, and this, once again, contrasted to the earlier Soviet policy. Thus in 1957 investment, the very keystone of China's economic policy, was slashed in the hope of restraining inflation.

One comes to the conclusion, then, that the Chinese monetary policy in the period was directed toward the provision of short-term flexibility and long-term stability. For brief intervals monetary fluctuations, pri-

[74] Socialization considerations not only contributed greatly toward the 1956 monetary expansion but also prevented the Bank from forestalling the 1953 inflation.

marily in the form of repressed inflation, served as a stop-gap to absorb the planning and macro-coordinating mistakes. Given time, however, monetary contractions as well as adjustments of the real factors were sought, and the residual pressures were then released as open inflation.

X

SUMMARY AND CONCLUSIONS

◐ THE OBJECTIVE of this study has been to investigate the role of money and banking in China, the nature of China's monetary policy as well as whether and how her monetary mechanism has helped to maintain stability under a high rate of economic development. These questions have been examined because they are important to the understanding of the Chinese economy and immediately relevant to the economics of development.

The study began with a survey of the banking institutions. It was found that during the early years of the Communist government, existing banks were quickly transformed and subordinated to the People's Bank. The banking structure was simplified and centralized while a wide diffusion of the monolithic financial network took place. By the end of 1957, the sole institution that could directly influence the domestic supply of money was the People's Bank, with its Main Office in Peking and 20,000 branches all over the country. These branches were in turn assisted in their operations by approximately 32,000 urban savings units plus 90,000 rural credit cooperatives.

The unification of the banking system and the extension of its influence in urban areas were carried out relatively smoothly. However, the creation of supplementary financial organs in the farm areas encountered serious difficulties. There were unsuccessful attempts to establish a bank specializing in agriculture, and the development of the credit cooperative was beset with problems both financial and administrative. But despite the confusion, the People's Bank gained entry into the countryside and, broadly speaking, a monopolistic banking structure penetrated the economy.

Parallel to the organizational expansion, controls over money were gradually gathered into the hands of the People's Bank. A series of measures was adopted to shape the monetary system according to the

254

Soviet pattern. The People's Bank was made the single creator of money; commercial debts between state enterprises were banned so that the Bank became the exclusive source of credit to these enterprises; units in the state sector, enterprises and government organs alike, were required to deposit all funds except a minimal sum in the People's Bank; and withdrawals of such deposits in the form of currency were permissible only for payments to individuals, while payments to other state units had to be made via accounting transfers.

Through the implementation of these measures, the People's Bank achieved the role of the "center of cash, credit and settlement" from which the supply of money originated, into which currency held in the state sector was deposited, and through which inter-state-unit payments were effected. In addition, the Bank aspired to be a supervisory organ over the state enterprises by virtue of its ability to oversee all their monetary transactions and consequently all their non-barter economic activities. However, the enforcement of the control measures generated resistance from the enterprises, and the People's Bank was at best partially successful in serving as the monetary center and the supervisory organ. On the other hand, the goals were made evident, and the foundation of a system necessary for their attainment was laid.

As a result of the 1953–1957 developments, the money circuit was by and large separated into two levels, a bank deposit flow circulating primarily within the state sector and a currency flow serving mainly individuals and semiprivate units. The creation of money began basically with credit granted to the state enterprises, which immediately became deposits in the same bank. This new money remained in the deposit flow if used as a means of payment for transactions involving other state units. Alternatively, the deposits might be withdrawn and thus become currency-in-circulation if used to discharge obligations relating to the private and semiprivate sectors. Such currency would once more revert to the form of deposits when it flowed back into the state sector as payments for taxes or for purchases from public enterprises.

Because the crucial determinant of the money supply was the availability of bank credit, it became necessary to examine how the latter was in turn determined. Under the new system the interest rate no longer performed an allocating function, and the apportionment of bank credit rested on certain rules. The mainstream of bank loans flowed to the state enterprises. Such credit was in principle limited to the financing of working capital that was not constant in nature, whereas the regularly required working captial was to be provided by the budget. In practice, however, the Bank was at times required to finance a portion of the regularly needed working capital (called quota working capital) in the form of quota loans; and the Bank's responsibility in this area appeared shifting and uncertain. But the bulk of the bank credit was used for the financing of temporary and fluctuating capital requirements (nonquota working capital) and was called nonquota loans. For this type of credit there was in fact no limit before 1955. Thus until that year, there was a lack of bank control over the majority of the loans granted; they were, in general, extended whenever requested by the state enterprises. In 1955, an intricate structure of bank loans was erected that aimed at making the flow of bank credit dependent on the size of inventory, and the People's Bank in effect adopted the "real bills" principle as a criterion for bank loans.

A survey of the available data on bank loans has suggested that, except in 1956, the lion's share went to state commercial enterprises. The remaining portion was granted to state industrial enterprises and to the agricultural sector, with only an insignificant fraction available to private and semiprivate firms. In 1956, however, the socialization drive led to an upsurge in agricultural loans and, to a lesser extent, also in loans to private and semiprivate enterprises.

The aggregate of outstanding bank loans appeared surprisingly large; at the end of 1957, it was more than three times the size of total loans granted annually. This divergence between the two series was contradictory to the stated principle of confining bank credit to short-term financing. In managing credit, the People's Bank encountered problems in two areas that apparently added to the steep rise in outstanding loans. First, there was the persistent problem of inventory accumulations that occurred in the state enterprises. The Bank attempted repeatedly to press for the liquidation of inventory so as to reduce outstanding loans, but it did not succeed. Second, the Bank also faced difficulties in the collection of overdue agricultural loans.

256

Thus in commerce and industry, as well as in agriculture, some bank loans were not repaid. In essence, they became concealed subsidies to the receiving units.

The components of money supply, deposits and currency, have been studied separately. With regard to deposits, they were held by both the state sector and the private sector, but the predominant share was held by the former. Inside the state sector, enterprise deposits were relatively stable. Budgetary deposits, however, formed the most important component, accounting for more than half of all bank deposits, and the proportion was rising over time. One reason for the growth of budgetary deposits was asserted to be the accumulation of budget surpluses, but there is evidence that the budget surplus reported during the earlier years was to some extent more apparent than real. Beginning in 1955, the fiscal and monetary systems became better integrated and a portion of the accumulated budget surplus was allocated as "credit fund" to the People's Bank. From 1957 on, an expected amount was assigned to this fund in the planned budget each year, and the entire *ex post* budget surplus was so assigned after the fiscal year was completed. In effect, then, after 1955 the budget surplus was formally used to neutralize some of the deposits, thereby paritally offsetting the money created by the People's Bank through its loans to state enterprises.

Deposits held by the private sector were mainly personal deposits. Those of the urban areas increased steeply, and they varied more with the intensity of the savings drive conducted by the Bank than with the changes in urban income. Personal deposits from the rural areas also climbed rapidly. They were at first propagated by the Bank in the form of "preferential deposits." In 1955, however, the management of rural personal deposits was delegated to the network of credit cooperatives, and the Bank received only rural redeposits from these cooperatives. In general, the expansion in personal deposits, urban and rural, was achieved through a combination of pecuniary incentives, ideological appeals, and semi-coercions; it was thus not entirely spontaneous. This series had the highest rate of growth, surpassing even the growth in budgetary deposits.

Unlike bank loans, which were in the main based on inventory and therefore not subject to an effective quantitative limit, the amount of currency in circulation was annually restricted by a target imposed by the central government. Since bank credit could be used for wage or agricultural payments that were made in cash, the Bank had no real control over the amount of currency that entered into circulation as a result of such payments. The Bank therefore relied on various measures to reduce the use of currency and to remove currency from circulation in order to stay within the limit set by the central government. Four measures for the minimization of currency have been examined. Only one of these, the savings drive, was found to be capable of serving as a permanent instrument; the currency-absorption effects of the others were transitory in nature. This finding, plus the data on the sharp rise of personal deposits, disclosed the pivotal position of the savings drive.

A synthesis of the findings has demonstrated the way in which money supply was regulated after 1955. Money sprang from bank loans, for which the real bills principle furnished an elastic limit. Suppleness in this limit was essential because of the rural character of the economy and the lack of planning experience. In addition, the real bills principle was analytically less objectionable in the Chinese framework than in an advanced country. It did, however, permit relatively easy credit, and to counterbalance this, absorption was used. Monetary absorption rested on two instruments: the offsetting credit fund and that portion of personal savings that the Bank was able to transform into time deposits. But even personal demand deposits performed an absorption function, for their continuous growth immobilized a part of the most liquid form of money: currency. This was of immediate significance in the private sector. Thus, the tools of monetary policy operated negatively through compensation, the process being inverse to that in a free economy. Nonetheless, it constituted a means of regulating and adjusting the money supply so as to achieve economic stabilization.

To determine the results of this monetary policy, we proceeded to investigate the extent of monetary disequilibrium that actually existed in the period. A rough indicator of changes in inflationary pressures in the consumer's market has been constructed on the basis of comparative movements in the estimated aggregate supply of currency and the corresponding transactional demand, the latter having been approximated by the volume of retail sales at constant prices. According to this indicator, inflationary pressures during 1953–1957 were consistently higher than those registered by the published retail price indexes. Even so, over the period as a whole, the average degree of inflation per year was mild when viewed with the concurrent high rate of investment. In a broad sense, then, the Chinese monetary mechanism and the Chinese authorities have been fairly successful in containing the inflationary tendency associated with rapid development and in preventing a disruptive degree of monetary disequilibrium.

This overall achievement was marred, however, by short-term fluctuations, for the period contained two interludes of strong inflationary pressures in 1953 and 1956. The causes of this inflation did not lie in the monetary mechanism and policy as such, but rather in the lack of them (as in 1953) and in the temporary subordination of the stability objective to other goals considered more urgent at the time (as in 1956). The correction of these inflationary spurts, however, was motivated by monetary considerations and the fear of prolonged inflation. It was achieved through a conglomeration of monetary, fiscal, and commercial actions. In 1953, the inflationary pressures triggered the complete monopoly of trading in basic agricultural products and the consequent development of credit cooperatives for the control of rural money. In 1956, the final cure included a retrenchment in the rate of investment and the rate of economic growth.

Certain generalizations relating to the part played by money and monetary policy in Communist China can be drawn from this study.

THE ROLE OF MONEY AND BANKING

A soviet-type money and banking system had been established by 1955. Ideally, the state bank under this system could perform two functions. It could exercise microfinancial serveillance over units in the state sector where activities were guided by plans; it could also provide a means of indirect centralized control over the non-state sector through macromonetary operations. During the period of the

First Five Year Plan, however, certain basic features of the Chinese economy shaped the actual role of the People's Bank. China was an agricultural, economically decentralized society with little background, skill, or experience in planning. Given the rudimentary and experimental nature of the plans, the Bank could not adequately fulfill its first aspiration without intervening with managerial decisions of individual enterprises; yet, in these enterprises production received more emphasis then finance. Thus the Bank had to abdicate partially its first role and devote itself to the second type of control, under which the aggregate money supply and monetary policy assumed importance. But even in this macromonetary approach, the nature of the Chinese economy left its marks. When the Bank was used as a buffer to absorb shocks from plan deviations or from natural bounty or calamity, the shocks were unusually severe and the burden heavy; this caused the People's Bank and its monetary policy to occupy a more influential position than their counterparts in other Soviet-type economies. The granting of credit in China had to be extraordinarily flexible. The resulting inflationary or deflationary gap was compensated for afterwards by a certain amount of automatic accommodation via the budget and by savings coaxed from the population. When these compensations were insufficient to close the gap, non-monetary measures, including the scaling down of investment, would then be called for.

In retrospect, bank credit in China was actually used for three different purposes. Besides meeting the unpredicted and unpredictable financial needs alluded to above, it also provided a large sum of the anticipated, regular working capital, especially trading capital; in addition, it was used to subsidize the transformation of private ownership into a socialistic economy. Thus the role of money and banking had several facets. First, the People's Bank furnished the necessary suppleness and continuity in the economy and was thus essential in preventing breakdowns that originated from unplanned activities. This role was closely related to and rendered important by the characteristics of the Chinese economy. Second, money and banking formed an indirect means of socializing private productive units. Through credit financing, the transition of ownership was made more palatable and hence more rapid. However, in this instance money and banking were merely used as a temporary expedient.

Third, the People's Bank served the traditional role of mobilizing savings for investment. It was especially important in encouraging and facilitating private personal saving. However, to the extent that personal depsoits were not entirely voluntary, they assumed the nature of an adjustable quasi-tax. Nevertheless, it was more pliable than a rigid tax, and perhaps less inequitable than open inflation. In providing for investment, the Bank was very much secondary to the budget, which supplied the bulk of funds for total investment. However, the Bank was important in commercial investment; it was also important in directing rural savings to rural investment until the collectives were formed in 1956.

Finally, underlying all these aspects, there was another more basic one: the bank ensured a degree of monetary equilibrium in the economy so as to avoid excessive inflationary pressures. This was achieved by absorbing personal savings, by demanding budget savings, and by raising sufficient warnings to force a slowdown in the rate of state investment. These four different facets of the role of money and banking were not completely harmonious, and the need to reconcile them led to a monetary performance characterized by short-run flexibility and fluctuations combined with long-run relative stability.

A FUNDAMENTAL ECONOMIC PROBLEM

Judging from the 1953–1957 experience, would it be possible to eliminate the short-term fluctuations so that, in time, the economy could follow a smooth path of rapid development at a full employment level? This question brings up a fundamental problem faced by the nation. Many of the short-term fluctuations in 1953–1957 were caused by such factors as a lack of macro-coordination, inexperienced planning, or temporary drives, all of which might feasibly be improved or removed in due course. However, a major cause of the fluctuations, the harvest, would remain as long as the nation was heavily dependent on agriculture. It was to forestall this kind of instability that the providing of a commodity reserve was emphasized in China. In turn, the creation of such a buffer stock, together with a budget surplus to finance it, would mean the diversion of a part of the nation's products from immediate use and hence a less than full utilization of the available resources. The maintenance of an adequate commodity reserve was therefore in conflict with the desire for the highest possible rate of investment. Thus, analogous to the Western dilemma of full employment versus price stability, China was confronted with a basic choice between the maximum use of resources and the prevention of monetary fluctuations. The People's Bank, due to the nature of its economic role, would of course prefer the second alternative even though it meant a slower rate of growth. Therefore, like Western banking circles, the People's Bank formed the center of the forces of restraint in the Chinese economy, warning against the danger of overcommitment of resources.

THE STATUS OF MONEY AND BANKING

Although this study deals with an economic aspect of the nation, it should be noted before closing that, in China, political considerations enter into all crucial decisions. In the contest between the two conflicting demands—maximum growth rate and stability—was the People's Bank able to maintain its position? In fact, during the First Five Year Plan, shifts in the status of the People's Bank were already visible. For example, in both 1953 and 1956 monetary restraints were sacrificed for a high rate of development and socialization. However, during the five-year period as a whole, the Bank generally strengthened its position and exerted considerable influence; and the period ended on a note of triumph for the Bank, since the nation retrenched in order to restore stability in 1957. The foundation of the Bank's influence appeared to be political as well as economic, for it was not only the fear of the economic consequences of inflation but fear of its political impacts as well that provided leverage for the People's Bank. The political impacts in turn rested on the historical inflationary experience in China and the economic conditions under which the Communist Party took over the Mainland. In short, the People's Bank was more influential than it otherwise might have been because serious inflation could have eroded the political position of the government.

262

Summary and Conclusions

The resiliency of the People's Bank was demonstrated during the Great Leap and post-Great Leap eras when the pendulum's swing between two opposing policies was widened. In 1958, as political cadres attempted to control and stimulate overfull production on the basis of ideology and mass enthusiasm, monetary considerations were abandoned and the Bank's status plummeted. But the aftermath of the Leap led to a resumption of economic coordination and macromonetary control by the Bank. The recent proletarian cultural revolution once again indicated a confrontation of forces of irrational passion with passionate rationality, of romanticism with realism, and of political zeal with economic calculation. At present neither the direction of change nor the outcome is clear. However, on the basis of developments during 1953–1957, the following statement may be ventured. Insofar as decentralized, direct physical control of economic activities by cadres is impracticable, and insofar as the political strength of a government in the final analysis requires an economic base, the People's Bank and monetary control are likely to retain an important position in the Chinese economy and to continue to act as a moderating and restraining economic force.

APPENDIXES

Appendix A
Major Accounting Classifications of the People's Bank[1]

The two sides of the statement of the People's Bank were labeled "sources of funds" and "uses of funds." The accounting classifications were revised with the assistance of Soviet advisers and became effective on January 1, 1955. There were 161 items (exclusive of foreign activities) that were grouped under 29 categories. The major categories were as follows. (Roman numerals indicate the category number in the People's Bank statement.)

1. Currency in Circulation (II). This category reflected the increase or decrease in the quantity of currency in circulation, respectively called the "issuance" and the "withdrawal" of currency.

2. Gold, Silver, and Precious Articles (IV). These were considered major materialistic assets owned by the Bank. Gold, silver, and silver coins, which previously had been listed separately, were combined into one item. (It is not clear what precious articles are; presumably they are articles made of precious metals.)

3. Deposits and Loans of the State Sector (V). This category was itemized by government departments. As a rule, each department had one deposit item and one loan item, but there were exceptions.

4. Deposits and Loans of the Cooperative Sector (VI). Included in this were the supply and marketing cooperatives, the handicraft cooperatives, and others, but not the credit cooperatives or the agricultural production cooperatives.

[1] This appendix is a summary of the following article: Hsuen, "The 1955 Accounting Classifications of the State Bank," *CKCJ*, no. 23, 1954, pp. 15–16. This article does not enumerate all categories, only the major ones.

5. Deposits and Loans of the Joint Public-Private Enterprise Sector, the Private Enterprise Sector, and the Individuals' Sector (VII, VIII, IX). Because the totals were small, the joint enterprise sector and the private enterprise sector had only one deposit and one loan item each. The individuals' sector did not include the peasantry. It had three items, deposits and loans of the handicraft workers and urban savings.

6. Deposits and Loans of the Agricultural Sector (X). To facilitate the establishment of the Agricultural Bank and to provide a unified management of the agricultural sector, all items relating to rural finance were grouped together in one category that was subdivided into the state, the cooperative, and the individuals' sectors. Loans to the cooperative sector were further classified according to the form of cooperation (i.e., collectives, production cooperatives, and mutual-aid teams) so as to coordinate with the agricultural policy of the time.[2] Rural savings deposits, including preferential deposits, formed another item.[3] The pre-1955 practice of separating long-term short-term agricultural loans was eliminated for the sake of simplicity.

7. Funds to be Collected (XII). This category contained two items, "overdue loans" and "interest to be collected." The objective was to strengthen the Bank's supervisory position. These items could promptly reflect any financial difficulties encountered by the state enterprises; such difficulties were in turn indicators of unfulfilled plans.

8. Accounts with Other Financial Institutions (XVI). This included the accounts of all special banks and credit cooperatives and also the People's Insurance Company.[4]

9. Deposits of Funds for Major Repairs (XVIII). The capital maintenance reserves put aside by the state enterprises were taken out of the enterprises' deposit accounts (Category V) to form a separate category

---

[2] The main purpose of agricultural loans granted in 1955–1956 was to promote the collectivization. Since this movement was completed in 1956, the classification of loans according to the form of cooperation was eliminated in 1957. Cheng Tsu-yao, "Reasons for the 1957 Revision of Accounting Classifications," *CKCJ,* no. 23, 1956, p. 18.

[3] It is not clear whether redeposits from the rural credit cooperatives were included here or listed under Category XVI. Since the unified management of agricultural finance was emphasized, it is possible that they were included here.

[4] The People's Insurance Company was state owned, subordinated in the early years to the People's Bank and later to the Ministry of Finance. Premiums from the national compulsory insurance system were considered budgetary receipts.

during the 1955 revision.[5] This step was taken in order to tighten the Bank's supervision over the use of these capital funds and to distinguish them from the enterprise working capital. If for any reason a given enterprise was short of funds for current operations, it could no longer avoid detection by drawing on these capital reserves.

10. Accounts with Branch Banks (XIX). Accounts with branch banks had been confusing in the past. The revision attempted to classify different items in such a way as to facilitate auditing.

11. Depreciations of Fixed Assets Owned by the People's Bank (XXVI).

12. Basic Construction Funds for the People's Bank Itself (XXVII).

13. Prepaid Expenditures (XXVIII). These were the Bank's disbursements paid in advance for various purposes. Previously, such advances formed a loophole through which uncontrolled bank expenditures were made. The scope of such expenditures was now narrowed and defined more sharply. They covered such items as traveling expenses for banking personnel.

Appendix B
Data on Agricultural Loans of the People's Bank

Data on agricultural loans are confusing; sometimes more than one series is available. Loans are presented in two different forms, one in terms of the total amount granted during a period of time and the other refering to the amount outstanding at the end of a period. In addition there are the annual planned targets of loans.

Two series are available that give the total amount of loans granted. One was published in *NTCJ* in 1957 and was later quoted by Yang P'ei Hsin; the other was released in *CKCJ* in 1959. The latter series was probably revised figures. They are presented in Table B-1.

There are also two series of data for outstanding loans. It is not clear what caused this discrepancy, but it could also be due to revisions.

---

[5] Out of this pool of major repair funds came the supply for the major repair loans to the enterprises.

267

Table B-1
Total Agricultural Loans Granted by the People's Bank, 1950–1958

Year	*CKCJ* Series Million yuan (1)	Yang P'ei-hsin Series Million yuan (2)	Index 1950 = 100 (3)
1950	212.4	212.4	100.0
1951	399.5	401.5	189.0
1952	966.2	1,076.3	506.7
1953	1,051.4	1,264.0	595.1
1954	788.2	840.6	395.7
1955	1,004.2	1,004.1	472.7
1956	3,408.4	3,387.1	1,590.4
1957	2,257.4	—	—
1958	3,837.4	—	—

Sources:

Col. (1): "Agricultural Loans of 1950–1958," *CKCJ,* September 25, 1959, p. 2.

Cols. (2) and (3): Yang P'ei-hsin, "Ways to Raise Funds for Agricultural Developments in Our Country," *CCYC,* no. 1, 1958, p. 32. (Data were taken by Yang from *NTCJ,* no. 19, 1957, p. 1.)

Table B-2
Outstanding Agricultural Loans of the People's Bank, 1950–1957

	Yang P'ei-hsin Series (million yuan) End of year (1)	Index 1950 = 100 (2)	Tseng Ling Series (million yuan) End of June (3)	Increase during first half year (4)	End of year (5)
1950	94.9	100.0	—	—	80.4
1951	204.8	215.8	165.5	85.1	205.9
1952	481.6	507.4	463.6	257.7	438.0
1953	666.2	702.0	833.9	395.9	569.6
1954	782.7	824.7	932.8	363.2	758.6
1955	1,000.7	1,054.5	1,168.4	409.8	1,008.0
1956	3,029.5	3,192.1	2,840.0	1,832.0	—
1957	2,759.5	—	—	—	—

Sources:

Cols. (1) and (2): 1950–1956: Yang P'ei-hsin, "Ways to Raise Funds . . . ," *CCYC,* no. 1, 1958, p. 32. (Data were taken by Yang from *NTCJ,* no. 19, 1957, p. 1.) 1957: Li Hsien-nien, the 1958 Budget Report, *FKHP,* VII, 119.

Cols. (3) and (4): 1951–1955: Tseng Ling, "The Rural Market in the Surging Tide of Agricultural Collectivization," *CCYC,* no. 2, 1956, p. 7. 1956: Tseng Ling, "The Effects of Agricultural Collectivization on the Rural Monetary Circulation," *CCYC,* no. 6, 1956, p. 43.

Col. (5): Computed on the basis of cols. (3) and (4).

Appendix C

Table C-1
The Estimated Working Capital of State Industrial Enterprises in 1957

	Billion ￥	Percent
(1) Total industrial output for 1957, at 1952 prices	78.39	
(2) The share of total industrial output produced by state industrial enterprises, 1956		54.5
(3) Assuming the 1956 ratio remained unchanged in 1957, the total of state industrial output in 1957 would be	42.72	
(4) The ratio of working capital to total output of state industrial enterprises, 1957		18.5
(5) Working capital of state industrial enterprises, 1957	7.90	

Sources:

(1) SSB, *The Ten Great Years*, p. 14.

(2) SSB, "Communiqué on the Results of the Implementation of the 1956 National Economic Plan," *FKHP*, VI (July-December, 1957), 584.

(3) The product of items (1) and (2). (4) *JMJP*, August 5, 1958, p. 6.

(5) The product of items (3) and (4).

Appendix D

Table D-1
The Accumulation of Working Assets in the State Sector, 1952–1957
(in million yuan at 1952 prices)

Year	Total working assets (1)	Share of accumulation by the state sector* (percent) (2)	Accumulation of working assets in the state sector (3)
1952	6,910	80	5,528
1953	7,281	80	5,825
1954	7,662	80	6,130
1955	6,855	80	5,468
1956	2,094	75.5	1,581
1957	5,986	75.5	4,519
			29,051

*The share of total accumulation undertaken by the state sector was given for the years 1953 and 1956. The 1953 proportion is here applied to 1952–1955, and the 1956 proportion to 1956–1957.

Sources:

Cols. (1) and (2): Nai-Ruenn Chen, *Chinese Economic Statistics: A Handbook for Mainland China* (Chicago: Aldine, 1967; copyright © 1967 Social Science Research Council). pp. 155–56.

Col. (3): Col. (1) × col. (2).

Appendix E

Table E-1
Bank Deposits in Shanghai, 1949–1950
(million yuan)*

| | The People's Bank | | | | |
End of	From public enterprises and orga- nizations	From private enterprises and indi- viduals	From others†	Total	Private banks
July 1949	—	—	—	2.05	0.58
Jan. 1950	22.94	18.38	4.51	45.83	27.70
Feb. 1950	23.88	26.97	13.52	64.37	25.07
Mar. 1950	42.83	28.22	—	—	—
Apr. 1950	108.96	28.02	31.50	168.48	24.09

*In post-1955 new currency.
†Not specified.
Source: Liu Lang, "The Public-Private Relationship in Banking," *HHYP*, II, no. 3 (July, 1950), 615–16.

This table shows that, in late 1949, deposits in private banks in Shanghai expanded along with those of the People's Bank; the former began to decline early in 1950. The disparity in growth between the private banks and the People's Bank was particularly evident in April, 1950. This was due to the promulgation of the cash control program that required all public units to deposit their funds in the People's Bank. This program was promulgated on March 3, but the detailed regulation was not announced until April 7.

Appendix F

Table F-1 presents an inflationary index that measures the percentage relationship between social purchasing power and social commodity retail value. For any one year, an index of 100 indicates equilibrium, when it is above (or below) 100, inflationary (or deflationary) pressures exist. The index in column (3) indicates that during 1950–1957, the overall tendency was deflationary. In addition, it is surprising to note

270

Table F-1

An Inflationary Index Based on Purchasing Power and Commodity Retail Sales, 1950–1957

Year	Social purchasing power (billion yuan) (1)	Social commodity retail sales (billion yuan) (2)	Inflationary index* (3)
1950	17.66	17.06	103.5
1951	22.08	23.43	94.2
1952	27.60	27.68	99.7
1953	33.12	34.80	95.2
1954	37.67	38.11	98.8
1955	40.24	39.22	102.6
1956	46.50	46.10	100.9
1957	47.00	47.42	99.1

*Index = 100 when there are neither inflationary nor deflationary pressures.
Sources:
Col. (1): Perkins, *Market Control and Planning in Communist China* (Cambridge: Harvard University Press, 1966), p. 255.
Col. (2): SSB, *Ten Great Years,* p. 146.   Col. (3): (Col. 1 ÷ Col. 2) × 100.

that 1953, which was generally known as an inflationary year (and this was shown by all four indexes in Table IX-1 in the text) registers a rather heavy deflation here. Similarly the reported inflationary pressures of 1956 do not show up strongly; there is a more severe one in 1955 instead. Thus this inflationary index, despite its theoretical validity, tends to contradict the general body of existing information on monetary development in China.

Two reasons can be given to explain this paradox. First, to the extent that price changes were possible under conditions of monetary disequilibrium, the retail sales series reflects *ex post* data. Thus whatever amount of excessive purchasing power might have existed would have driven up prices and, consequently, the value of retail sales also. In other words, open inflation cannot be registered by this index. This may be part of the reason why the inflation of 1953 does not show up in Table F-1,[1] in that year private trade was still important and, as indicated in the first two inflationary indexes of Table IX-1, prices did rise.[2] A

[1] However, this alone does not explain why 1953 should register a deflation in the index.
[2] This argument can also be applied to 1957 when there was a price rise and for which the index shows a slight deflation.

271

second reason may be found in the way the social purchasing power is computed in China. This series is derived by deducting "non-commodity expenditures" and savings from the money income of the residents (i.e., the population). Non-commodity expenditures refer to both service expenditures (such as rent, transportation, cultural activities, and recreation) and the purchase of government bonds.[3] It is possible that in computing the social purchasing power, the planning authorities take into account the amount of goods available for retail sales so as to strike an approximate balance between the two. If so, that part of money income that could represent excessive purchasing power would not be included as "social purchasing power," but would be left as a part of non-commodity expenditures or savings instead.[4]

While the lack of data on the population's total money income and noncommodity expenditures prevents a detailed exploration into this area, the available fragments of information for 1956 and 1957 tend to substantiate the above hypothesis relating to the computation of social purchasing power. Table F-2 combines the relevant materials for these two years in order to show the broad relationships among social purchasing power, non-commodity expenditures and money income. In this table service expenditures is derived as a residual. It can be seen that, for urban residents, service expenditures amounted to between 28 and 29 percent of money income in 1956 and 1957. When bond purchase is included, the resulting non-commodity expenditures represented more than 30 percent of money income in urban areas. The question arises as to whether the amount of services actually available in the retail market was sufficient to absorb this portion of money income. There is no direct information on this point. But the actual or realized proportion of non-commodity expenditures relative to income can be broadly determined from various family budget studies undertaken in China. Table F-3 presents some of these data. Based on these data, the impression cannot be avoided that the amount of non-com-

---

[3] Nai-Ruenn Chen, *Chinese Economic Statistics,* p. 89.

[4] The government not only encouraged savings and the purchase of government bonds as anti-inflationary devices, it also emphasized an increased supply of services, such as cultural activities or recreation (concerts, opera, movies, etc.), as an anti-inflationary measure. The purchase of such services was voluntary.

Table F-2
Money Income, Purchasing Power, and Non-commodity
Expenditures, 1956 and 1957
(*in billion yuan*)

	1956	1957
A. Purchasing power:		
(1) Social purchasing power	46.5	47.0
(2) Less purchasing power of collective units*	−5.3†	−4.9†
(3) Purchasing power of residents (incl. agricultural cooperatives)	41.2	42.1
(4) Less rural purchasing power	−24.5	−25.0
(5) Purchasing power of urban residents	16.7	17.1
B. Urban residents: Money income and non-commodity expenditures:		
(6) Money income of urban residents	24.7	25.5
(7) Less bond purchase by urban residents and	−.47	−.43
(8) Increase in personal deposits	−.54	−.55
(9) Money income minus bond purchase and savings	23.7	24.5
(10) Less purchasing power of urban residents (item 5)	−16.7	−17.1
(11) Service expenditures of urban residents	7.0	7.4
(12) Service expenditures as proportion of money income, for urban residents (item 11 ÷ 6)	28.3%	29.0%
(13) Non-commodity expenditures (i.e., service expenditures plus bond purchase) as proportion of money income (the sum of items 7 and 11 ÷ item 6)	30.2%	30.7%

* Collective units include government agencies, public organizations, schools, and economic enterprises. The purchasing power of collective units refers to their monetary expenditures on consumption goods.

† These were the actual commodity purchases of collective units, with the 1956 figure computed from percentage change from 1957. A different source gives more general information and states that the collective units account for 16 percent of social purchasing power. Nai-Ruenn Chen, *Chinese Economic Statistics,* pp. 428–29. If the latter source is used, the purchasing power for collective units would be larger than shown and the resulting purchasing power of urban residents would be smaller, further accentuating the inflationary gap discussed in the text.
Sources:

(1) Table IX-2.

(2) "A Survey of the Commodity Circulation in the Domestic Market in 1957," *Stat. Res.,* no. 4, 1958, p. 24.

(4) and (7) Perkins, *Market Control and Planning in Communist China* (Cambridge, Harvard University Press, 1966), pp. 161 and 170.

(6) and (8): Table VI-9, cols. (1) and (4)

Table F-3
Selected Data on theProportion of Non-commodity Expenditures
Relative to Income, 1955 and 1956

A. National average, 1955:

    (1) Per capita income, including non-commodity expenditures — ￥183.0

    (2) Per capita income, excluding non-commodity expenditures — 148.0

    (3) Per capita non-commodity expenditures (item 1 — item 2) — ￥ 35.0

    (4) Non-commodity expenditures as percent of income (item 3 ÷ item 1) — 19.1%

B. Workers and employees in Kirin Province, 1956:

    (5) Per capita income — ￥173.0

    (6) Per capita non-commodity expenditures — 25.6

    (7) Non-commodity expenditures as percent of income (item 6 ÷ item 5) — 14.8%

C. Workers in Shanghai, 1956:

    (8) Service expenditures as percent of consumption expenditures* — 23.0%

D. Workers and employees compared with peasants, 1955:

    (9) Per capita service expenditures as percent of consumption expenditures:

        Workers and employees — 20.0%

        Peasants — 5.0%

*Consumption expenditures is presumably smaller than money income by the amount of savings.

Source: Nai-Ruenn Chen, *Chinese Economic Statistics* (Chicago: Aldine, 1967; copyright © 1967 Social Science Research Council), pp. 430, 433, 435–36.

modity expenditures actually spent was less than 20 percent of money income for the nation as a whole. The proportion was higher for urban residents, but even in this category, the ratio could not be more than 25 percent, and this is considerably lower than the percentage presented in item 13 of Table F-2. Thus the evidence suggests that the portion of money income available for non-commodity expenditures during 1956 and 1957 was higher than the portion of money income so spent. In other words, there was a gap of excessive purchasing power in the service (or non-commodity) market that was excluded from the official social purchasing power series. Under the circumstances, an inflationary index based on this series of purchasing power would be meaningless.[5]

To sum up, the purchasing-power approach to measuring inflationary pressures is sterile. Logically, open inflation involving price changes will not be reflected by it. While this approach can theoretically register repressed inflation, in practice it is rendered inapplicable by the nature of the Chinese data on social purchasing power.

[5] Possibly it is more correct to consider the social purchasing power as a series of planned, *ex ante* commodity retail sales, while the social commodity retail sales represent the realized sales. In that case the inflationary index computed above would become an index of accuracy in planning in the commodity retail market.

275

1921–1957 (Collection of Shanghai Price Data before and after the Liberation: 1921–1957). Shanghai: People's Press, 1958.

State Council. *Chung-hua jen-min kung-ho-kuo fa-kuei huei-pien (Collection of Laws and Regulations of the People's Republic of China).* Volume I covers the period of September, 1954 to June, 1955; thereafter semiannual. Peking: Legal Press.

State Statistical Bureau. *Wei-ta ti shih-nien (The Ten Great Years).* Peking: People's Press, 1959.

Su Yuan-lei. *Kuo-min ching-chi shih-yung tz'u-tien (Practical Dictionary on the National Economy).* Shanghai: Ch'un-ming Press, 1953.

Ti-i wu-nien-chi-hua chiang-hua (Talks on the First Five Year Plan). Prepared by the Editorial Department of *Ta Kung Pao.* Peking: Common Readers Press, 1955.

Tseng Ling. *Chung-hua jen-min kung-ho-kuo huo-pi chih-tu ti you-yueh-hsing (The Superiority of the Currency System of the People's Republic of China).* Peking: Financial and Economic Press, 1955.

Tsi Ch'ün. *Jen-min yin-hang ti hsien-chin chi-hua (The Cash Plan of the People's Bank).* Peking: Financial and Economic Press, 1964.

Wo-kuo she-huei chu-i chien-she-chung ti jo-kan ching-chi wen-t'i (Certain Economic Questions on the Socialist Construction of China). Peking: Chinese Youth Press, 1959.

Wu Ch'eng-hsi. *Chung-kuo ti yin-hang (Banks in China).* Shanghai: Commercial Press, 1935.

B. GOVERNMENT DIRECTIVES AND REGULATIONS

The Agricultural Bank of China. "Temporary Measures on the Management of Loans to Agricultural Collectives," *FKHP* (July–December, 1955), II, 545–46.

Government Administration Council. "Decision on the Implementation of Cash Control over State Organs," *Central TCCT* (1950), I, 237–38.

———. "Decision on the System of Final Accounts, the Auditing of Budgetary Estimates, Engineering Plans for Capital Investments, and Monetary Control," *Central TCCT* (1951), II, 271–73.

———. "Decision on the Unification of State Financial and Economic Work," *Central TCCT* (1950), I, 30.

———. "Directive on Certain Questions Relating to the Settlement of Agricultural Loans," *JMST,* 1955, pp. 441–42.

———. "Directive on Measures for 'the Implementation of Monetary Control' and 'Measures for the Compilation of Monetary Receipt and Expenditure Plan,'" *Central TCCT* (1951), II, 549–76.

"Joint Directive of the Central Ministry of Commerce and the Main Office of the People's Bank," *CKCJ,* no. 11 (1953), pp. 1–5.

Ministry of Finance. "Report on the Nature of Organization and the Problems of Administration and Decentralization Regarding the Bank of Construction and the Bank of Communications," *FKHP* (January–June, 1958), VII, 279–80.

——. Ministry of Finance and the People's Bank. "Notice on the Disposition of Several Major Problems Regarding the Authorization of Quota Working Capital," *FKHP* (July–December, 1959), X, 252–53.

——. "Regulations on the Abolition of Existing Commercial Credit within the State Commercial Network and between This Network and Other Organs," *FKHP* (September, 1954–June, 1955), I, 278–83.

——. "Supplementary Regulations on the Transfer to the People's Bank of the Unified Management of State Enterprise Working Capital," *FKHP* (January–June, 1959), IX, 121–27.

Ministry of Trade, The Chinese National Federation of Cooperatives, and the People's Bank. "Directive on the Extension of Credit to Public-Private Stores, Cooperative Stores and Mutual-Aid Teams," *FKHP* (July–December, 1956), IV, 292–95.

National Economic Commission. "Report on the Adjustments of Surplus Inventory of the Enterprises," *FKHP* (January–June, 1957), V, 87–90.

"Order of the GAC of the Central People's Government on the Strengthening of Supervision and Control over the Bank of China," *Central TCCT* (1950), I, 267.

People's Bank. "Directive on the Collection of Loans in 1957," *FKHP* (January–June, 1957), V, 153–56.

——. "Directive on Rural Financial Works in the Second Quarter of 1953," *CJFKHP* (1953), pp. 90–91.

——. "Notice on the Question of Covering the 1959 Quota Working Capital of Local Enterprises with Budgetary Grants," *FKHP* (July–December, 1959), X, 270–71.

——. "Notice on State Council Regulations Regarding Improvements of Financial Administration in Respect to Capital Construction," *CJFKHP* (1958–60), *JPRS* #19,499, pp. 257–259.

——. "Report on the Abolition of Commercial Credit among State Industrial Enterprises and between State Industrial Enterprises and Other State Enterprises, Substituting These Credits with Bank Settlement," *FKHP* (September, 1954–June, 1955), I, 270–73.

——. "Report on the Adjustment on Prevailing Interest Rates for Loans," *FKHP* (July–December, 1957), VI, 344–47.

——. "Report on the Need to Further Strengthen Planning in Cash Receipts and Expenditures," *FKHP* (July–December, 1959), X, 275–77.

———. "Supplementary Regulations on the Reduction of Interest Rates for Savings Deposits and the Unification of Interest Rates on Bank Loans," *JMST,* 1959, p. 379.

———. "The Task of the State Bank in 1950," *Central TCCT* (1952), III, 183–190.

———. Shanghai Branch. "Regulations on Fixed Amount Deposit," *East China TCCT* (1951), pp. 496–97.

State Council. "Communiqué on the Abolition of the Agricultural Bank of China," *CJFKHP* (1957), pp. 87–88.

———. "Decision on the Establishment of the People's Bank of Construction of China," *JMST,* 1955, pp. 440–41.

———. "Decision on Wage Reform," *HHPYK,* no. 15, 1956, pp. 175–76.

———. "Directive on Certain Questions Regarding Rural Financial Works," *FKHP* (July–December, 1956), IV, 302–305.

———. "Directive on the Compilation of the 1958 State Draft Budget," *FKHP* (July–December, 1957), VI, 330.

———. "Directive on the Correction of Compulsory Phenomena in the Works of Banks and Credit Cooperatives," *HHPYK,* no. 15, 1956, pp. 4–5.

———. "Directive on the People's Bank's Report Relating to the Settlement of Agricultural Loans," *CKCJ,* no 23, 1957, pp. 4–5.

———. "Directive on Strengthening the Bank's Leadership in Savings and Positively Developing Personal Deposits," *FKHP* (January–June, 1959), IX, 137.

———. "Order on the Issuance of the New People's Currency and the Withdrawal of Existing People's Currency," *JMST,* 1956, pp. 531–32.

———. "Regulation on the Standard of Classification of Urban and Rural Areas," *FKHP* (July–December, 1955), II, 411–17.

———. "Regulations on the Implementation of Fixed Dividend Rate in Public-Private Joint Enterprise," *HHPYK,* no. 5, 1956, p. 70.

———. "Regulations on Several Problems Relating to the Credit Departments of the People's Communes and on the Question of Working Capital for State Enterprise," *FKHP* (July–December, 1958), VIII, 156–58.

———. "Resolution Concerning Spring Ploughing and Production," *FKHP* (September, 1954–June, 1955), I, 368–76.

———. "Supplementary Regulations," *FKHP* (January–June, 1959), IX, 121–27.

"Temporary Measures on the Control of Private Monetary Enterprises in North China," *Central TCCT* (1950), I, 267–70.

C. OFFICIAL REPORTS AND SPEECHES

Ch'en Hsi-yü. "Report to the Conference on Financial Works during the Brisk Season" (excerpts), *CKCJ,* no. 18, 1957, pp. 1–5.

————. "Report to the Conference of Branch Bank Managers on Last Year's Conditions and This Year's Tasks," *CKCJ,* no. 6, 1957, pp. 1–3.

Chou En-lai. "Report on Government Work," (1) June, 1957: *FKHP* (July–December, 1957), VI, 61–108; (2) April, 1959: *FKHP* (January–June, 1959), IX, 3–44.

————. "Report on the Proposal for the Second Five Year Plan for Development of the National Economy," *Literature of the Eighth National Congress of the Communist Party of China.* Peking: People's Press, 1956, pp. 120–21.

Hu Ching-yün. "Concluding Report Delivered at the Conference on State Industrial Credit and Settlement," *HHYP,* no. 4, 1955, pp. 146–49.

————. "Further Implement Currency Control," *HHYP,* no. 3, 1951, pp. 616–17.

————. "Report to the National Conference of Outstanding Worker's Representatives on Savings," *CKCJ,* no. 8, 1956, pp. 5–9.

————. "Report to the Second National Conference on the State Commercial Credit System," *HHYP,* no. 7, 1955, pp. 192–96.

————. "Speech at the Conference of Monetary Workers for the Exchange of Advanced Experiences," *CKCJ,* no. 8, 1953, pp. 6–7.

Li Hsien-nien. Annual report on the implementation of the previous year's budget and on the draft budget for the current year: (1) The 1955 Budget Report, *FKHP,* (July–December, 1955), II, 489–522; (2) The 1956 Report, *FKHP,* (January–June, 1956), III, 206–32; (3) The 1957 Budget Report, *FKHP,* (July–December, 1957), VI, 108–44; (4) The 1958 Budget Report, *FKHP,* (January–June, 1958), VII, 113–41; (5) The 1959 Budget Report, *FKHP,* (January–June, 1959), IX, 63–74; (6) The 1960 Budget Report, *FKHP,* (January–June, 1960), XI, 33–49.

Li Shao-yü. "Report to the National Conference of Outstanding Workers' Representatives on Rural Finance," (excerpts) *CKCJ,* no. 15, 1956, pp. 2–4.

————. "Speech Delivered at the National Conference of Branch Bank Managers (excerpts)," *CKCJ,* no. 6, 1957, pp. 7–9.

Liu Cho-fu. "Concluding Report to the Second National Conference on the State Commercial Credit System (excerpts)," *HHYP,* no. 7, 1955, pp. 196–99.

Nan Han-ch'en. "Report to the Conference Commemorating the Second Anniversary of the People's Bank of China," *HHYP,* January, 1951, pp. 617–19.

————. "Report to the First National Conference on Rural Finance, May 10 1951," *Central TCCT* (1952), III, 240–57.

————. "Report regarding the National Joint Financial Conference," *Central TCCT* (1951), II, 538.

Po I-po. "Report on the Draft 1958 National Economic Plan," *FKHP,* (January–June, 1958), VII, 143–76.

————. "Report on the Results of Implementation of the 1956 National Economic Plan and the Draft 1957 National Economic Plan," *FKHP* (July–December, 1957), VI, 145–79.

————. Reports on the State Budget: (1) "The Planned Budget for 1950," *Central TCCT* (1950), I, 90–93; (2) "The Estimated Results of the 1951 Budget and the Planned Budget for 1952," *JMJP*, August 11, 1952; (3) "The Estimated Results of the 1952 Budget and the Planned Budget for 1953," *JMST*, 1955, pp. 279–86.

State Statistical Bureau. Annual communiques on the previous year's achievements or on the fulfillments of the previous year's plan: (1) for 1952, *JMST*, 1955, pp. 419–23; (2) for 1953, *JMST*, 1955, pp. 424–28; (3) for 1954, *FKHP* (July–December, 1955), II, 858–72; (4) for 1955, *FKHP* (January–June, 1956), III, 603–13; (5) for 1956, *FKHP* (July–December, 1957), VI, 583–94; (6) for the First Five Year Plan (1953–1957), *FKHP* (January–June, 1959), IX, 288–300; (7) for 1958, *FKHP* (January–June, 1959), IX, 300–11.

————. "Report on the Results of Implementation of the First Five Year Plan (1953–1957) of National Economic Development," *FKHP* (January–June, 1959), IX, 288–300.

Teng Hsiao-p'ing. "Report on the Planned Budget for 1954," *JMST*, 1955, pp. 428–33.

Teng Tzu-hui. "Speech Delivered at the National Conference of Outstanding Workers' Representatives on Rural Finance," *HHPYK*, no. 19, 1956, pp. 78–82.

Ts'ao Chü-ju. "Concluding Report Delivered at the Conference of Branch Bank Managers," *CKCJ*, no. 1, 1958, pp. 3–5.

————. "Summary Report at the Conference of Branch Bank Managers," *CKCJ*, no. 7, 1957, pp. 1–3.

D. ARTICLES

Only articles cited in the text are included.

"Absorb Personal Deposit from the Peasants," editorial, *TKP*, December 12, 1957.

"The Actual Policy of Basic Construction Loans to the Agricultural Collectives," CKCJ, no. 7, 1956, p. 2.

"The Agricultural Bank of China Formally Inaugurated in Peking," *TKP*, March 26, 1955.

"Agricultural Loans of 1950–1958," *CKCJ*, September 25, 1959, p. 2.

"The Basic Situation of the Implementation of the 1956 National Economic Plan and an Explanation of the 1957 Draft Plan," *CHCC*, no. 4, 1957, p. 3.

"A Brief Summary of Works on Savings During the Period of the First Five Year Plan," *CKCJ*, no. 5, 1958, pp. 24–26.

Bureau of Rural Finance of the People's Bank. "Opinions on the Several Procedures for the Development of Preferential Deposits from Grain Sales," *CKCJ*, no. 2, 1954, p. 6.

———. "Positively Develop Preferential Savings for Grain Sales," *CKCJ,* no. 23, 1953, p. 4.

Bureau of State Enterprise Credit, People's Bank. "How to Begin to Implement the 'Temporary Measures on Short-Term Loans to State Commerce,'" *CKCJ,* no. 8, 1953, pp. 14–15.

Bureau of State Industrial Credit, People's Bank. "The Condition of Industrial Credits in 1957 and the Arrangements for 1958," *CKCJ,* no. 3, 1958, pp. 11–14.

———. "Summary of Work on the Experimentations of the New Draft Regulation on Industrial Credit and on the Classification of Loans," *CKCJ,* no. 11, 1955, pp. 11–13.

Chan Wu. "How the Bank of China Coordinated the Drive to Develop Private Business," *CKCJ,* no. 9, 1951, p. 24.

Chang P'ing-tzu. "Strengthen Financial Supervision over Public-Private Enterprises," *TKP,* September 18, 1955.

Chang Yuan-yuan. "Rural Credit Cooperatives Urgently Needed Further Development," *CCCP,* no. 8, 1952, pp. 5–6.

"The Change of the Shanghai Financial Market in the Past Four Years," *CCCP,* no. 22, 1953, p. 23.

"The Change in Workers' Standard of Living in Shanghai during the Past Twenty-Seven Years," *TCKT,* no. 13, 1957, pp. 6–7.

Chao Chih-ch'eng. "Abolish Commercial Credit, Improve the Settlements of Payments of State Enterprises," *TKP,* May 7, 1955.

———. "On the Question of Credit to State Enterprises," *CKCJ,* no. 10, 1953, pp. 3–4.

CHCC Data Office. "The Situation of Labor Wages in 1956," *HHPYK,* no. 10, 1957, p. 116.

Ch'en Hsi-yü. "Notes from Studying 'Soviet Credit Reform,'" *CJCK,* no. 79, in *TKP,* June 20, 1955.

Ch'en Ju-lung, "On the Question of Balancing State Budget and Bank Credit," *TC,* no. 4, 1957, p. 4.

Ch'en Yang-ch'ing. "On the Nature of the State Bank," *CKCJ,* no. 21, 1953, pp. 17–18, 26.

———. "On the Work of the State Bank," *CKCJ,* no. 11, 1953, p. 1.

———. "On the Work of the State Bank from the Viewpoint of Materialism," *CKCJ,* no. 12, 1955, pp. 12–22.

Cheng K'ang-ning. "Improve Labor Wages Planning Works by Summarizing the 1956 Experience," *CHCC,* no. 8, 1957, pp. 1–12.

Cheng Po-pin. "The Role of State Loan on the Promotion of Agricultural Collectivization," *HCS,* no. 12, 1956, pp. 8–12.

Cheng Tsu-yao. "Reasons for the 1957 Revision of Accounting Classifications," *CKCJ,* no. 23, 1956, p. 18.

Ch'i Hsien and Liu Shan-chu. "On Bank Expenditures and Actual Expenditures," *TC,* no. 8, 1957, pp. 17–18.

Chiang Shih-Tsi. "Pay Attention to the Problem of Loan Repayments from the Cadres," *NTCJ,* no. 24, 1956, pp. 14–15.

Chiang T'ieh-shui. "Bank Credit Must Serve the Accelerated Developments of Production," *TCYC,* no. 7, 1958, pp. 36–38.

Ch'ü Shen. "Problems and Conditions of Rural Credit Works," *CKCJ,* no. 13, 1956, p. 8.

————. "Work on the Payments of This Year's Grain and Cotton Preferential Deposits Must Be Performed Well," *CJCK,* no. 67, in *TKP,* February 28, 1955.

"Commodity Turnover in the Domestic Market in 1957," *Stat. Res.,* no. 4, 1958, p. 24.

"Conditions in the Past Half Year; Requirements for the Next Half Year," *CKCJ,* no. 14, 1958, pp. 1–2.

"Conference of Branch Bank Managers of the People's Bank," *CKCJ,* no. 4, 1956, p. 3.

"Continue to Struggle for the Fulfillment of the Bank's Tasks during the Brisk Season," *CKCJ,* no. 22, 1957, pp. 1–3.

"Correctly Develop the Supervisory Function of the Bank," *JMST,* 1962, pp. 211–12.

"Credit Cooperative Enterprises Are Rapidly Growing," *JMST,* 1955, pp. 443–44.

"Data on China's Population, 1949–1956," *TCKT,* no. 11, 1957, p. 24.

"Data from a Survey of Rural Family Income and Expenditures in 1954," *TCKT,* no. 10, 1957, pp. 31–32.

"The Discussion of Commercial Credit Work in the Conference of Branch Bank Managers," *CKCJ,* no. 6, 1957, pp. 3–6.

"The Distribution of State Allocated Resources during the Past Years," *TCKT,* no. 13, 1957, pp. 29 and 31.

"Do Well in the Work of Currency Conversion," *JMJP,* March 1, 1955.

"Does the People's Currency Serve as a Store of Value?," *CKCJ,* no. 4, 1957, pp. 4–5.

"Endeavor to Recall Expired Agricultural Loans and to Absorb Rural Deposits," *CKCJ,* no. 24, 1956, pp. 2–4.

"Excerpts of Discussions on This Year's Bank Tasks in the National Conference of Branch Bank Managers," *CKCJ,* no. 2, 1958, pp. 1–6.

"Explanations of Several Questions on Preferential Savings for Grain Sales," *CKCJ,* no. 1, 1954, p. 3.

"Extend the New System of Credit and Settlement for State Industry; Promote Enterprise Economic Accounting," (editorial) *TKP,* February 17, 1955.

Fei Chin-jen. "Help the Commercial Department to Implement Quota Control," *CKCJ,* no. 5, 1958, pp. 15–16.

Feng Hsi-hsi. "The Rise of Our National Economy as Seen through the State Budget," *TCKT,* no. 12, 1957, pp. 28–33.

Feng Li-ti'en. "Financial Planning," *CHCC,* no. 8, 1956, pp. 29–33.

"The First Meeting of Branch Bank Managers of the Agricultural Bank of China," *JMST,* 1964, pp. 523–24.

"Further Improve Cash Control," *CKCJ,* no. 9, 1957, pp. 10–11.

"The General Development of Credit Cooperatives and Their Operations," *CKCJ,* September 25, 1959, p. 2.

"The Glorious Performance of Fiscal and Financial Works in 1958," *JMST,* 1959, p. 360.

"Great Developments in People's Monetary Affairs," *JMST,* 1958, p. 571.

Han Ch'uan. "Independent Credit Cooperatives Are Still Necessary after the Agricultural Collectivization," *CKCJ,* no. 6, 1957, p. 21.

Han Lei. "The Meaning and Functions of the Currency Conversion," *HH,* February, 1955, pp. 23–24.

He Li-Ch'iu. "Who Should Manage the Credit Cooperative?" *CKCJ,* no. 6, 1957, pp. 23–24.

Ho Chuan. "An Opinion on the Improvement of State Industrial Loans," *CKCJ,* no. 18, 1956, pp. 20–21.

Ho Wei. "The Real Nature of the Rightist Opposition to the Policy of State Monopoly in Purchases and Sales," *HH,* no. 14, 1957, pp. 14–16.

"How to Manage the Productive Expenditure Loans to the Agricultural Collectives," *CKCJ,* no. 7, 1956, p. 3.

Hsiao Fu. "Is It the Business of Bank Credit to Serve or to Supervise?" *TCYC,* no. 5, 1958, pp. 15–17.

Hsin. "Contradictions in the Works of Commercial Credits," *CKCJ,* no. 13, 1957, pp. 9–10.

Hsin Chin. "Do Well in the Work of State Enterprises' Credit and Agricultural Loans," *CCCP,* no. 23, 1953, p. 6.

Hsü Yi *et al.* "On the Present System of Management of Working Capital," *CCYC,* no. 7, 1958, pp. 161–68.

Hsüen Sheng. "The 1955 Accounting Classification of the State Bank," *CKCJ,* no. 23, 1954, pp. 15–16.

Hu Ching-yün. "Improve Credit Work, Help Enterprises to Economize Capital," *HHYP,* no. 9, 1955, pp. 183–84.

———. "Strengthen Credit Supervision, Endeavor to Enforce Austerity, and Oppose Waste," *CJCK,* no. 15, 1955, pp. 4–5.

Hu Hou-jen. "The Relationship between the Cash Plan and the Credit Plan," *CKCJ,* no. 1, 1957, pp. 12–14.

Hu Li-chiao. "Do Well the Rural Financial Works; Effectively Support the Collective Economic Sector," *JMST,* 1963, pp. 349–52.

Huang Ju-chi. "A Talk on the Contradiction between the Bank and the Enterprises," *CKCJ,* no. 15, 1957, p. 15.

Huang Ta. "Principles of Bank Credit and the Circulation of Money," *CCYC,* no. 9, 1962, pp. 1–7.

————. "The People's Currency Is a Symbol of a Commodity Currency with Intrinsic Value," *CCYC,* no. 4, 1957, pp. 64–73.

Huang Ya-kuang. "A Lecture Delivered at the Training Class for the Administration of State Budgetary Receipts and Expenditures (Excerpts)," *CKCJ,* no. 22, 1955, pp. 2–3.

"An Important Measure on the State's Support to Agricultural Production," editorial, *TKP,* March 27, 1955.

"An Important Measure on the Strengthening of Control over Enterprise Working Capital," *JMST,* 1961, pp. 216–17.

"Improve the Supply of Producer's Goods through Works on Bank Credit," *NTCJ,* no. 10, 1956, pp. 18–19.

"Increase in Urban Savings in the Past Two Years Equals That of Previous Five Years," *JMST,* 1960, p. 373.

"Interest Rates on Deposits and Loans Are Lowered," *JMST,* 1956, pp. 536–37.

"Issue Rural Loans Correctly," editorial, *CKCJ,* no. 6, 1957, pp. 10–11.

Jen Hsi-peng and Kung Sung-chou. "An Understanding of the Measures on Loans for Agricultural Purchases to Basic-Level Supply and Marketing Cooperatives," *CKCJ,* no. 10, 1955, pp. 8–9.

Jung Tzu-ho. "A Lecture Delivered at the Training Class for the Administration of State Budgetary Receipts and Expenditures (Excerpts)," *CKCJ,* no. 22, 1955, pp. 1–2.

————. "On the Balance of State Budgetary Receipts and Expenditures, State Credit Receipts and Expenditures, and Commodity Supply and Demand," *TC,* no. 6, 1957, pp. 1–3.

Kao Chi-min and Wang Chung-ho. "Views on the Revision of Loans for Prepayments of Commodity Purchases," *CKCJ,* no. 15, 1955, pp. 11–13.

Kao Hsiang. "On the Function of the State Bank in Socialist Construction," *CCYC,* no. 10, 1962, pp. 12–23.

Ko Chih-ta. "The Arrangement and Control of Budgetary Funds and Credit Funds," *JMST,* 1961, p. 216.

————. "The Nature of the National Budget in Our Country and Its Function in the Transitional Period," *CCYC,* no. 3, 1956, pp. 67–80.

————. "On the Connection between the State Budget and the Credit Plan," *TKP,* May 31, 1955.

————. "On the Inter-Connection and Equilibrium of Budget, Credit and Material Goods," *CCYC,* no. 1, 1958, pp. 8–17.

—— and Wang T'uan. "On Several Relationships in Fiscal and Monetary Works," *JMST*, 1962, p. 201.

Kuan Chung-yün and Tai Ch'ien-ting. "The Great Monetary Achievements in China under the Guidance of Marxism-Leninism," *CJYC*, no. 1, 1958, pp. 52–65.

Kuo Kuang Ts'ung. "Views on the State Budgetary Surplus," *CCYC*, no. 8, 1959, pp. 58–62.

"Laxity in Cash Control," *CKCJ*, no. 9, 1957, pp. 10–11.

Li Ch'ang-ch'in. "The 'Circulation Notes' Should Not Be Legalized," *CKCJ*, no. 23, 1956, pp. 19–20.

Li Cho-wen. "From the Principle of Credit Repayment to the Supervisory Function of the Bank," *JMST*, 1962, pp. 212–13.

Li Hsien-nien. "On Several Questions of Fiscal and Monetary Works," *HC*, no. 1, 1960, pp. 9–11; also in *JMST*, 1960, pp. 359–60.

Li Shao-yü. "Improve Rural Financial Works and Support Agricultural Collectivization," *HH*, March, 1956, pp. 27–28.

——. "Several Questions on Credit to State Commerce," *CKCJ*, no. 17, 1955, pp. 9–11.

——. "Tasks of Rural Finance in 1958," *CKCJ*, no. 2, 1958, pp. 6–8.

—— and Ch'en Shih. "Correctly Implement the New State Commercial Credit System," *JMJP*, August 7, 1955.

Liang Li-po. "The Condition and Problems of the 'Three Cooperatives in One' Experiment in Lientang County," *CKCJ*, no. 20, 1957, pp. 22–24.

Lieh Jung. "Subsidiary Agricultural Loans Should Not Be Granted Blindly," *CKCJ*, no. 24, 1956, pp. 6–7.

Lin Lang-t'ien. "Do Well in This Year's Work on Foodgrains Credits," *CKCJ*, no. 12, 1955, pp. 23–24.

Lin Tsi-k'eng. "On the Function of the Law of Circulation of Money under Socialism," *CCYC*, no. 2, 1963, pp. 24–30.

——. "On the Determination of the Required Quantity of Currency," *TCYC*, no. 9, 1958, pp. 38–43.

Lin Tsi-tsin. "Views on the Investigation and Analysis of the Aggregate Credit Plan," *CKCJ*, no. 13, 1955, pp. 11–13.

"Listen to the Opinions of the Enterprises on the Improvements of the Credit and Settlement Systems," *CKCJ*, no. 16, 1956, pp. 19–20.

Liu Lang. "The Public-Private Relationship in Banking," *HHYP*, no. 3, 1950, 615–16.

Liu Yung Hua. "Public Finance in Communist China, 1963," *China Monthly* (Union Research Institute, Hong Kong), 1964, pp. 54–56.

Lo Chün. "Certain Questions on the Credit System of the Supply and Marketing Cooperatives," *CKCJ*, no. 14, 1955, pp. 4–7.

Lu Han Ch'uan. "On the Equilibrium of Budgetary Receipts and Expenditures,

Credit Receipts and Expenditures, and the Supply of Commodities," *CKCJ*, no. 10, 1957, pp. 2–5.

Lu T'ai. "Conditions of Rural Currency Circulation during the First Half Year," *CKCJ*, no. 14, 1956, pp. 10–11.

Ma Yin-ch'u. "The Superiority and Characteristics of the New Chinese Currency System," *JMJP*, March 9, 1955.

Main Office, Agricultural Bank. "How to Manage Loans to Agricultural Producer's Cooperatives," *CKCJ*, no. 6, 1956, p. 5.

Main Office, People's Bank. "Major Tasks of the State Bank in 1951," *Central TCCT* (1952), III, 199.

—— "The Task of the State Bank in 1950," *Central TCCT* (1952), III, 183–200.

"The Main Task of the People's Bank in 1955," *HHYP*, no. 6, 1955, pp. 142–44.

"The Mushroom Growth of Credit Cooperation Enterprises during the First Five Year Plan," *CKCJ*, no. 3, 1958, p. 22.

"National Conference of Branch Bank Managers Convened by the Main Office of the People's Bank," *CKCJ*, no. 4, 1956, pp. 2–3.

"New Measures Are Implemented on the Management of Commercial Enterprise Working Capital," *JMST*, 1962, p. 210.

"The Objects, Uses, Amounts, and Durations of the Poor Peasant Cooperation Fund Loans," *CKCJ*, no. 7, 1956, pp. 3–4.

"On the Goal and Functions of Credit to State Commerce," *CKCJ*, no. 5, 1957, pp. 13–15.

"On the Policy of Capital Supply through Commercial Credit and Other Questions," *CKCJ*, no. 6, 1957, pp. 19–20.

"On Public Welfare Loans to the Agricultural Collective and Individual Members," *CKCJ*, no. 7, 1956, p. 5.

"The People's Bank Lowers the Interest Rate for Agricultural Loans," *JMST*, 1961, p. 226.

Po Hsiang. "Why Do We Establish the Agricultural Bank of China?" *HHYP*, no. 5, 1955, pp. 176–78.

"Positively Participate in Social Savings," editorial, *JMJP*, March 4, 1957, reprinted in *HHPYK*, no. 7, 1957, pp. 86–87.

"The Present Conditions of Loans to the State Commercial System (Summarized Report)," *CKCJ*, no. 11, 1953, pp. 17–18.

"Press Conference Held by Spokesman of the State Council on the Question of Market Price," *HHPYK*, no. 7, 1957, pp. 109–10.

"Private Monetary Enterprises in Various Areas Formed Loan Syndicates," *HHYP*, no. 2 1950, p. 376.

"Put Temporarily Unused Fund into Savings," *HHPYK*, no. 18, 1959, p. 129.

"The Quality and Quantity of Works on the Allocation of Funds and the Supervision of Basic Construction Must Be Raised," editorial, *TKP*, March 6, 1955.

"Quickly Correct the Phenomenon of Wasting Agricultural Loans," *NTCJ*, no. 8, 1956, pp. 6–7.

"A Review of Market Price in the First Quarter of 1957," *TCKT*, no. 11, 1957, pp. 26–27.

Shao Ch'iu-ming. "The Management of Industrial Loans for Major Repairs," *CKCJ*, no. 2, 1956, pp. 19–20.

——— . "Prevent Industrial Enterprises from Purchasing and Stocking Materials Blindly," *CKCJ*, no. 4, 1957, p. 13.

Shen Chi-yen. "An Opinion on the Present Work of Loans to the State Commercial System," *CKCJ*, no. 11, 1953, pp. 7–11.

——— . "Strengthen the Credit and Settlement Works of State Commerce, Help Enterprises to Economize in the Use of State Capital," *CKCJ*, no. 15, 1955, pp. 5–8.

——— . "The Superiority of Socialist Credit Principles Was Revealed through the Implementation of New Measures on Commercial Loans," *CKCJ*, no. 13, 1955, pp. 7–9.

Shen Ch'ün. "To Exert Leadership in Rural Deposit Work," *CKCJ*, no. 1, 1954, p. 1.

Shen Yü-chieh. "The Meaning and Functions of the Special Loan for Accumulated Inventory to State Industries," *CJCK*, #98 in *TKP*, Decempber 29, 1955.

——— . "Work on the Extension of the New Regulations of State Industrial Loans," *CJCK*, #97 in *TKP*, December 22, 1955.

Shih Tzu-kuang. "The Main Task of State Commercial Credit and Settlements in 1958," *CKCJ*, no. 2, 1958, pp. 9–10.

Shih Wu. "A Discussion on the Foundation of the People's Currency and the Marxian Theory of Money," *CCYC*, no. 2, 1957, pp. 36–50.

Shu. "An Understanding of the Starting Amounts for Settlements," *CJCK*, #78 in *TKP*, May 30, 1955.

"The State Bank Granted Eight Billion Yuan of Agricultural Loans during the Period of the First Five Year Plan," *CKCJ*, no. 2, 1958, p. 23.

"State Bank Personnel Should Endeavor to Complete the Central Tasks of the Second Half Year," *CJCK*, no. 86, in *TKP*, September 22, 1955.

State Statistical Bureau. "Statistical Materials on Agricultural Collectivization of the Distribution of Products in Cooperatives in 1955," *HHPYK*, no. 20, 1956, pp. 63–65.

"The State's Important Assistance to the Peasants," *SSST*, no. 7, 1956, p. 39.

"Statistical Data on the Improvement of Living Conditions of Workers and Employees," *TCKT*, no. 14, 1957, pp. 13–14.

"Stop the Accumulations and Wastes of Commodities," editorial, *JMJP*, May 21, 1955. Reprinted in *HHYP*, no. 6, 1955, pp. 102–103.

"Striving to Develop Credit Cooperation Enterprises," *HHYP*, no. 9, 1955, pp. 132–33.

"Summary Records of the First National Conference on Rural Finance," *CKCJ,* no. 7, 1951, pp. 21–34.

Sun Wei-ch'i and Kuo chu. "Why Is It Necessary to Adjust the Interest Rates," *CKCJ,* no. 24, 1957, pp. 17–18.

"A Survey of the Commodity Circulation in the Domestic Market in 1957," *Stat. Res.,* no. 4, 1958, p. 24.

Ta Wu. "The Development and Functions of Credit Cooperatives in Our Country," *HH,* no. 2, 1954, pp. 31–32.

Tai Ch'ien-ting. "A Discussion of the Purchase Loan and Expenditure Loan under the Regulation of Loans for Agricultural Purchases," *CJCK,* #111 in *TKP,* June 11, 1956.

────── and Peng Wang-p'ei. "An Understanding of the Regulations on Short-Term Loans to State Foodgrains Units," *CKCJ,* no. 12, 1955, pp. 25–28.

T'an Chen-lin. "A Preliminary Study of the Income and the Standard of Living of the Chinese Peasant," *HHPYK,* no. 11, 1957, pp. 105–11.

T'ao Ta-hung. "The Sale of Public Bonds and Economic Development," *HCS,* I, no. 7 (December 4, 1949), 4-6.

"The Task of Credit Withdrawal Has Been Completed; Works during the Brisk Season Require Further Efforts," *CKCJ,* no. 2, 1958, p. 14.

TCKTTH Data Office. "The Condition of Domestic Market Prices in 1956," *HHPYK,* no. 10, 1957, pp. 114–15.

────── . "The Great Achievement on Socialist Construction and Socialist Transformation during the First Half Year of 1956," *TCKTTH,* no. 5, 1956, p. 6.

────── . "Rapid Progress Was Made by Various Sectors of the National Economy in the Third Quarter of 1956," *TCKTTH,* no. 21, 1956, p. 2.

Teng Tzu-hui. "The Historic Mission of the Credit Cooperatives during the Present Stage of Our Country," *HC,* no. 23, 1963, pp. 1–29.

"Thoroughly Implement the Policy of Economy, Further Improve the Works on Industrial Credit and Settlement," *CKCJ,* no. 16, 1955, pp. 3–4.

T'ieh Ying. "An Understanding of the Three Lending Procedures under 'Temporary Measures on Short-Term Loans to Basic Level Supply and Marketing Cooperatives,'" *CKCJ,* no. 11, 1955, pp. 7–8.

Ts'ai Chin. "On the Question of Working Capital," *JMST,* 1962, pp. 208–10.

Ts'ao Chü-ju. "Monetary Affairs in the Past Ten Years," *JMST,* 1960, pp. 87–91.

────── . "Repeated Leaps in Bank Works," *TKP,* October 1, 1958.

────── . "Two Links in Solving the Problems of Agricultural Funds," *HHPYK,* no. 23, 1956, p. 85.

Tseng Ling. "A Year's Planning Begins in the Winter," *CKCJ,* no. 11, 1951, pp. 1–3.

────── . "The Effects of Agricultural Collectivization on the Rural Monetary Circulation," *CCYC,* no. 6, 1956, pp. 39–58.

———. "Is There Inflation in China at the Present?" *CCYC,* no. 5, 1957, pp. 26–49.

———. "The Rural Market in the Surging Tide of Agricultural Collectivization," *CCYC,* no. 2, 1956, pp. 1–27.

———. "Special Features of the 1953 Economic Conditions and the Bank's Task in Planning," *CKCJ,* no. 10, 1953, p. 1.

——— and Han Lei. "Money in Circulation in the Liberated Areas. 1948–1949," *CCYC,* no. 3, 1955, pp. 109–23.

——— and Yang P'ei-hsin. "On the Leap of Monetary Works," *HH,* no. 9, 1958, pp. 14–15.

Tuan Yün. "Several Questions on the Work of the Socialistic Bank in Our Country," *HH,* no. 1, 1964, pp. 21–33.

Wang Chao, "Contradictions in the Work of Collecting Bank Loans," *NTCJ,* no. 14, 1957, pp. 19–20.

Wang Ching-jan. "Important Achievements in the Country's Financial Structure during the Past Three Years," *CCCP,* XIII, no. 24 (December, 1951), 463–65.

Wang Ch'uan-lun. "The Two Fundamentally Different Attitudes on the Question of Budget Deficits," *CHYYC,* no. 5, 1958, pp. 11–18.

Wang Ken-shu. "The Significance of the Granting of Quota Loans to Industrial Enterprises by the Bank," *CKCJ,* no. 5, 1958, p. 21.

Wang Lan. "Financial Planning in the Past Three Years," *CKCJ,* no. 14, 1956, pp. 3–5.

———. "Credit Planning during the Period of the First Five Year Plan," *CKCJ,* no. 1, 1958, p. 10.

Wang P'ing. "The Scope and Changes of the Free Market in Our Country," *TCKT,* no. 11, 1957, pp. 28–29.

Wang T'uan. "Fiscal and Monetary Works and the Policy of Emphasizing Agriculture," *JMST,* 1962, pp. 197–98.

Wang Tzu-ch'in. "The Role and Functions of Credit and Settlement of the State Bank in the Rural Market," *CKCJ,* no. 10, 1955, pp. 4–7.

Wang Tzu-ying. "The Experience and Lessons from the Compilation and Implementation of the 1956 State Budget," *HHPYK,* no. 5, 1957, pp. 91–93.

Wang Wei-ts'ai. "To Further Develop People's Deposits," *HHYP,* no. 3, 1955, p. 147.

———. "Guidelines for Works on Urban Savings in 1955," *CKCJ,* no. 3, 1955, pp. 5–6.

"Why Were Prices for These Commodities Raised," *HHPYK,* no. 10, 1957, pp. 110–11.

"The Work of Currency Conversion Was Successfully Accomplished," *JMST,* 1956, p. 536.

"Work Hard to Accomplish the Task of Currency Withdrawal during This First Half Year," *CKCJ,* no. 8, 1957, pp. 1–2.

Wu Ch'ing-you. "Is the Socialist State Bank an Organization or an Enterprise?," *HH,* no. 1, 1957, p. 8.

Wu Yi-t'ang *et al.* "The Slow Progress in Rural Financial Works Must Be Changed," *CKCJ,* no. 24, 1956, p. 7.

Yang Li-hsiao. "On the Meaning and Function of the Administration by the People's Bank of State Budgetary Receipts and Expenditures," *CKCJ,* no. 22, 1955, pp. 3–5.

Yang Ming. "My Understanding of the Contradictions in the Present Rural Financial Works," *CKCJ,* no. 11, 1957, pp. 12–13.

Yang P'ei-hsin. "The Meaning and Functions of the Currency Conversion," *JMST,* 1956, pp. 533–35.

——— . "On Interest Rates in Our Country," *JMST,* 1956, pp. 537–39.

——— . "Prices, Money and Public Bonds," *HCS,* I, no. 11 (January 29, 1950), 8–11.

——— . "On the Question of the Balancing of the Fiscal Receipts and Expenditures, the Monetary Receipts and Expenditures, and the Commodity Supply and Demand," *CCYC,* no.5, 1957, pp. 50–63.

——— . "Ways to Raise Funds for Agricultural Developments in Our Country," *CCYC,* no. 1, 1958, pp. 22–37.

Yang Po. "A Preliminary Analysis of the Process of Socialist Transformation of Private Trade in China," *TCKTTH,* no. 15, 1956, pp. 7–10.

Yang Yin-fu. "After Reading the New Measures on the Supervision of Private Monetary Enterprises," *HHYP,* no. 1, 1949, pp. 137–38.

Yin Yi. "On the Experimentation of '100% Credit,'" *TCYC,* no. 8, 1958, pp. 9–11.

Yü. "Absorb More Deposit to Support Agricultural Production," *TKP,* January 22, 1958.

Yü Jui-Hsiang. "On Several Questions Relating to the Balance of the Monetary Circulation and the Commodity Circulation," *CCYC,* no. 3, 1963, pp. 17–24.

II. English-Language Sources

A. BOOKS AND DISSERTATIONS

Angell, James W. *The Behavior of Money.* New York: McGraw-Hill, 1936.

Arnold, Arthur Z. *Banks, Credit and Money in Soviet Russia.* New York: Columbia University Press, 1937.

Barnett, A. Doak. *Communist China and Asia.* New York: Harper and Brothers for the Council on Foreign Relations, 1960.

Beckhart, B. H. ed. *Banking Systems.* New York: Columbia University Press, 1954.

Bergson, Abram. *The Economics of Soviet Planning.* New Haven: Yale University Press, 1964.

Bowie, Robert R., and John K. Fairbank. *Communist China: Policy Documents with Analysis.* Cambridge: Harvard University Press, 1962.

Brzeski, Andrzej. *Inflation in Poland, 1945–1960.* Unpublished dissertation, University of California, Berkeley, 1964.

Chang Kia-ngau. *The Inflationary Spiral: The Experience in China, 1939–1950.* New York: The Technological Press of MIT and John Wiley & Sons, 1958.

Chao, Kang. *The Rate and Pattern of Industrial Growth in Communist China.* Ann Arbor: The University of Michigan Press, 1965.

Chao Kuo-chun. *Economic Planning and Organization in Mainland China, a Documentary Study (1949–1957).* 2 vols. Cambridge: Harvard University Press, 1959–1960.

Chen, Nai-Ruenn ed. *Chinese Economic Statistics: A Handbook for Mainland China.* Chicago: Aldine Publishing Co., 1967.

———, and Galenson, Walter. *The Chinese Economy under Communism.* Chicago: Aldine Publishing Co., 1969.

Cheng Chu-yuan. *Communist China's Economy 1949–1962: Structural Changes and Crisis.* South Orange, New Jersey: Seton Hall University Press, 1963.

Chou Shun-hsin. *The Chinese Inflation 1937–1949.* New York: Columbia University Press, 1963.

The Common Program and Other Documents of the First Plenary Session of the Chinese People's Political Consultation Conference. Peking: Foreign Language Press, 1950.

Ecklund, George. *Financing the Chinese Government Budget: Mainland China 1950–1959.* Chicago: Aldine Publishing Co., 1966.

Eckstein, Alexander. *Communist China's Economic Growth and Foreign Trade.* New York: McGraw-Hill, 1966.

———. *The National Income of Communist China.* Glencoe: The Free Press, 1961.

———, Galenson, Walter, and Liu, Ta-chung, ed., *Economic Trends in Communist China.* Chicago: Aldine Publishing Co., 1968.

An Economic Profile of Mainland China. 2 vols. Studies prepared for the Joint Economic Committee, U.S. Congress. Washington, D.C.: Government Printing Office, 1967.

Garvy, George. *Money, Banking and Credit in Eastern Europe.* New York: Federal Reserve Bank of New York, 1966.

Government of India Planning Commission. *Third Five Year Plan.* New Delhi: Government of India Press, 1961.

Selected Bibliography: English-Language Sources

Grossman, Gregory. *Economic Systems.* Englewood Cliffs: Prentice-Hall, 1967.

———. ed. *Value and Plan.* Berkeley: University of California Press, 1960.

Hollister, William W. *China's Gross National Product and Social Accounts 1950–1957.* Glencoe: Glencoe Free Press, 1958.

Holzman, Franklyn D. ed. *Readings on the Soviet Economy.* Chicago: Rand McNally and Company, 1962.

———. *Soviet Taxation: The Fiscal and Monetary Problems of a Planned Economy.* Cambridge: Harvard University Press, 1955.

Hsia, Ronald. *Price Control in Communist China.* New York: Institute of Pacific Relations, 1953 (Mimeograph).

Hubbard, L. E. *Soviet Money and Finance.* London: McMillan, 1936.

Hughs, T. J., and D. E. T. Lurad. *The Economic Development of Communist China, 1949–1958.* London: Oxford University Press, 1959.

Ishikawa, Shigeru. *National Income and Capital Formation in Mainland China.* Tokyo: The Institute of Asian Economic Affairs, 1965.

Kirby, E. S. ed. *Contemporary China.* 5 vols. Hong Kong: Hong Kong University Press, 1955–1963.

Li, Choh-ming. *Economic Development of Communist China.* Berkeley: University of California Press, 1959.

———. *The Statistical System of Communist China.* Berkeley: University of California Press, 1962.

Liu, Ta-chung and Kung-chia Yeh. *The Economy of the Chinese Mainland: National Income and Economic Development, 1933–1959.* Princeton: Princeton University Press, 1965.

Ma, James Chao-seng. *A Study of the People's Bank of China.* Unpublished dissertation, University of Texas, Austin, 1960.

Miyashita, Tadao. *The Currency and Financial System of Mainland China.* Tokyo: The Institute of Asian Economic Affairs and Seattle: The University of Washington Press, 1966.

Neuberger, Egon. *Central Banking in Semi-Planned Economies, Yugoslav Case.* Unpublished dissertation, Harvard University, Cambridge, 1957.

Nove, Alec. *The Soviet Economy.* New York: Frederick A. Praeger, 1961.

People's Bank, Main Office. *Collection of Fiscal Laws and Regulations, 1958–1960.* Peking, 1962. Translated into English, *JPRS*, #19,499. Washington, 1963.

Perkins, Dwight H. *Market Control and Planning in Communist China.* Cambridge: Harvard University Press, 1966.

Powell, Raymond P. *Soviet Monetary Policy.* Unpublished dissertation, University of California, Berkeley, 1952.

Robertson, D. H. *Banking Policy and the Price Level.* London: P. S. King and Son, Ltd., 1926.

———. *Money.* Chicago: The University of Chicago Press, 1962.

Rostow, Walt W. *The Prospects for Communist China.* Cambridge: Technology Press of MIT, 1954.

Starlight, Lawrence L. *Fiscal and Monetary Policies in Communist China, 1949–1954.* Unpublished dissertation, Harvard University, Cambridge, 1956.

Tang, Peter S. H. *Communist China Today.* Washington, D. C.: Research Institute on the Sino-Soviet Bloc, 1961.

Tseng Ling and Han Lei. *The Circulation of Money in the People's Republic of China.* Peking, 1956. Translated into English from the Russian translation, *JPRS* #3317, New York, 1960.

United Nations, Economic Commission of Asia and the Far East. *Economic Survey of Asia and the Far East, 1949.* Bankok, 1949.

Walker, Kenneth R. *Planning and Chinese Agriculture.* Chicago: Aldine Publishing Co., 1967.

Wellisz, Stanislaw. *The Economics of the Soviet Bloc.* New York: McGraw-Hill, 1964.

Wu, Yuan-li. *The Economy of Communist China.* New York: Frederick A. Praeger, 1966.

——— . *An Economic Survey of Communist China.* New York: Bookman Associates, 1956.

Yin, Helen. *The Reporting of Industrial Statistics in Communist China.* Unpublished dissertation, Columbia University, 1966.

——— , and Yin, Yi-chang. *Economic Statistics of Mainland China (1949–1957).* Cambridge: Harvard University Press, 1960.

Young, Arthur H. *China's Wartime Finance and Inflation, 1937–1945.* Cambridge: Harvard University Press, 1965.

B. ARTICLES

Ch'en Hsi-yü. "The 1958 Banking Work and the 1959 Tasks" (excerpts of a report delivered at the National Conference of Managers of Branches of the People's Bank of China), *CKCJ,* May 25, 1959. Translation by U.S. Consulate, Hong Kong, *ECMM* #178, pp. 28–34.

"Circulation Notes in Rural China," *Far Eastern Economic Review,* April 11, 1957, pp. 466–67.

Chou, S. H. "Prices in Communist China," *Journal of Asian Studies,* XXV, no. 4 (August, 1966), pp. 645–63.

Grossman, Gregory. "Union of Soviet Socialist Republics," in B. H. Beckhart, ed., *Banking Systems.* New York: Columbia University Press, 1954.

Hodgman, Donald. "Soviet Monetary Control Through the Banking System," in Franklyn D. Holzman, ed., *Readings on the Soviet Economy.* Chicago: Rand McNally, 1962.

——— . "Financing Soviet Economic Development," in Moses Abramovitz, ed. *Capital Formation and Economic Growth.* Pp. 229–87. Reprinted in *Readings on the Soviet Economy.* Chicago: Rand McNally, 1962.

Hoffman, Charles. "The Basis of Communist China's Incentive Policy," *Asian Survey,* III, no. 5 (May, 1963), pp. 245–57.

Holzman, Franklyn D. "Soviet Inflationary Pressure, 1928–1957; Causes and Cures," *Quarterly Journal of Economics,* LXXIV, no. 2 (May, 1960), pp. 167–88.

Hooton, G. L. V. "The Planning Structure and the Five Year Plan in China," in E. S. Kirby, ed., *Contemporary China,* I (1955).

Kaufman, George G. "More On An Empirical Definition of Money," *American Economic Review,* LIX, no. 1 (March, 1969), pp. 78–87.

Liu, John Y. W. "Monetary System of Communist China," *Proceedings of the Symposium on Economic and Social Problems of the Far East.* Hong Kong: University Press, 1961. Pp. 72–81.

Liu, Ta-chung. "The Tempo of Economic Development of the Chinese Mainland, 1949–65," *An Economic Profile of Mainland China.* Studies prepared for the Joint Economic Committee. U.S. Congress. Washington, D.C.: Government Printing Office, 1967. I, 45–76.

"Notice on State Council Regulations Regarding Improvements of Financial Administration in Respect to Capital Construction," *CJFK* 1958–1960. Translation: *JPRS* #19,499. Washington, D.C.: 1963.

Powell, Raymond P. "Soviet Monetary Institutions and Policies," in *The Economy of the U.S.S.R.* National Academy of Economics and Political Science Proceeding of October, 1957. Washington, D.C.

———. "Recent Developments in Soviet Monetary Policy," in Franklyn D. Holzman, ed., *Readings on the Soviet Economy.* Chicago: Rand McNally, 1962.

Robertson, D. H. "Theories of Banking Policy," *Economica,* VIII, no. 23 (June, 1928), pp. 131–46.

Schurmann, Franz. "Economic Policy and Political Power in Communist China," *The Annals of the American Academy of Political and Social Science,* September, 1963, pp. 49–69.

"There Is Still the Need for Credit Cooperatives," *TKP,* August 21, 1956. Translation by U.S. Consulate. Hong Kong: *SCMP* #1369, pp. 5–7.

Tsiang, S. C. "Money and Banking in Communist China," in *An Economic Profile of Mainland China.* Studies prepared for the Joint Economic Committee, U.S. Congress. Washington: Government Printing Office, 1967. I, 323–39.

U.S. Department of Agriculture. *Report of the China-United States Agricultural Mission.* Washington, D.C.: Government Printing Office, 1947.

Wiles, Peter. "Soviet Economics," *Soviet Studies,* October, 1952, pp. 133–38.

Wyczalkowski, M. R. "The Soviet Price System and the Ruble Exchange Rate," *Staff Papers, International Monetary Fund,* Vol. I, no. 2.

Selected Bibliography: English-Language Sources

Yang P'ei-Hsin. "Rural Finance," *Peking Review,* April 17, 1964, no. 16, pp. 17–19.

Zauberman, Alfred. "Gold in Soviet Economic Theory and Policies," *American Economic Review,* XLI, no. 5 (December, 1951), pp. 879–90.

INDEX

299

302

Studies of the East Asian Institute

The Ladder of Success in Imperial China, by Ping-ti Ho. New York: Columbia University Press, 1962.

The Chinese Inflation, 1937–1949, by Shun-hsin Chou. New York: Columbia University Press, 1963.

Reformer in Modern China: Chang Chien, 1853–1926, by Samuel Chu. New York: Columbia University Press, 1965.

Research in Japanese Sources: A Guide, by Herschel Webb with the assistance of Marleigh Ryan. New York: Columbia University Press, 1965.

Society and Education in Japan, by Herbert Passin. New York: Bureau of Publications, Teachers College, Columbia University, 1965.

Agricultural Production and Economic Development in Japan, 1873–1922, by James I. Nakamura. Princeton, N.J.: Princeton University Press, 1966.

Japan's First Modern Novel: Ukigumo of Futabatei Shimei, by Marleigh Ryan. New York: Columbia University Press, 1967.

The Korean Communist Movement, 1918–1948, by Dae-sook Suh. Princeton, N.J.: Princeton University Press, 1967.

The First Vietnam Crisis, by Melvin Gurtov. New York: Columbia University Press, 1967.

Cadres, Bureauracy, and Political Power in Communist China, by A. Doak Barnett. New York: Columbia University Press, 1967.

The Japanese Imperial Institution in the Tokugawa Period, by Herschel Webb. New York: Columbia University Press, 1968.

The Recruitment of University Graduates in Big Firms in Japan, by Koya Azumi. New York: Teachers College Press, Columbia University, 1968.

The Communists and Chinese Peasant Rebellion: A Study in the Rewriting of Chinese History, by James P. Harrison, Jr. New York: Atheneum Publishers, 1969.

How the Conservatives Rule Japan, by Nathaniel B. Thayer. Princeton, N.J.: Princeton University Press, 1969.

Studies of the East Asian Institute

Aspects of Chinese Education, edited by C. T. Hu. New York: Teachers College Press, Columbia University, 1969.

Economic Development and the Labor Market in Japan, by Koji Taira. New York: Columbia University Press, 1970.

The Japanese Oligarchy and the Russo-Japanese War, by Shumpei Okamoto. New York: Columbia University Press, 1970.

Documents on Korean Communism, by Dae-sook Suh. Princeton, N.J.: Princeton University Press, 1970.

Japan's Postwar Defense Policy, 1947-1968, by Martin E. Weinstein. New York: Columbia University Press, 1971.

Imperial Restoration in Medieval Japan, by H. Paul Varley. New York: Columbia University Press, 1971.

Election Campaigning Japanese Style, by Gerald L. Curtis. New York: Columbia University Press, 1971.

Money and Monetary Policy in Communist China, by Katharine Huang Hsiao. New York: Columbia University Press, 1971.

Li Tsung-Jen, A Memoir. Edited by T. K. Tong. University of California Press (forthcoming).

Law and Policy in China's Foreign Relations, by James C. Hsiung. New York: Columbia University Press (forthcoming).